Second Edition

London Railway
atlas

Second Edition

London Railway
atlas

Joe Brown

Ian Allan PUBLISHING

First published 2009

ISBN 978 0 7110 3397 9

Published by Ian Allan Publishing

an imprint of Ian Allan Publishing Ltd, Hersham,
Surrey KT12 4RG.
Printed in England by Ian Allan Printing Ltd,
Hersham, Surrey KT12 4RG.

Code: 0907/B

Visit the Ian Allan Publishing website at:
www.ianallanpublishing.com

Front cover: The combined 09.57 Ramsgate /
10.04 Margate to Charing Cross service arrives
at its destination, led by Class 375/6 Electrostar
No 375604. *Brian Morrison*

PREFACE

London, more than possibly any other city on Earth, owes its growth and continuing success to its intricate network of railways, which have been a part of the landscape for over 170 years and show no sign of losing their relevance or importance. Unlike much of the United Kingdom, London had lost relatively little of its passenger infrastructure during the 20th century and it could indeed be argued that with the recent additions of the Docklands Light Railway and Croydon Tramlink to the scene along with 'Heavy Rail' developments such as the Channel Tunnel Rail Link and East London Line Extension, London's passenger rail network is today at its zenith. Despite this, there are many long-forgotten branch lines and abandoned stations dotted around London; casualties of World Wars, route duplication, trams, buses and the car. London's freight and industrial facilities did not fare anywhere near as well as the passenger facilities during the late 20th century; changes to the way that freight was carried combined with industrial decline decimated the hundreds of goods and coal yards and rail-served industrial sites in London.

I commenced this project in 2004 after searching for a publication like this one to no avail: one that provided a diagrammatic representation of London's railway history. What began as a light-hearted hobby has since become a serious project, which has taken up hundreds of hours' work through map-drawing, indexing and research. Publication of the first edition 3 years ago was a personal triumph, but within weeks I began work on this second edition as London's railway geography continued to change apace. I took the opportunity to make the biggest change to the format, which is the depiction of each track and platform. I feel the cartography is greatly improved, and hope those of you who possess the first edition agree. For this edition I have also made extensive use of satellite images and old Ordnance Survey maps so feel this is a far more accurate depiction, both currently and historically.

Despite many hours of research I am the first to acknowledge that there are quite probably some omissions, particularly regarding freight facilities on which available information is often scant. I have endeavoured to provide a hopefully near-complete history of London's passenger railways, although I have chosen to omit a handful of temporary, excursion and unadvertised stations which have had little bearing on London's railway history or for which I have been unable to find any significant information.

I very much regard this as a work in progress, and I would be delighted to hear from anyone who can provide me with further information. There are question marks against some dates in the index (all freight facilities), and I would be very happy to receive locations and relevant dates for other goods, freight and industrial facilities that have been omitted, although I have had to be mindful in more complex areas not to overload the map with detail to the extent that it becomes a distraction.

Please feel free to email me with any further information at: atlasupdate@blueyonder.co.uk

Regarding future developments, I have included those under construction such as the East London Line extension as well as squeezing in the proposed 'Crossrail 1', which has as good a chance as ever of coming to fruition. As before I have chosen to omit the Post Office Railway and London's first piece of railway infrastructure, the Surrey Iron Railway, as I do not feel them to fit into the concept of railways in the modern sense.

THANKS / DEDICATIONS

I would firstly like to thank Gary James for his never-ending patience and support during the five years that it has taken for this second edition to be realised. Secondly a huge thank you to a multitude of people who offered feedback and information by email and post following publication of the first edition; I cannot thank you all but special mention to James Tinkler, Brian Polley, Andy Cope, David Burnell, Simon Moore, Ken Weston, Phil Jones, John Sketcher, John Groves, Claude Hart, John Edser, Colin Hills, A Porter & D Roberts.

For my Nephews and Godsons Max & Felix Brown and Nephew and Niece Oscar & Jemima Thiagaraj.

In loving memory of Ruth Brown 1945-1989.

Joe Brown,
London,
April 2009

About the Author

Joe Brown

Joe was born in Preston, Lancashire in February 1977 but before his first birthday his family had moved south to London where he has remained ever since.

Growing up a stone's throw from the District / North London lines and the British Rail Hounslow Loop evidently made a very early impression and like many little boys Joe was obsessed with all things railways, combining this with his other great love; drawing.

Daily journeys to school in Hammersmith on the District Line began to raise questions in Joe's mind about the traces of abandoned railways he saw, which prompted library research and culminated at the age of 12 in the first version of this book, which was a sprawling mass of A4 sheets of paper, black ink and sellotape taking up most of a bedroom wall. It used the humble A to Z as a guide, just as this book does now.

Following the premature loss of his mother in 1989, Joe filled long Summer holiday days by purchasing a zone 1-6 travelcard and roving London's railway network, curious to find traces of the abandoned lines and stations his research was uncovering. He'd also cycle around West London, camera in hand, photographing the remnants of these lines and stations perhaps with a book in the distant future in mind.

By his mid-teens Joe had pretty much lost all outward interest in railways and turned his sights to the usual pursuits of teenage boys, whilst still maintaining a keen interest in drawing and design. After a very short university career (1 term studying Biology at King's College London) and 18 months working London's club scene as well as bit-parts acting Joe's former interest came back to the fore one day in the form of a poster recruiting for Northern Line Guards at Old Street Tube station.

That was in late 1997, and after initially joining London Underground on a 6 month short-term contract as a stop-gap (the Guard role's days were numbered), a whole career has since ensued.

After 9 months working out of East Finchley Depot as a Guard, Joe successfully passed 'motors' and spent a further 6 months driving 1959 and 1962 Stock trains on the Northern Line before transferring to Parson's Green Depot on the District Line in March 1999. After 2 years driving on the District Line, Joe was promoted to Duty Manager (Trains) at Earl's Court, and it was whilst in this role that he appeared in 'The Tube' Series 1 on television.

After 6 years as a Duty Manager at Earl's Court, Joe was again promoted to the role of Train Operations Manager, currently in charge of the day-to-day operations of Elephant & Castle Depot on the Bakerloo Line. This work and the 2006 First edition are a revival of Joe's childhood interest and have been gradually spawned on a home PC using pretty basic software and many hundreds of hours' endeavour. Despite job demands Joe is still keen to continue periodically updating this work as London's railways continue to evolve, and has some future projects in mind to complement this book.

ABBREVIATIONS:

BAK	Bakerloo Line	Abbreviated form of BS&WR
BER	Blackwall Extension Railway	Absorbed by GER 1866
BR	British Rail ('Railways' until 1966)	Formed 1948 (Nationalisation of all Main Line companies), became Railtrack 1994
BS&WR	Baker Street & Waterloo Railway	Part of UERL from opening, name later shortened to Bakerloo Line
CCE&HR	Charing Cross, Euston & Hampstead Railway	Part of UERL from opening, Merged with C&SLR to form Northern Line 1926 *
CEN	Central Line	Originally Central London Railway
CLR	Central London Railway	Absorbed by LT 1933 (Became Central Line)
CR	Caterham Railway	Taken over by SER 1859 after going bankrupt
C&SLR	City & South London Railway	Absorbed by UERL 1913, merged with CCE&HR to form Northern Line 1926 *
CTL	London Tramlink Croydon	Opened 2000. 'Croydon Tramlink' until 2008
DBS	Deutsche Bahn Schenker	Freight operator (formerly English, Welsh & Scottish Railway / EWS)
DIS	District Line	Originally Metropolitan District Railway, absorbed by UERL 1902
DLR	Docklands Light Railway	Opened 1987
ECR	Eastern Counties Railway	Absorbed by Great Eastern Railway 1862
ELL	East London Line	Originally "Metropolitan Line-East London Section", name began being used in 1980s
ELR	East London Railway	Absorbed by LT 1948 (Became Metropolitan Line-East London Section)
ES	Eurostar	In operation since 1994
EWS	English, Welsh & Scottish Railway	Freight operator, became DBS 2009
GCR	Great Central Railway	Absorbed by LNER 1923
GER	Great Eastern Railway	Absorbed by LNER 1923
GN&CR	Great Northern & City Railway	Absorbed by Metropolitan Railway 1913
GNP&BR	Great Northern, Piccadilly & Brompton Railway	Part of UERL from opening, name later shortened to Piccadilly Line
GNR	Great Northern Railway	Absorbed by LNER 1923
GWR	Great Western Railway	Became part of BR 1948
H&C	Hammersmith & City Line	Created 1990 (formerly part of Metropolitan Line)
HEX	Heathrow Express	Opened 1998, British Airports Authority and Railtrack joint venture
HJR	Hampstead Junction Railway	Absorbed by LNWR 1867
JUB	Jubilee Line	Opened 1979, incorporating Bakerloo Line Stanmore Branch
L&B	London & Birmingham Railway	Became LNWR 1846
L&BR	London & Brighton Railway	Became LBSCR 1846
LBR	London & Blackwall Railway	Absorbed by GER 1866
LBSCR	London, Brighton & South Coast Railway	Formed 1846 from merging L&BR with LCR. Became part of SR 1923
LCC	London County Council	Operated Becontree Estate Railway
LCDR	London, Chatham & Dover Railway	Became SECR 1899
LCR	London & Croydon Railway	Became LBSCR 1846
L&CR	London & Continental Railway	Consortium building Channel Tunnel Rail Link
LGR	London & Greenwich Railway	Absorbed by SER 1845
LMS	London, Midland & Scottish Railway	Formed 1923 from MID, LNWR, N&SWJR, T&FG & LTSR. Became part of BR 1948
LNER	London & Northeastern Railway	Formed 1923 from GNR, GER & GCR. Became Part of BR 1948
LNWR	London & Northwestern Railway	Formed 1846, absorbed by LMS 1923.
LOROL	London Overground Railway Operations Ltd	Formed 2007, TFL subsidiary operating services over Network Rail infrastructure
LSWR	London & Southwestern Railway	Absorbed by SR 1923
LT	London Transport	Formed 1933 **
LTSR	London, Tilbury & Southend Railway	Absorbed by LMS 1923
LUL	London Underground Limited	Formed 1985 from LT
MDR	Metropolitan District Railway	Absorbed by UERL 1902
MET	Metropolitan Railway	Absorbed by LT 1933
MID	Midland Railway	Absorbed by LMS 1923
NLR	North London Railway ***	Absorbed by LNWR 1922
NOR	Northern Line	Formed 1926 by amalgamating C&SLR and CCE&HR *
NR	Network Rail	Formed 2002 from Railtrack
N&SWJR	North & Southwestern Junction Railway	Absorbed by LMS 1923
PIC	Piccadilly Line	Abbreviated form of GNP&BR
PLA	Port of London Authority	Operated some railways in London and West India Docks
PRIV	Private	Private sidings / Industrial Railways etc
RT	Railtrack	Formed 1994 from British Rail, became Network Rail 2002
SECR	Southeastern & Chatham Railway	Formed 1899 from merging LCDR with SER. Became part of SR 1923
SER	Southeastern Railway	Became SECR 1899. Includes Bexley Heath Railway & Mid Kent Railway
SR	Southern Railway	Formed 1923 from merging LSWR, SECR & LBSCR. Became part of BR 1948
T&FG	Tottenham & Forest Gate Railway	Absorbed by LMS 1923
T&HJ	Tottenham & Hampstead Junction Railway	Became LNER & LMS joint after 1923, BR after 1948
UERL	Underground Electric Railways of London	Formed 1902 from MDR and the then unopened CCE&HR, GNP&BR and BS&WR
VIC	Victoria Line	Opened 1968
W&C	Waterloo & City Line	Owned & operated by LSWR (later SR then BR), transferred to LUL in 1994
WCR	Wimbledon & Croydon Railway	Absorbed by LBSCR 1866
WLER	West London Extension Railway	GWR, LNWR, LSWR & LBSCR Joint. Became LMS, GWR & SR joint after 1923
WLR	West London Railway	Became LMS & GWR joint after 1923
XRAIL	Crossrail 1	Proposed cross-London Network Rail line, estimated opening 2017

* When the C&SLR and CCE&HR were merged in 1926, "Morden - Edgware Line" was used, "Northern Line" was not coined until 1937

** London Passenger Transport Board formed 1933, became London Transport Executive 1948, then London Transport Board 1963, again London Transport Executive 1970, then London Regional Transport 1984. All are referred to as "LT"

*** North London Railway originally "East & West India Docks & Birmingham Junction Railway", renamed 1853

KEY TO MAP PAGES

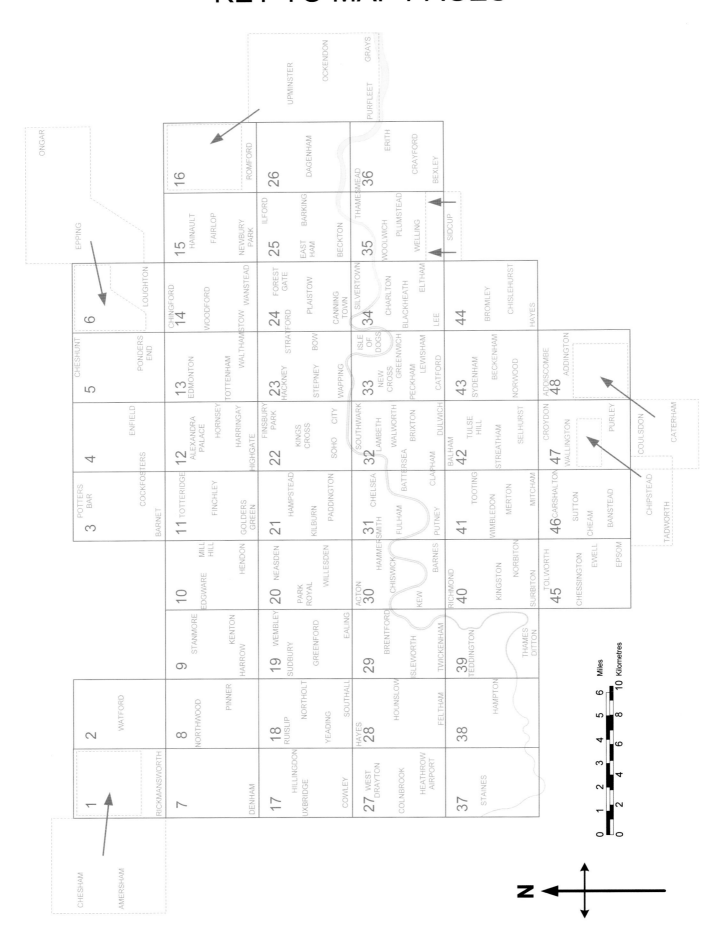

KEY TO MAP SYMBOLS

DATES INDICATE YEAR OF OPENING FOR OPEN STATIONS / LINES AND YEARS OF OPENING AND CLOSING FOR CLOSED STATIONS / LINES.
IF THE YEARS ARE FOLLOWED BY YEARS IN ITALICS, THIS INDICATES THE STATION / LINE WAS OPEN FOR FREIGHT TRAFFIC BEFORE AND /
OR AFTER IT WAS OPEN FOR PASSENGER TRAFFIC. GOODS STATIONS OPENED IN SAME YEAR AS ASSOCIATED PASSENGER STATIONS
UNLESS OTHERWISE STATED, YEAR QUOTED IS YEAR OF CLOSURE.

STATION SYMBOLS:

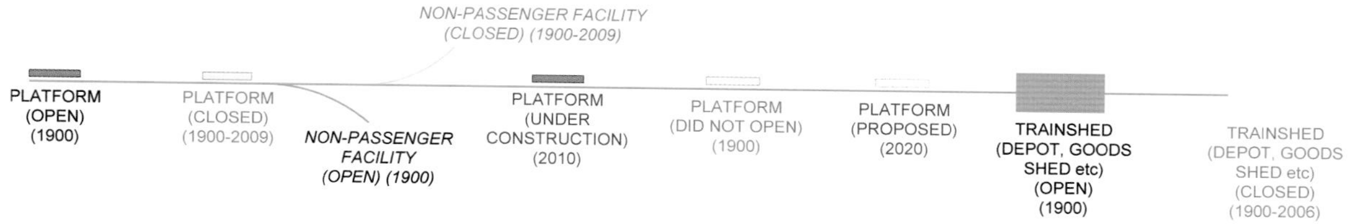

NON-PASSENGER FACILITY
(CLOSED) (1900-2009)

PLATFORM (OPEN) (1900)

PLATFORM (CLOSED) (1900-2009)

NON-PASSENGER FACILITY (OPEN) (1900)

PLATFORM (UNDER CONSTRUCTION) (2010)

PLATFORM (DID NOT OPEN) (1900)

PLATFORM (PROPOSED) (2020)

TRAINSHED (DEPOT, GOODS SHED etc) (OPEN) (1900)

TRAINSHED (DEPOT, GOODS SHED etc) (CLOSED) (1900-2006)

LINE SYMBOLS:

1900 — SINGLE TRACK, OPEN, WITH YEAR OF OPENING

2010 — SINGLE TRACK, UNDER CONSTRUCTION, WITH YEAR OF OPENING

1900-2009 — SINGLE TRACK, CLOSED, WITH YEAR OF OPENING FOLLOWED BY YEAR OF CLOSING

1900 — RAILWAY WHERE CONSTRUCTION COMMENCED BUT WAS ABANDONED, WITH YEAR OF ABANDONMENT

2020 — PROPOSED RAILWAY WITH ANTICIPATED YEAR OF OPENING

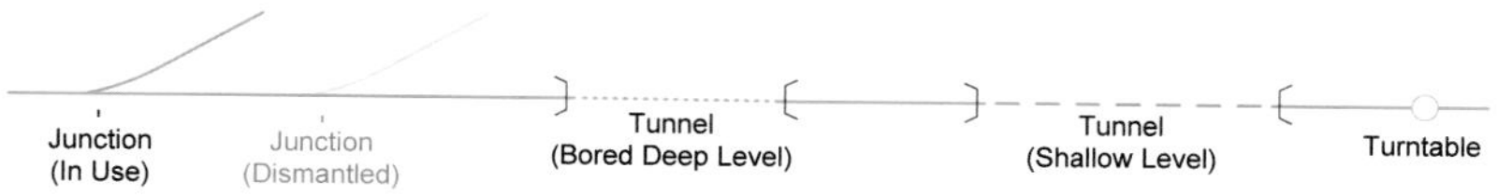

Junction (In Use)

Junction (Dismantled)

Tunnel (Bored Deep Level)

Tunnel (Shallow Level)

Turntable

NETWORK RAIL (FORMERLY RAILTRACK, BRITISH RAIL, AND PRE-NATIONALISATION MAINLINE COMPANIES)

NETWORK RAIL LINE SERVED BY LUL DISTRICT LINE TRAINS

NETWORK RAIL LINE SERVED BY LUL BAKERLOO LINE TRAINS

NETWORK RAIL LINE FORMERLY SERVED BY LUL BAKERLOO LINE TRAINS

NETWORK RAIL LINE FORMERLY OWNED AND SERVED BY LUL METROPOLITAN LINE

LUL DISTRICT LINE

LUL DISTRICT LINE SERVED BY PICCADILLY LINE TRAINS

LUL DISTRICT LINE SERVED BY CIRCLE LINE TRAINS

LUL DISTRICT LINE SERVED BY HAMMERSMITH & CITY LINE TRAINS

LUL METROPOLITAN LINE

LUL METROPOLITAN LINE SERVED BY HAMMERSMITH & CITY AND CIRCLE LINE TRAINS

LUL METROPOLITAN LINE SERVED BY MAINLINE TRAINS

LUL METROPOLITAN LINE SERVED BY PICCADILLY LINE TRAINS

LUL CIRCLE LINE

LUL HAMMERSMITH & CITY LINE

LUL HAMMERSMITH & CITY LINE SERVED BY CIRCLE LINE TRAINS

LUL EAST LONDON LINE (ALL CLOSED)

LUL PICCADILLY LINE

LUL VICTORIA LINE

LUL NORTHERN LINE

LUL BAKERLOO LINE

LUL JUBILEE LINE

LUL CENTRAL LINE

DOCKLANDS LIGHT RAILWAY (DLR)

ABANDONED DLR ON ABANDONED MAINLINE TRACK BED

LUL WATERLOO & CITY LINE

LONDON TRAMLINK CROYDON

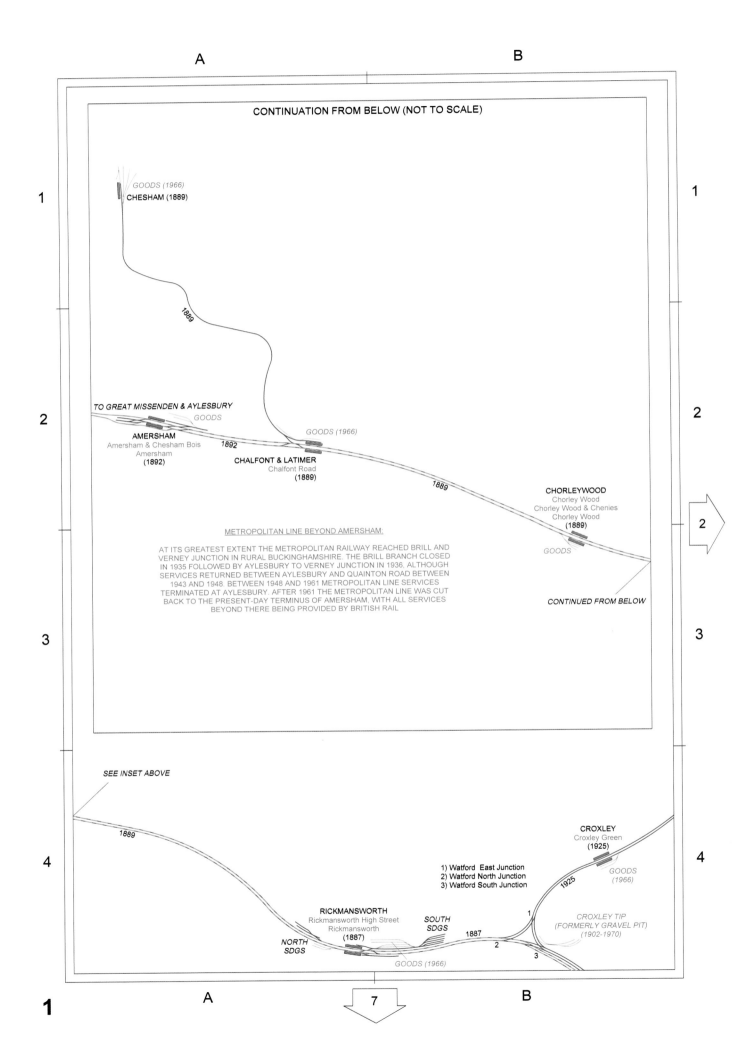

CONTINUATION FROM BELOW (NOT TO SCALE)

GOODS (1966)
CHESHAM (1889)

1889

TO GREAT MISSENDEN & AYLESBURY
GOODS
AMERSHAM
Amersham & Chesham Bois
Amersham
(1892)
1892
GOODS (1966)
CHALFONT & LATIMER
Chalfont Road
(1889)
1889
CHORLEYWOOD
Chorley Wood
Chorley Wood & Chenies
Chorley Wood
(1889)
GOODS

METROPOLITAN LINE BEYOND AMERSHAM:

AT ITS GREATEST EXTENT THE METROPOLITAN RAILWAY REACHED BRILL AND
VERNEY JUNCTION IN RURAL BUCKINGHAMSHIRE. THE BRILL BRANCH CLOSED
IN 1935 FOLLOWED BY AYLESBURY TO VERNEY JUNCTION IN 1936, ALTHOUGH
SERVICES RETURNED BETWEEN AYLESBURY AND QUAINTON ROAD BETWEEN
1943 AND 1948. BETWEEN 1948 AND 1961 METROPOLITAN LINE SERVICES
TERMINATED AT AYLESBURY. AFTER 1961 THE METROPOLITAN LINE WAS CUT
BACK TO THE PRESENT-DAY TERMINUS OF AMERSHAM, WITH ALL SERVICES
BEYOND THERE BEING PROVIDED BY BRITISH RAIL

CONTINUED FROM BELOW

SEE INSET ABOVE

1889

CROXLEY
Croxley Green
(1925)
GOODS
(1966)
1) Watford East Junction
2) Watford North Junction
3) Watford South Junction
1925
CROXLEY TIP
(FORMERLY GRAVEL PIT)
(1902-1970)
RICKMANSWORTH
Rickmansworth High Street
Rickmansworth
(1887)
SOUTH
SDGS
1887
1
NORTH
SDGS
2
3
GOODS (1966)

A   B

1   1

2   2

2

3   3

4   4

1   A   7   B

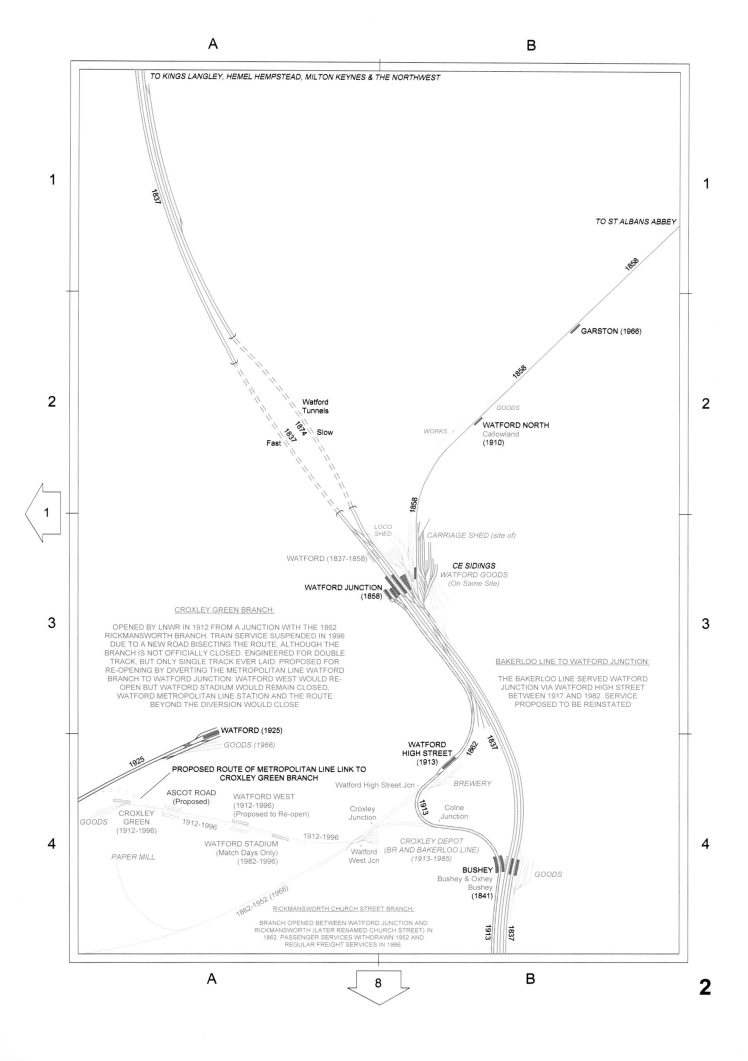

A   B

1   1

TO KINGS LANGLEY, HEMEL HEMPSTEAD, MILTON KEYNES & THE NORTHWEST

TO ST ALBANS ABBEY

1837

1858

GARSTON (1966)

1858

2   2

Watford
Tunnels

1874   Slow

1837

Fast

GOODS

WORKS   **WATFORD NORTH**
Callowland
(1910)

1858

1

*LOCO
SHED*

CARRIAGE SHED (site of)

WATFORD (1837-1858)

CE SIDINGS
WATFORD GOODS
(On Same Site)

WATFORD JUNCTION
(1858)

3   3

<u>CROXLEY GREEN BRANCH:</u>

OPENED BY LNWR IN 1912 FROM A JUNCTION WITH THE 1862
RICKMANSWORTH BRANCH. TRAIN SERVICE SUSPENDED IN 1996
DUE TO A NEW ROAD BISECTING THE ROUTE, ALTHOUGH THE
BRANCH IS NOT OFFICIALLY CLOSED. ENGINEERED FOR DOUBLE
TRACK, BUT ONLY SINGLE TRACK EVER LAID. PROPOSED FOR
RE-OPENING BY DIVERTING THE METROPOLITAN LINE WATFORD
BRANCH TO WATFORD JUNCTION: WATFORD WEST WOULD RE-
OPEN BUT WATFORD STADIUM WOULD REMAIN CLOSED,
WATFORD METROPOLITAN LINE STATION AND THE ROUTE
BEYOND THE DIVERSION WOULD CLOSE

<u>BAKERLOO LINE TO WATFORD JUNCTION:</u>

THE BAKERLOO LINE SERVED WATFORD
JUNCTION VIA WATFORD HIGH STREET
BETWEEN 1917 AND 1982. SERVICE
PROPOSED TO BE REINSTATED

WATFORD (1925)

GOODS (1966)

**WATFORD
HIGH STREET
(1913)**

1862   1837

1925

**PROPOSED ROUTE OF METROPOLITAN LINE LINK TO
CROXLEY GREEN BRANCH**

ASCOT ROAD
(Proposed)

WATFORD WEST
(1912-1996)
(Proposed to Re-open)

Watford High Street Jcn -

BREWERY

CROXLEY
GREEN
(1912-1996)

1912-1996

Croxley
Junction

Colne
Junction

1913

GOODS

1912-1996

1912-1996

CROXLEY DEPOT
(BR AND BAKERLOO LINE)
(1913-1985)

4   4

PAPER MILL

WATFORD STADIUM
(Match Days Only)
(1982-1996)

Watford
West Jcn

BUSHEY
Bushey & Oxhey
Bushey
(1841)

GOODS

1862-1952 (1966)

<u>RICKMANSWORTH CHURCH STREET BRANCH:</u>

BRANCH OPENED BETWEEN WATFORD JUNCTION AND
RICKMANSWORTH (LATER RENAMED CHURCH STREET) IN
1862. PASSENGER SERVICES WITHDRAWN 1952 AND
REGULAR FREIGHT SERVICES IN 1966.

1913   1837

A   B

8

2

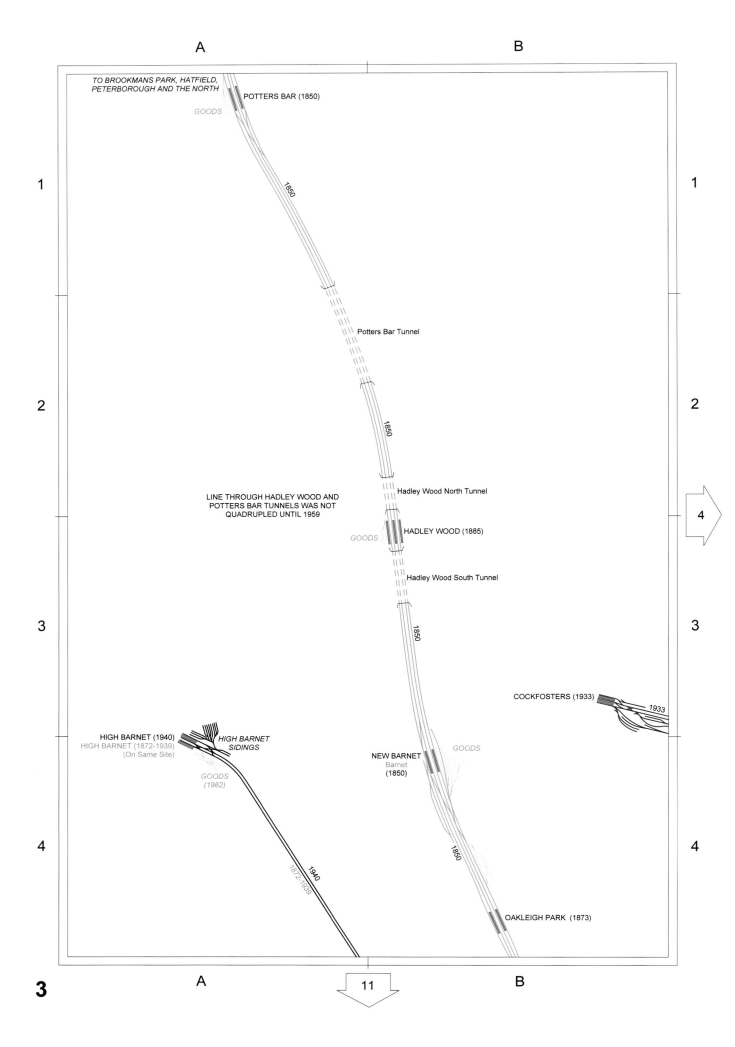

TO BROOKMANS PARK, HATFIELD,
PETERBOROUGH AND THE NORTH

POTTERS BAR (1850)

GOODS

1850

1

Potters Bar Tunnel

2

1850

LINE THROUGH HADLEY WOOD AND
POTTERS BAR TUNNELS WAS NOT
QUADRUPLED UNTIL 1959

Hadley Wood North Tunnel

HADLEY WOOD (1885)

GOODS

4

Hadley Wood South Tunnel

3

1850

COCKFOSTERS (1933)

1933

HIGH BARNET (1940)
HIGH BARNET (1872-1939)
(On Same Site)

HIGH BARNET
SIDINGS

GOODS
(1962)

NEW BARNET
Barnet
(1850)

GOODS

4

1940

1872-1939

1850

OAKLEIGH PARK (1873)

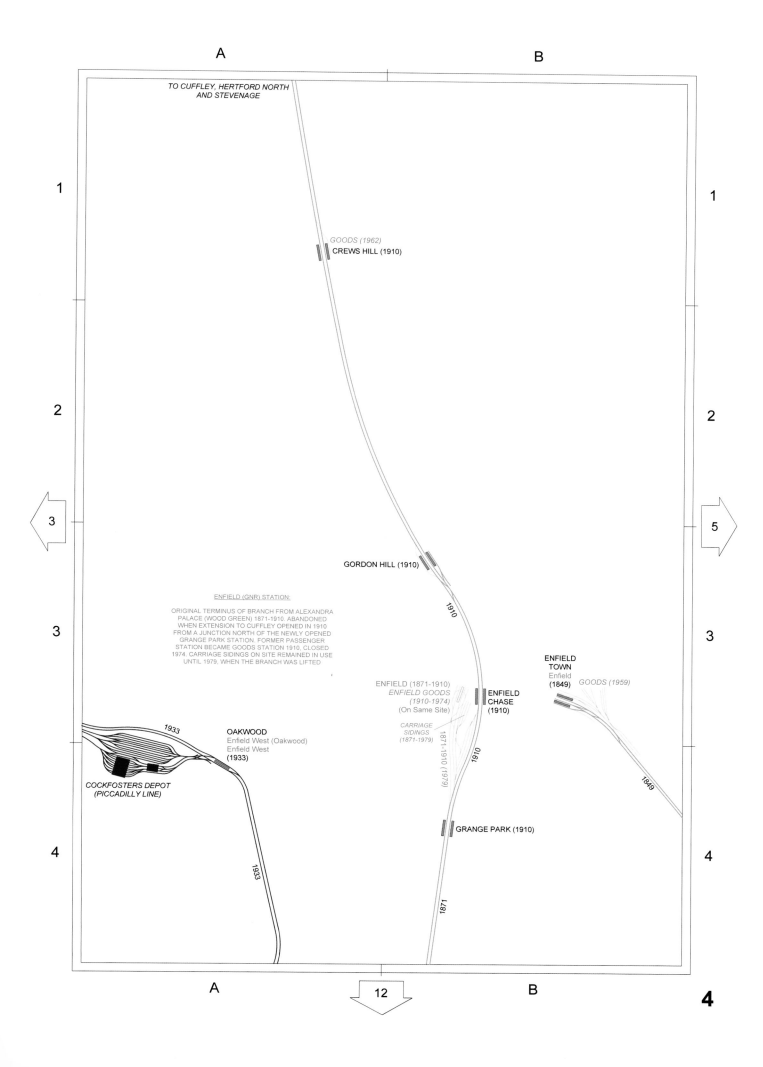

A B

1 1

2 2

3 5

3 3

4 4

4

TO CUFFLEY, HERTFORD NORTH
AND STEVENAGE

GOODS (1962)
CREWS HILL (1910)

GORDON HILL (1910)

1910

ENFIELD (GNR) STATION:

ORIGINAL TERMINUS OF BRANCH FROM ALEXANDRA
PALACE (WOOD GREEN) 1871-1910. ABANDONED
WHEN EXTENSION TO CUFFLEY OPENED IN 1910
FROM A JUNCTION NORTH OF THE NEWLY OPENED
GRANGE PARK STATION. FORMER PASSENGER
STATION BECAME GOODS STATION 1910, CLOSED
1974. CARRIAGE SIDINGS ON SITE REMAINED IN USE
UNTIL 1979, WHEN THE BRANCH WAS LIFTED

ENFIELD (1871-1910)
*ENFIELD GOODS
(1910-1974)*
(On Same Site)

*CARRIAGE
SIDINGS
(1871-1979)*

1871-1910 (1979)

ENFIELD
CHASE
(1910)

ENFIELD
TOWN
Enfield
(1849)

GOODS (1959)

1933

OAKWOOD
Enfield West (Oakwood)
Enfield West
(1933)

*COCKFOSTERS DEPOT
(PICCADILLY LINE)*

1933

1910

1849

GRANGE PARK (1910)

1871

A B

12

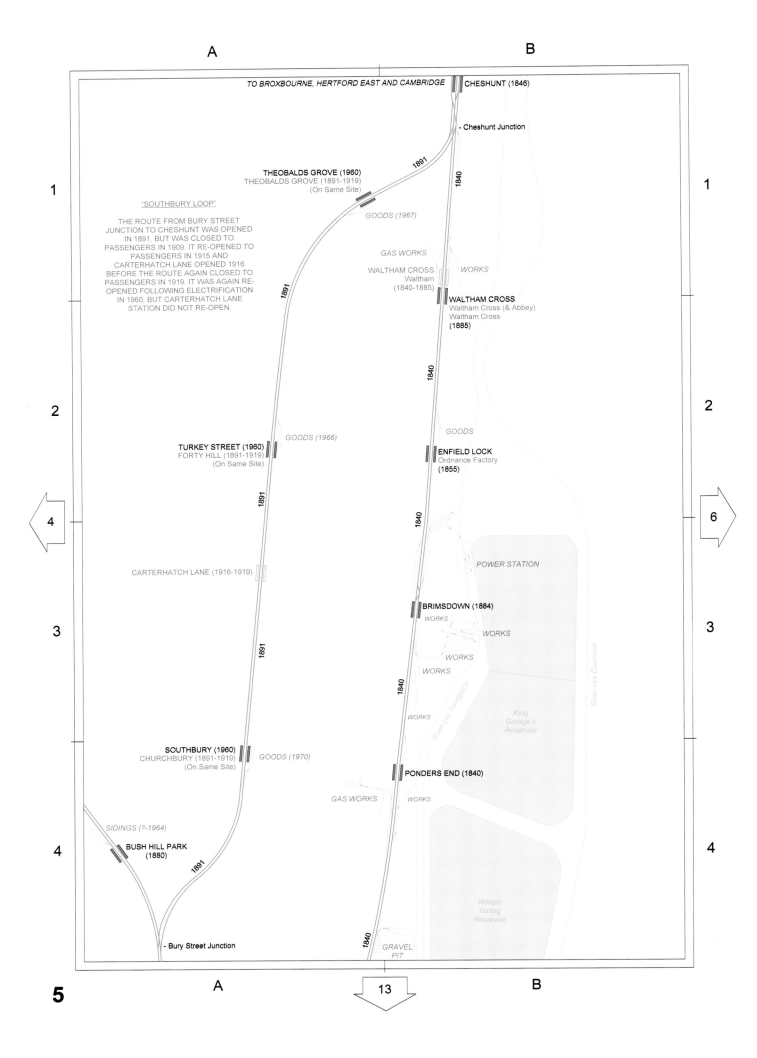

TO BROXBOURNE, HERTFORD EAST AND CAMBRIDGE   CHESHUNT (1846)

- Cheshunt Junction

1891

1840

THEOBALDS GROVE (1960)
THEOBALDS GROVE (1891-1919)
(On Same Site)

GOODS (1967)

"SOUTHBURY LOOP"

THE ROUTE FROM BURY STREET
JUNCTION TO CHESHUNT WAS OPENED
IN 1891, BUT WAS CLOSED TO
PASSENGERS IN 1909. IT RE-OPENED TO
PASSENGERS IN 1915 AND
CARTERHATCH LANE OPENED 1916
BEFORE THE ROUTE AGAIN CLOSED TO
PASSENGERS IN 1919. IT WAS AGAIN RE-
OPENED FOLLOWING ELECTRIFICATION
IN 1960, BUT CARTERHATCH LANE
STATION DID NOT RE-OPEN.

GAS WORKS

WORKS

WALTHAM CROSS
Waltham
(1840-1885)

WALTHAM CROSS
Waltham Cross (& Abbey)
Waltham Cross
(1885)

1840

1891

GOODS (1966)

GOODS

TURKEY STREET (1960)
FORTY HILL (1891-1919)
(On Same Site)

ENFIELD LOCK
Ordnance Factory
(1855)

1891

1840

CARTERHATCH LANE (1916-1919)

POWER STATION

1891

1840

BRIMSDOWN (1884)

WORKS

WORKS

WORKS

WORKS

River Lee Navigation

River Lee Diversion

King
George's
Reservoir

SOUTHBURY (1960)
CHURCHBURY (1891-1919)
(On Same Site)

GOODS (1970)

PONDERS END (1840)

GAS WORKS

WORKS

SIDINGS (?-1964)

BUSH HILL PARK
(1880)

1891

William
Girtling
Reservoir

1840

- Bury Street Junction

GRAVEL
PIT

1

2

4

3

4

1

2

6

3

4

A

B

A

B

5

13

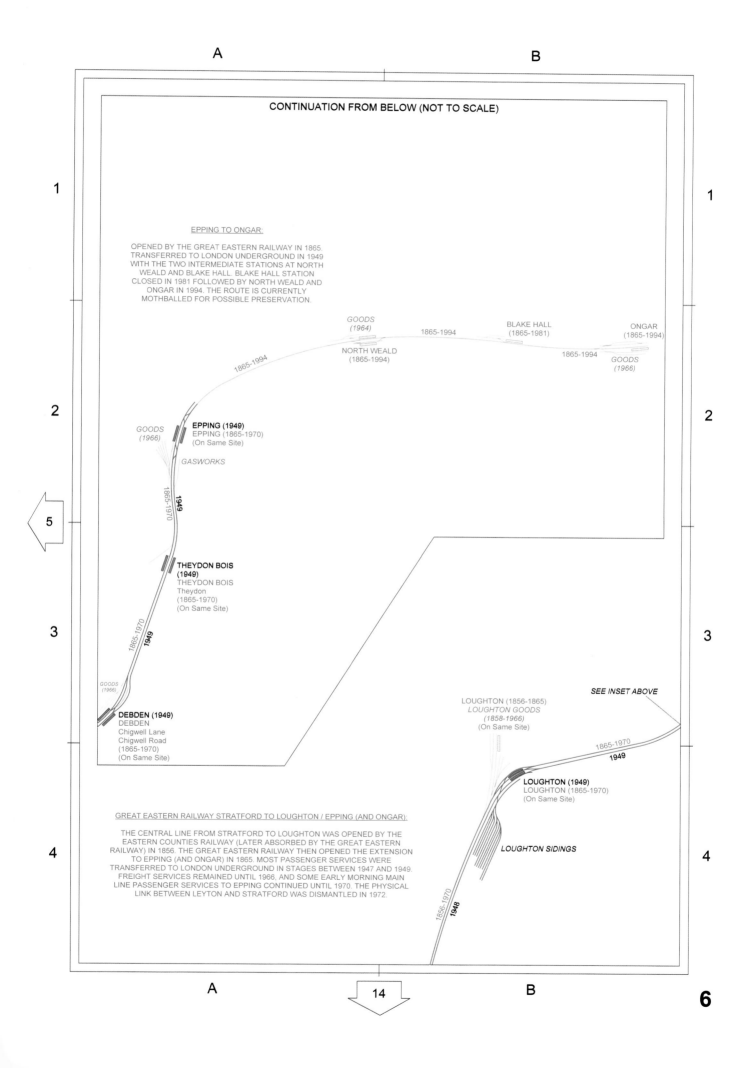

CONTINUATION FROM BELOW (NOT TO SCALE)

EPPING TO ONGAR:

OPENED BY THE GREAT EASTERN RAILWAY IN 1865.
TRANSFERRED TO LONDON UNDERGROUND IN 1949
WITH THE TWO INTERMEDIATE STATIONS AT NORTH
WEALD AND BLAKE HALL. BLAKE HALL STATION
CLOSED IN 1981 FOLLOWED BY NORTH WEALD AND
ONGAR IN 1994. THE ROUTE IS CURRENTLY
MOTHBALLED FOR POSSIBLE PRESERVATION.

GOODS
(1964)   1865-1994   BLAKE HALL   ONGAR
                 (1865-1981)   (1865-1994)
  NORTH WEALD   1865-1994
1865-1994 (1865-1994)   *GOODS*
                      (1966)

GOODS **EPPING (1949)**
(1966) EPPING (1865-1970)
    (On Same Site)

GASWORKS

1865-1970 1949

THEYDON BOIS
(1949)
THEYDON BOIS
Theydon
(1865-1970)
(On Same Site)

1865-1970 1949

GOODS
(1966)

DEBDEN (1949)
DEBDEN
Chigwell Lane
Chigwell Road
(1865-1970)
(On Same Site)

LOUGHTON (1856-1865)
LOUGHTON GOODS
(1858-1966)
(On Same Site)

SEE INSET ABOVE

1865-1970
1949

LOUGHTON (1949)
LOUGHTON (1865-1970)
(On Same Site)

LOUGHTON SIDINGS

GREAT EASTERN RAILWAY STRATFORD TO LOUGHTON / EPPING (AND ONGAR):

THE CENTRAL LINE FROM STRATFORD TO LOUGHTON WAS OPENED BY THE
EASTERN COUNTIES RAILWAY (LATER ABSORBED BY THE GREAT EASTERN
RAILWAY) IN 1856. THE GREAT EASTERN RAILWAY THEN OPENED THE EXTENSION
TO EPPING (AND ONGAR) IN 1865. MOST PASSENGER SERVICES WERE
TRANSFERRED TO LONDON UNDERGROUND IN STAGES BETWEEN 1947 AND 1949.
FREIGHT SERVICES REMAINED UNTIL 1966, AND SOME EARLY MORNING MAIN
LINE PASSENGER SERVICES TO EPPING CONTINUED UNTIL 1970. THE PHYSICAL
LINK BETWEEN LEYTON AND STRATFORD WAS DISMANTLED IN 1972.

1856-1970 1948

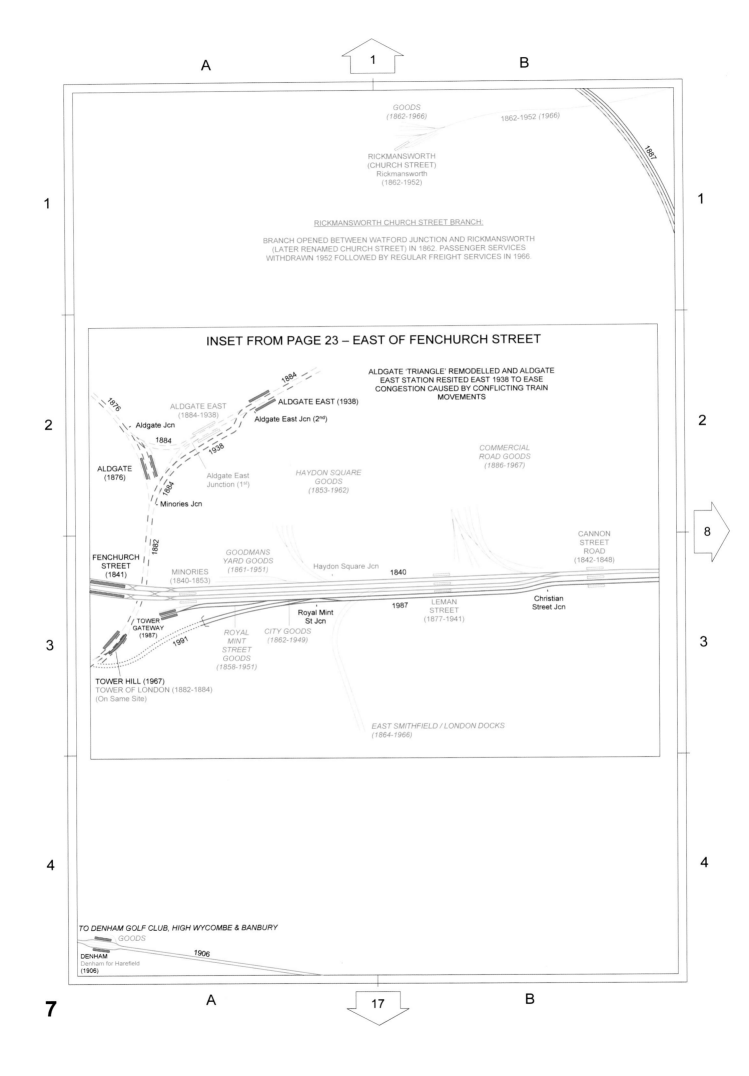

GOODS
(1862-1966)

1862-1952 *(1966)*

1887

RICKMANSWORTH
(CHURCH STREET)
Rickmansworth
(1862-1952)

RICKMANSWORTH CHURCH STREET BRANCH:

BRANCH OPENED BETWEEN WATFORD JUNCTION AND RICKMANSWORTH
(LATER RENAMED CHURCH STREET) IN 1862. PASSENGER SERVICES
WITHDRAWN 1952 FOLLOWED BY REGULAR FREIGHT SERVICES IN 1966.

INSET FROM PAGE 23 – EAST OF FENCHURCH STREET

ALDGATE 'TRIANGLE' REMODELLED AND ALDGATE
EAST STATION RESITED EAST 1938 TO EASE
CONGESTION CAUSED BY CONFLICTING TRAIN
MOVEMENTS

1876

1884

ALDGATE EAST
(1884-1938)

ALDGATE EAST (1938)

Aldgate East Jcn (2nd)

Aldgate Jcn

1884

1938

COMMERCIAL
ROAD GOODS
(1886-1967)

ALDGATE
(1876)

1884

Aldgate East
Junction (1st)

HAYDON SQUARE
GOODS
(1853-1962)

Minories Jcn

1882

CANNON
STREET
ROAD
(1842-1848)

FENCHURCH
STREET
(1841)

MINORIES
(1840-1853)

GOODMANS
YARD GOODS
(1861-1951)

Haydon Square Jcn

1840

1987

LEMAN
STREET
(1877-1941)

Christian
Street Jcn

Royal Mint
St Jcn

TOWER
GATEWAY
(1987)

1991

ROYAL
MINT
STREET
GOODS
(1858-1951)

CITY GOODS
(1862-1949)

TOWER HILL (1967)
TOWER OF LONDON (1882-1884)
(On Same Site)

EAST SMITHFIELD / LONDON DOCKS
(1864-1966)

8

TO DENHAM GOLF CLUB, HIGH WYCOMBE & BANBURY

GOODS

DENHAM
Denham for Harefield
(1906)

1906

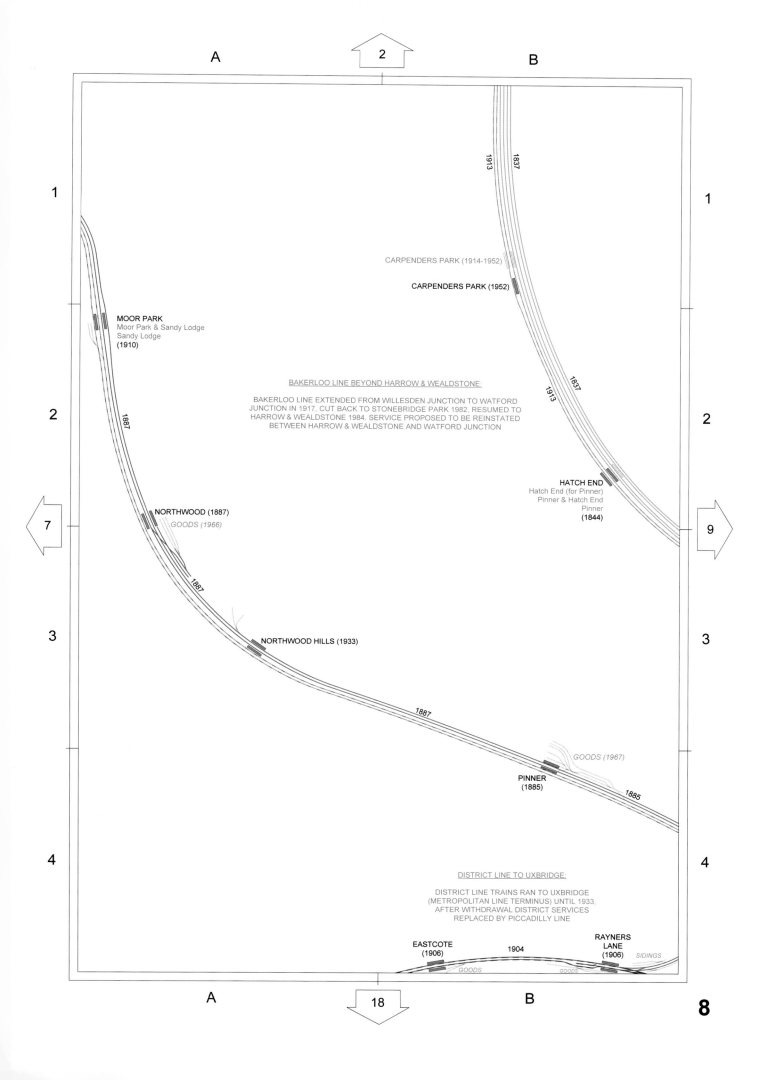

A

2

B

1913   1837

1

CARPENDERS PARK (1914-1952)

CARPENDERS PARK (1952)

MOOR PARK
Moor Park & Sandy Lodge
Sandy Lodge
(1910)

2

BAKERLOO LINE BEYOND HARROW & WEALDSTONE:

BAKERLOO LINE EXTENDED FROM WILLESDEN JUNCTION TO WATFORD
JUNCTION IN 1917, CUT BACK TO STONEBRIDGE PARK 1982, RESUMED TO
HARROW & WEALDSTONE 1984. SERVICE PROPOSED TO BE REINSTATED
BETWEEN HARROW & WEALDSTONE AND WATFORD JUNCTION

1837

1913

1887

HATCH END
Hatch End (for Pinner)
Pinner & Hatch End
Pinner
(1844)

NORTHWOOD (1887)
GOODS (1966)

7

9

1887

NORTHWOOD HILLS (1933)

3

1887

GOODS (1967)

**PINNER
(1885)**

1885

4

DISTRICT LINE TO UXBRIDGE:

DISTRICT LINE TRAINS RAN TO UXBRIDGE
(METROPOLITAN LINE TERMINUS) UNTIL 1933,
AFTER WITHDRAWAL DISTRICT SERVICES
REPLACED BY PICCADILLY LINE

**EASTCOTE
(1906)**   1904   **RAYNERS
LANE
(1906)**   *SIDINGS*

GOODS   *GOODS*

A

18

B

8

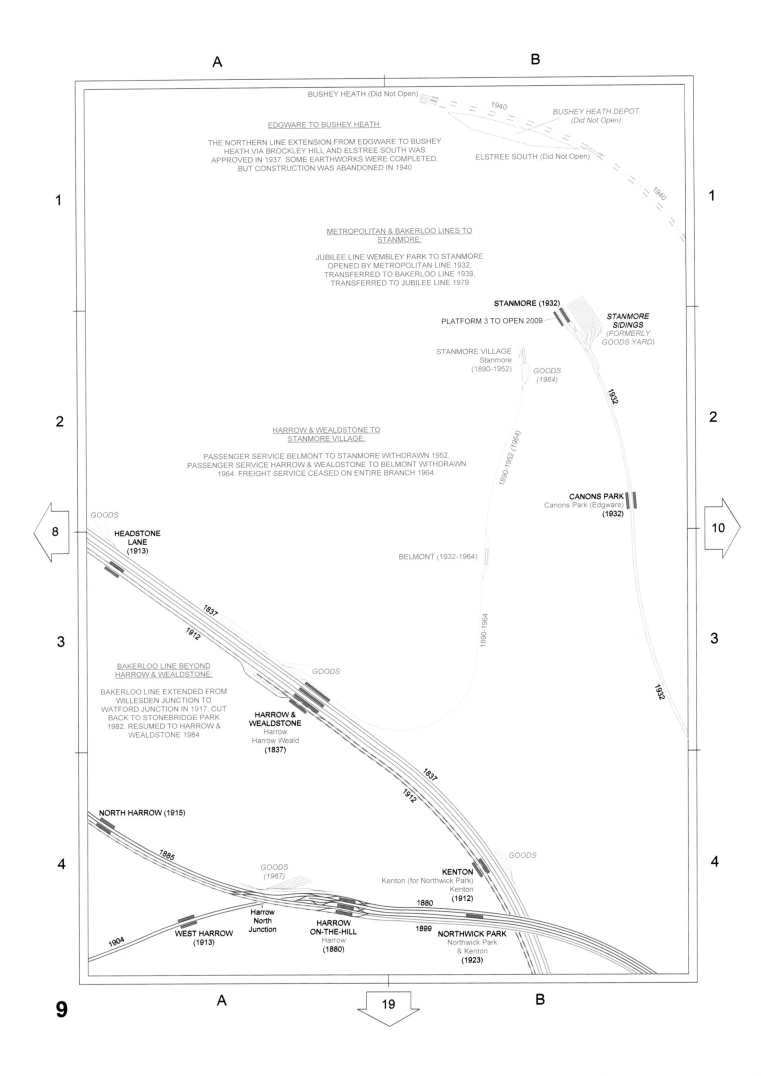

BUSHEY HEATH (Did Not Open)

1940

BUSHEY HEATH DEPOT
(Did Not Open)

ELSTREE SOUTH (Did Not Open)

1940

EDGWARE TO BUSHEY HEATH:

THE NORTHERN LINE EXTENSION FROM EDGWARE TO BUSHEY
HEATH VIA BROCKLEY HILL AND ELSTREE SOUTH WAS
APPROVED IN 1937. SOME EARTHWORKS WERE COMPLETED,
BUT CONSTRUCTION WAS ABANDONED IN 1940

**METROPOLITAN & BAKERLOO LINES TO
STANMORE:**

JUBILEE LINE WEMBLEY PARK TO STANMORE
OPENED BY METROPOLITAN LINE 1932,
TRANSFERRED TO BAKERLOO LINE 1939,
TRANSFERRED TO JUBILEE LINE 1979

STANMORE (1932)

PLATFORM 3 TO OPEN 2009

*STANMORE
SIDINGS*
*(FORMERLY
GOODS YARD)*

STANMORE VILLAGE
Stanmore
(1890-1952)

*GOODS
(1964)*

1932

1890-1952 (1964)

**HARROW & WEALDSTONE TO
STANMORE VILLAGE:**

PASSENGER SERVICE BELMONT TO STANMORE WITHDRAWN 1952,
PASSENGER SERVICE HARROW & WEALDSTONE TO BELMONT WITHDRAWN
1964. FREIGHT SERVICE CEASED ON ENTIRE BRANCH 1964.

CANONS PARK
Canons Park (Edgware)
(1932)

GOODS

**HEADSTONE
LANE
(1913)**

BELMONT (1932-1964)

1890-1964

1837

1912

**BAKERLOO LINE BEYOND
HARROW & WEALDSTONE:**

BAKERLOO LINE EXTENDED FROM
WILLESDEN JUNCTION TO
WATFORD JUNCTION IN 1917, CUT
BACK TO STONEBRIDGE PARK
1982, RESUMED TO HARROW &
WEALDSTONE 1984

GOODS

**HARROW &
WEALDSTONE**
Harrow
Harrow Weald
(1837)

1932

1837

1912

NORTH HARROW (1915)

1885

*GOODS
(1967)*

GOODS

KENTON
Kenton (for Northwick Park)
Kenton
(1912)

Harrow
North
Junction

**WEST HARROW
(1913)**

**HARROW
ON-THE-HILL**
Harrow
(1880)

1880

1899

NORTHWICK PARK
Northwick Park
& Kenton
(1923)

1904

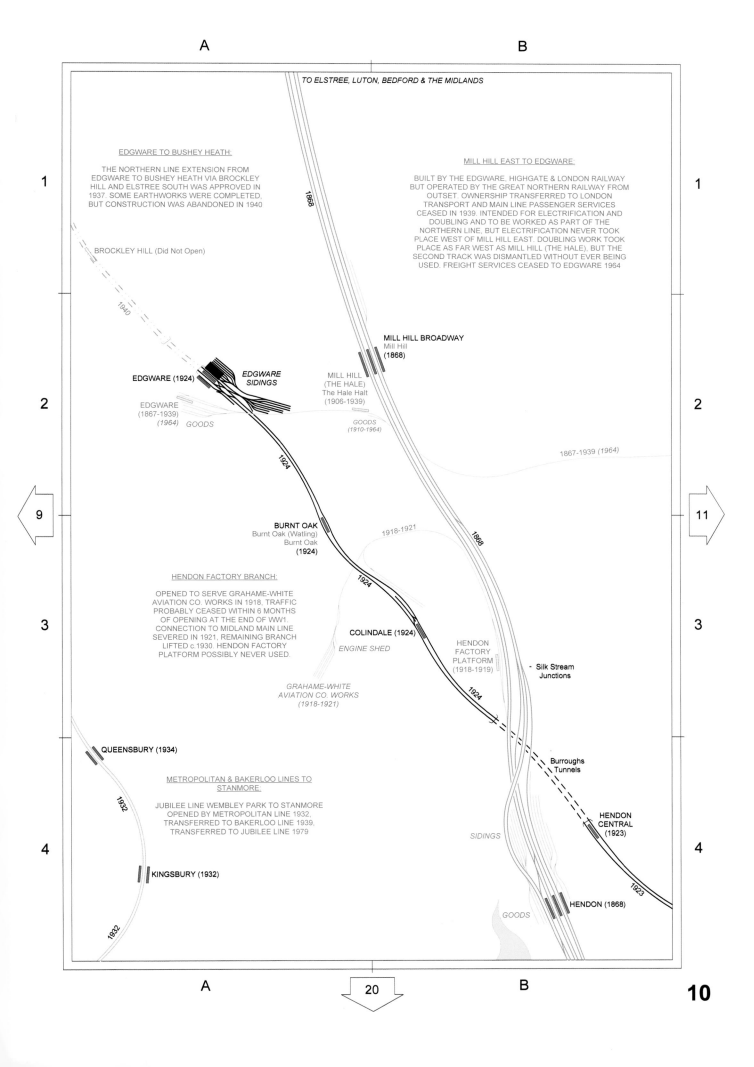

TO ELSTREE, LUTON, BEDFORD & THE MIDLANDS

1868

EDGWARE TO BUSHEY HEATH:

THE NORTHERN LINE EXTENSION FROM
EDGWARE TO BUSHEY HEATH VIA BROCKLEY
HILL AND ELSTREE SOUTH WAS APPROVED IN
1937. SOME EARTHWORKS WERE COMPLETED,
BUT CONSTRUCTION WAS ABANDONED IN 1940

MILL HILL EAST TO EDGWARE:

BUILT BY THE EDGWARE, HIGHGATE & LONDON RAILWAY
BUT OPERATED BY THE GREAT NORTHERN RAILWAY FROM
OUTSET. OWNERSHIP TRANSFERRED TO LONDON
TRANSPORT AND MAIN LINE PASSENGER SERVICES
CEASED IN 1939. INTENDED FOR ELECTRIFICATION AND
DOUBLING AND TO BE WORKED AS PART OF THE
NORTHERN LINE, BUT ELECTRIFICATION NEVER TOOK
PLACE WEST OF MILL HILL EAST. DOUBLING WORK TOOK
PLACE AS FAR WEST AS MILL HILL (THE HALE), BUT THE
SECOND TRACK WAS DISMANTLED WITHOUT EVER BEING
USED. FREIGHT SERVICES CEASED TO EDGWARE 1964

BROCKLEY HILL (Did Not Open)

1940

MILL HILL BROADWAY
Mill Hill
(1868)

EDGWARE (1924)

*EDGWARE
SIDINGS*

MILL HILL
(THE HALE)
The Hale Halt
(1906-1939)

EDGWARE
(1867-1939)
(1964)   *GOODS*

*GOODS
(1910-1964)*

1924

1867-1939 *(1964)*

BURNT OAK
Burnt Oak (Watling)
Burnt Oak
(1924)

1918-1921

1868

HENDON FACTORY BRANCH:

OPENED TO SERVE GRAHAME-WHITE
AVIATION CO. WORKS 1918, TRAFFIC
PROBABLY CEASED WITHIN 6 MONTHS
OF OPENING AT THE END OF WW1.
CONNECTION TO MIDLAND MAIN LINE
SEVERED IN 1921, REMAINING BRANCH
LIFTED c.1930. HENDON FACTORY
PLATFORM POSSIBLY NEVER USED.

1924

COLINDALE (1924)

ENGINE SHED

HENDON
FACTORY
PLATFORM
(1918-1919)

- Silk Stream
Junctions

*GRAHAME-WHITE
AVIATION CO. WORKS
(1918-1921)*

1924

QUEENSBURY (1934)

Burroughs
Tunnels

1932

METROPOLITAN & BAKERLOO LINES TO
STANMORE:

JUBILEE LINE WEMBLEY PARK TO STANMORE
OPENED BY METROPOLITAN LINE 1932,
TRANSFERRED TO BAKERLOO LINE 1939,
TRANSFERRED TO JUBILEE LINE 1979

SIDINGS

HENDON
CENTRAL
(1923)

KINGSBURY (1932)

1923

1932

GOODS   HENDON (1868)

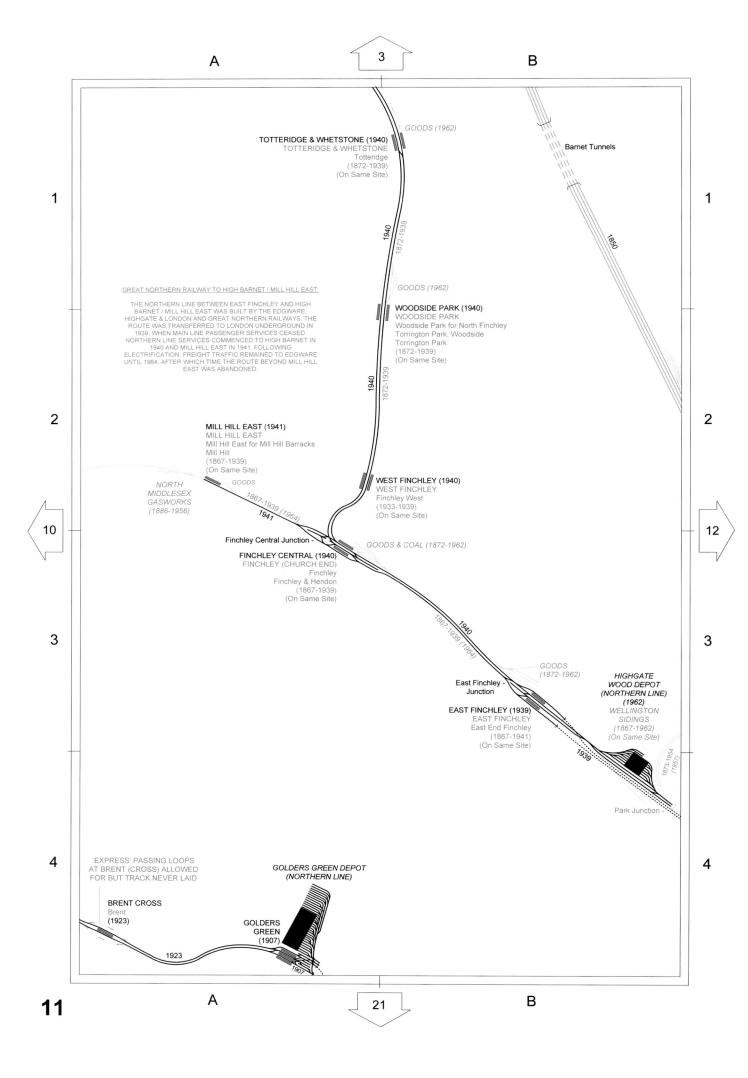

A

3

B

1

1

GOODS (1962)

TOTTERIDGE & WHETSTONE (1940)
TOTTERIDGE & WHETSTONE
Totteridge
(1872-1939)
(On Same Site)

Barnet Tunnels

1940

1872-1939

1850

GREAT NORTHERN RAILWAY TO HIGH BARNET / MILL HILL EAST:

THE NORTHERN LINE BETWEEN EAST FINCHLEY AND HIGH
BARNET / MILL HILL EAST WAS BUILT BY THE EDGWARE,
HIGHGATE & LONDON AND GREAT NORTHERN RAILWAYS. THE
ROUTE WAS TRANSFERRED TO LONDON UNDERGROUND IN
1939, WHEN MAIN LINE PASSENGER SERVICES CEASED.
NORTHERN LINE SERVICES COMMENCED TO HIGH BARNET IN
1940 AND MILL HILL EAST IN 1941, FOLLOWING
ELECTRIFICATION. FREIGHT TRAFFIC REMAINED TO EDGWARE
UNTIL 1964, AFTER WHICH TIME THE ROUTE BEYOND MILL HILL
EAST WAS ABANDONED.

GOODS (1962)

WOODSIDE PARK (1940)
WOODSIDE PARK
Woodside Park for North Finchley
Torrington Park, Woodside
Torrington Park
(1872-1939)
(On Same Site)

1940

1872-1939

2

2

MILL HILL EAST (1941)
MILL HILL EAST
Mill Hill East for Mill Hill Barracks
Mill Hill
(1867-1939)
(On Same Site)

NORTH
MIDDLESEX
GASWORKS
(1886-1956)

GOODS

WEST FINCHLEY (1940)
WEST FINCHLEY
Finchley West
(1933-1939)
(On Same Site)

1867-1939 (1964)

1941

Finchley Central Junction -

FINCHLEY CENTRAL (1940)
FINCHLEY (CHURCH END)
Finchley
Finchley & Hendon
(1867-1939)
(On Same Site)

GOODS & COAL (1872-1962)

10

12

3

3

HIGHGATE
WOOD DEPOT
(NORTHERN LINE)
(1962)
WELLINGTON
SIDINGS
(1867-1962)
(On Same Site)

GOODS
(1872-1962)

East Finchley -
Junction

1867-1939 (1964)

1940

EAST FINCHLEY (1939)
EAST FINCHLEY
East End Finchley
(1867-1941)
(On Same Site)

1939

1873-1954
(1957)

Park Junction -

4

4

'EXPRESS' PASSING LOOPS
AT BRENT (CROSS) ALLOWED
FOR BUT TRACK NEVER LAID

GOLDERS GREEN DEPOT
(NORTHERN LINE)

BRENT CROSS
Brent
(1923)

GOLDERS
GREEN
(1907)

1923

1907

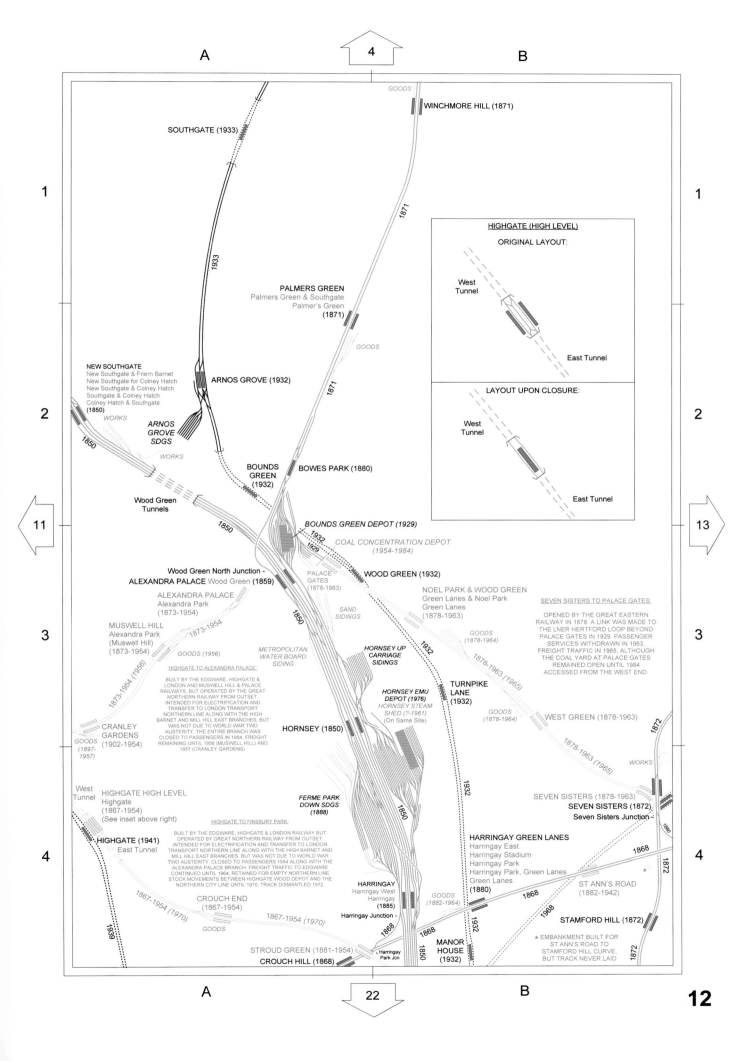

GOODS

WINCHMORE HILL (1871)

SOUTHGATE (1933)

1871

1933

PALMERS GREEN
Palmers Green & Southgate
Palmer's Green
(1871)

GOODS

NEW SOUTHGATE
New Southgate & Friern Barnet
New Southgate for Colney Hatch
New Southgate & Colney Hatch
Southgate & Colney Hatch
Colney Hatch & Southgate
(1850)

ARNOS GROVE (1932)

1871

HIGHGATE (HIGH LEVEL)

ORIGINAL LAYOUT:

West
Tunnel

East Tunnel

WORKS

1850

*ARNOS
GROVE
SDGS*

WORKS

LAYOUT UPON CLOSURE:

West
Tunnel

East Tunnel

BOUNDS
GREEN
(1932)

BOWES PARK (1880)

Wood Green
Tunnels

1850

BOUNDS GREEN DEPOT (1929)

1932
1929

*COAL CONCENTRATION DEPOT
(1954-1984)*

Wood Green North Junction -
ALEXANDRA PALACE Wood Green (1859)

PALACE
GATES
(1878-1963)

WOOD GREEN (1932)

NOEL PARK & WOOD GREEN
Green Lanes & Noel Park
Green Lanes
(1878-1963)

ALEXANDRA PALACE
Alexandra Park
(1873-1954)

1850

*SAND
SIDINGS*

GOODS
(1878-1964)

SEVEN SISTERS TO PALACE GATES:

MUSWELL HILL
Alexandra Park
(Muswell Hill)
(1873-1954)

1873-1954

1932

OPENED BY THE GREAT EASTERN
RAILWAY IN 1878. A LINK WAS MADE TO
THE LNER HERTFORD LOOP BEYOND
PALACE GATES IN 1929. PASSENGER
SERVICES WITHDRAWN IN 1963,
FREIGHT TRAFFIC IN 1965, ALTHOUGH
THE COAL YARD AT PALACE GATES
REMAINED OPEN UNTIL 1984
ACCESSED FROM THE WEST END.

1873-1954 (1956)

GOODS (1956)

*METROPOLITAN
WATER BOARD
SIDING*

1878-1963 (1965)

*HORNSEY UP
CARRIAGE
SIDINGS*

TURNPIKE
LANE
(1932)

GOODS
(1878-1964)

WEST GREEN (1878-1963)

HIGHGATE TO ALEXANDRA PALACE:

BUILT BY THE EDGWARE, HIGHGATE &
LONDON AND MUSWELL HILL & PALACE
RAILWAYS, BUT OPERATED BY THE GREAT
NORTHERN RAILWAY FROM OUTSET.
INTENDED FOR ELECTRIFICATION AND
TRANSFER TO LONDON TRANSPORT
NORTHERN LINE ALONG WITH THE HIGH
BARNET AND MILL HILL EAST BRANCHES, BUT
WAS NOT DUE TO WORLD WAR
TWO AUSTERITY. THE ENTIRE BRANCH WAS
CLOSED TO PASSENGERS IN 1954, FREIGHT
REMAINING UNTIL 1956 (MUSWELL HILL) AND
1957 (CRANLEY GARDENS).

*HORNSEY EMU
DEPOT (1976)*
*HORNSEY STEAM
SHED (?-1951)*
(On Same Site)

1872

CRANLEY
GARDENS
(1902-1954)

GOODS
(1897-
1957)

HORNSEY (1850)

1878-1963 (1965)

WORKS

1932

West
Tunnel

HIGHGATE HIGH LEVEL
Highgate
(1867-1954)
(See inset above right)

*FERME PARK
DOWN SDGS
(1888)*

1850

SEVEN SISTERS (1878-1963)
SEVEN SISTERS (1872)
Seven Sisters Junction -

HIGHGATE TO FINSBURY PARK:

BUILT BY THE EDGWARE, HIGHGATE & LONDON RAILWAY BUT
OPERATED BY GREAT NORTHERN RAILWAY FROM OUTSET.
INTENDED FOR ELECTRIFICATION AND TRANSFER TO LONDON
TRANSPORT NORTHERN LINE ALONG WITH THE HIGH BARNET AND
MILL HILL EAST BRANCHES, BUT WAS NOT DUE TO WORLD WAR
TWO AUSTERITY. CLOSED TO PASSENGERS 1954 ALONG WITH THE
ALEXANDRA PALACE BRANCH. FREIGHT TRAFFIC TO EDGWARE
CONTINUED UNTIL 1964. RETAINED FOR EMPTY NORTHERN LINE
STOCK MOVEMENTS BETWEEN HIGHGATE WOOD DEPOT AND THE
NORTHERN CITY LINE UNTIL 1970. TRACK DISMANTLED 1972.

HIGHGATE (1941)
East Tunnel

1880

HARRINGAY GREEN LANES
Harringay East
Harringay Stadium
Harringay Park
Harringay Park, Green Lanes
Green Lanes
(1880)

1868

1867-1954 (1970)

CROUCH END
(1867-1954)

1867-1954 (1970)

GOODS
(1882-1964)

1868

1932

ST ANN'S ROAD
(1882-1942)

1872

1968

1939

GOODS

HARRINGAY
Harringay West
Harringay
(1885)

Harringay Junction -

STROUD GREEN (1881-1954)
CROUCH HILL (1868)

Harringay
Park Jcn

1850

1868

1868

MANOR
HOUSE
(1932)

1932

STAMFORD HILL (1872)

* EMBANKMENT BUILT FOR
ST ANN'S ROAD TO
STAMFORD HILL CURVE,
BUT TRACK NEVER LAID

1872

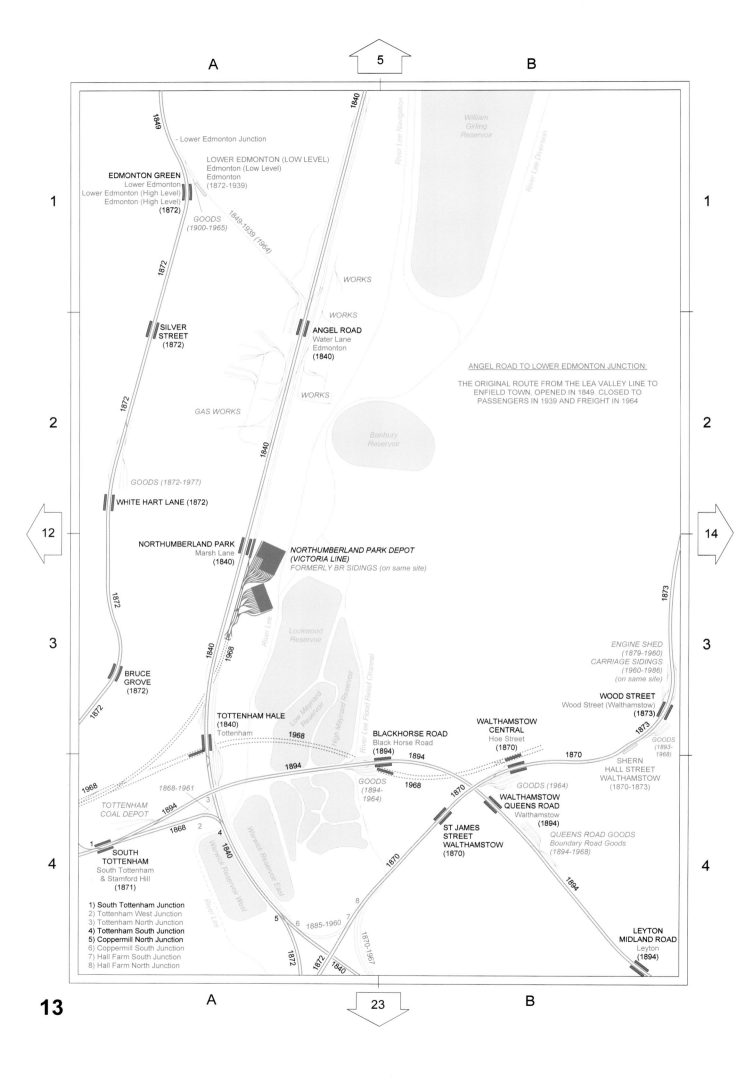

A

B

1

1

- Lower Edmonton Junction

LOWER EDMONTON (LOW LEVEL)
Edmonton (Low Level)
Edmonton
(1872-1939)

EDMONTON GREEN
Lower Edmonton
Lower Edmonton (High Level)
Edmonton (High Level)
(1872)

GOODS
(1900-1965)

1849
1840
1849-1939 (1964)

1872

William
Girling
Reservoir

River Lee Navigation

River Lee Diversion

SILVER
STREET
(1872)

WORKS

ANGEL ROAD
Water Lane
Edmonton
(1840)

ANGEL ROAD TO LOWER EDMONTON JUNCTION:

THE ORIGINAL ROUTE FROM THE LEA VALLEY LINE TO
ENFIELD TOWN, OPENED IN 1849. CLOSED TO
PASSENGERS IN 1939 AND FREIGHT IN 1964

WORKS

2

2

1872

GAS WORKS

WORKS

Banbury
Reservoir

1840

GOODS (1872-1977)

WHITE HART LANE (1872)

12

NORTHUMBERLAND PARK
Marsh Lane
(1840)

NORTHUMBERLAND PARK DEPOT
(VICTORIA LINE)
FORMERLY BR SIDINGS (on same site)

14

1872

1840

1968

River Lee

Lockwood
Reservoir

1873

3

ENGINE SHED
(1879-1960)
CARRIAGE SIDINGS
(1960-1986)
(on same site)

3

1872

BRUCE
GROVE
(1872)

Low Maynard Reservoir

High Maynard Reservoir

River Lee Flood Relief Channel

WOOD STREET
Wood Street (Walthamstow)
(1873)

1873

1872

TOTTENHAM HALE
(1840)
Tottenham

1968

1968

BLACKHORSE ROAD
Black Horse Road
(1894)

1894

WALTHAMSTOW
CENTRAL
Hoe Street
(1870)

1870

SHERN
HALL STREET
WALTHAMSTOW
(1870-1873)

GOODS
(1893-
1968)

1968

1894

GOODS
(1894-
1964)

1968

GOODS (1964)

1868-1961

TOTTENHAM
COAL DEPOT

1894

1870

WALTHAMSTOW
QUEENS ROAD
Walthamstow
(1894)

1868

3

1870

QUEENS ROAD GOODS
Boundary Road Goods
(1894-1968)

1

2

4

ST JAMES
STREET
WALTHAMSTOW
(1870)

4

SOUTH
TOTTENHAM
South Tottenham
& Stamford Hill
(1871)

1840

1870

1894

Warwick Reservoir West

Warwick Reservoir East

8

1) South Tottenham Junction
2) Tottenham West Junction
3) Tottenham North Junction
4) Tottenham South Junction
5) Coppermill North Junction
6) Coppermill South Junction
7) Hall Farm South Junction
8) Hall Farm North Junction

River Lee

5

6

1885-1960

7

1870-1967

LEYTON
MIDLAND ROAD
Leyton
(1894)

1872

1872

1840

A

B

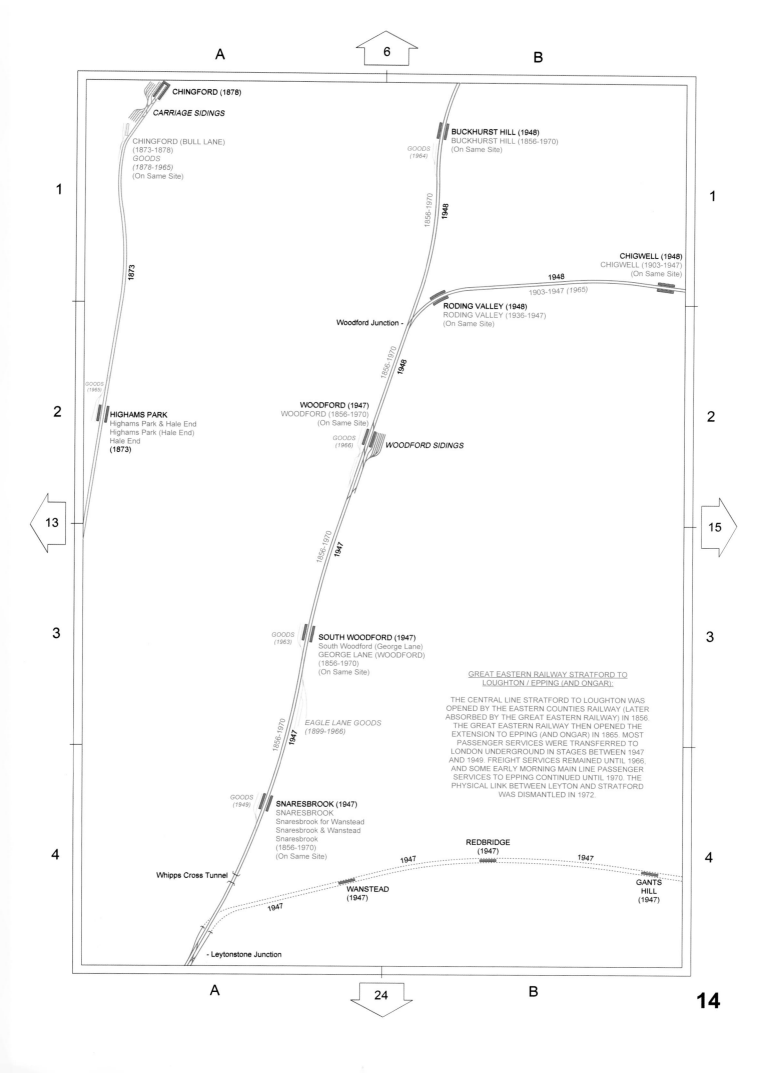

CHINGFORD (1878)

CARRIAGE SIDINGS

CHINGFORD (BULL LANE)
(1873-1878)
GOODS
(1878-1965)
(On Same Site)

BUCKHURST HILL (1948)
BUCKHURST HILL (1856-1970)
(On Same Site)

GOODS
(1964)

1856-1970

1948

1

1873

CHIGWELL (1948)
CHIGWELL (1903-1947)
(On Same Site)

1948

1903-1947 (1965)

RODING VALLEY (1948)
RODING VALLEY (1936-1947)
(On Same Site)

Woodford Junction -

1856-1970

1948

GOODS
(1965)

HIGHAMS PARK
Highams Park & Hale End
Highams Park (Hale End)
Hale End
(1873)

WOODFORD (1947)
WOODFORD (1856-1970)
(On Same Site)

GOODS
(1966)

WOODFORD SIDINGS

2

13

1856-1970

1947

15

3

GOODS
(1963)

SOUTH WOODFORD (1947)
South Woodford (George Lane)
GEORGE LANE (WOODFORD)
(1856-1970)
(On Same Site)

3

<u>GREAT EASTERN RAILWAY STRATFORD TO
LOUGHTON / EPPING (AND ONGAR):</u>

THE CENTRAL LINE STRATFORD TO LOUGHTON WAS
OPENED BY THE EASTERN COUNTIES RAILWAY (LATER
ABSORBED BY THE GREAT EASTERN RAILWAY) IN 1856.
THE GREAT EASTERN RAILWAY THEN OPENED THE
EXTENSION TO EPPING (AND ONGAR) IN 1865. MOST
PASSENGER SERVICES WERE TRANSFERRED TO
LONDON UNDERGROUND IN STAGES BETWEEN 1947
AND 1949. FREIGHT SERVICES REMAINED UNTIL 1966,
AND SOME EARLY MORNING MAIN LINE PASSENGER
SERVICES TO EPPING CONTINUED UNTIL 1970. THE
PHYSICAL LINK BETWEEN LEYTON AND STRATFORD
WAS DISMANTLED IN 1972.

1856-1970

1947

EAGLE LANE GOODS
(1899-1966)

GOODS
(1949)

SNARESBROOK (1947)
SNARESBROOK
Snaresbrook for Wanstead
Snaresbrook & Wanstead
Snaresbrook
(1856-1970)
(On Same Site)

REDBRIDGE
(1947)

4

4

Whipps Cross Tunnel

1947

WANSTEAD
(1947)

1947

GANTS
HILL
(1947)

1947

- Leytonstone Junction

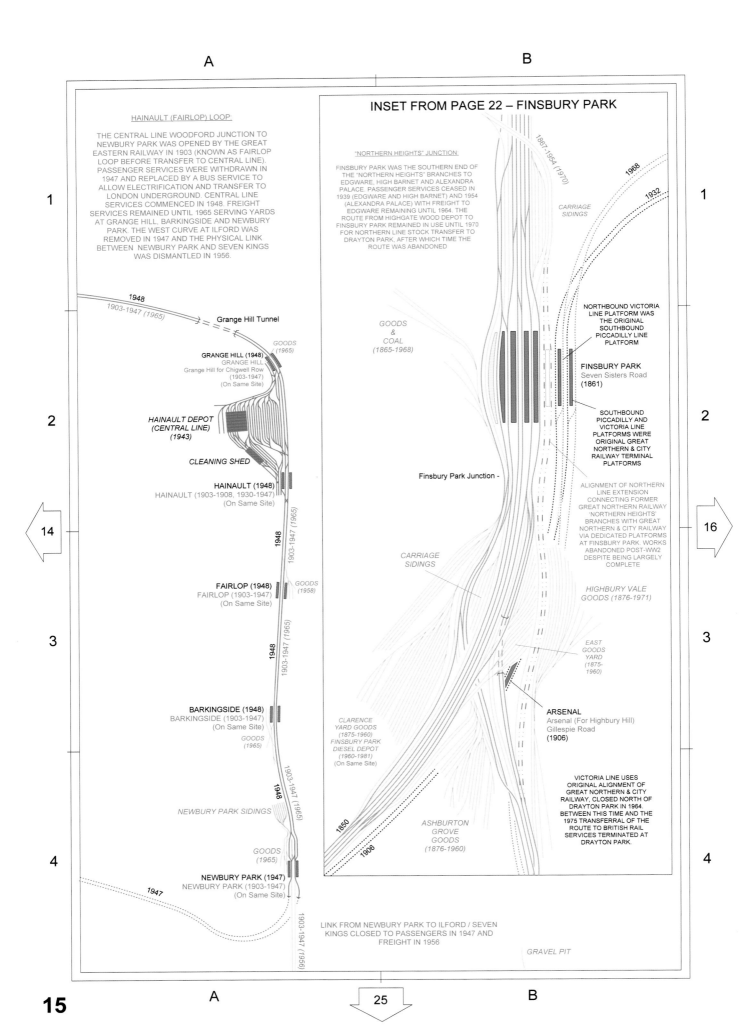

HAINAULT (FAIRLOP) LOOP:

THE CENTRAL LINE WOODFORD JUNCTION TO NEWBURY PARK WAS OPENED BY THE GREAT EASTERN RAILWAY IN 1903 (KNOWN AS FAIRLOP LOOP BEFORE TRANSFER TO CENTRAL LINE). PASSENGER SERVICES WERE WITHDRAWN IN 1947 AND REPLACED BY A BUS SERVICE TO ALLOW ELECTRIFICATION AND TRANSFER TO LONDON UNDERGROUND. CENTRAL LINE SERVICES COMMENCED IN 1948. FREIGHT SERVICES REMAINED UNTIL 1965 SERVING YARDS AT GRANGE HILL, BARKINGSIDE AND NEWBURY PARK. THE WEST CURVE AT ILFORD WAS REMOVED IN 1947 AND THE PHYSICAL LINK BETWEEN NEWBURY PARK AND SEVEN KINGS WAS DISMANTLED IN 1956.

INSET FROM PAGE 22 – FINSBURY PARK

"NORTHERN HEIGHTS" JUNCTION:

FINSBURY PARK WAS THE SOUTHERN END OF THE "NORTHERN HEIGHTS" BRANCHES TO EDGWARE, HIGH BARNET AND ALEXANDRA PALACE. PASSENGER SERVICES CEASED IN 1939 (EDGWARE AND HIGH BARNET) AND 1954 (ALEXANDRA PALACE) WITH FREIGHT TO EDGWARE REMAINING UNTIL 1964. THE ROUTE FROM HIGHGATE WOOD DEPOT TO FINSBURY PARK REMAINED IN USE UNTIL 1970 FOR NORTHERN LINE STOCK TRANSFER TO DRAYTON PARK, AFTER WHICH TIME THE ROUTE WAS ABANDONED

1948
1903-1947 (1965)   Grange Hill Tunnel

1867-1954 (1970)

1968

1932

CARRIAGE SIDINGS

GOODS (1965)

GRANGE HILL (1948)
GRANGE HILL
Grange Hill for Chigwell Row
(1903-1947)
(On Same Site)

GOODS & COAL (1865-1968)

NORTHBOUND VICTORIA LINE PLATFORM WAS THE ORIGINAL SOUTHBOUND PICCADILLY LINE PLATFORM

FINSBURY PARK
Seven Sisters Road
(1861)

HAINAULT DEPOT (CENTRAL LINE) (1943)

CLEANING SHED

SOUTHBOUND PICCADILLY AND VICTORIA LINE PLATFORMS WERE ORIGINAL GREAT NORTHERN & CITY RAILWAY TERMINAL PLATFORMS

HAINAULT (1948)
HAINAULT (1903-1908, 1930-1947)
(On Same Site)

Finsbury Park Junction -

1948
1903-1947 (1965)

ALIGNMENT OF NORTHERN LINE EXTENSION CONNECTING FORMER GREAT NORTHERN RAILWAY 'NORTHERN HEIGHTS' BRANCHES WITH GREAT NORTHERN & CITY RAILWAY VIA DEDICATED PLATFORMS AT FINSBURY PARK. WORKS ABANDONED POST-WW2 DESPITE BEING LARGELY COMPLETE

14

16

HIGHBURY VALE GOODS (1876-1971)

FAIRLOP (1948)
FAIRLOP (1903-1947)
(On Same Site)

GOODS (1958)

CARRIAGE SIDINGS

EAST GOODS YARD (1875-1960)

1948
1903-1947 (1965)

BARKINGSIDE (1948)
BARKINGSIDE (1903-1947)
(On Same Site)

GOODS (1965)

ARSENAL
Arsenal (For Highbury Hill)
Gillespie Road
(1906)

*CLARENCE YARD GOODS (1875-1960)
FINSBURY PARK DIESEL DEPOT (1960-1981)
(On Same Site)*

VICTORIA LINE USES ORIGINAL ALIGNMENT OF GREAT NORTHERN & CITY RAILWAY, CLOSED NORTH OF DRAYTON PARK IN 1964. BETWEEN THIS TIME AND THE 1975 TRANSFERRAL OF THE ROUTE TO BRITISH RAIL SERVICES TERMINATED AT DRAYTON PARK.

1948
1903-1947 (1965)

NEWBURY PARK SIDINGS

1850

1906

ASHBURTON GROVE GOODS (1876-1960)

GOODS (1965)

NEWBURY PARK (1947)
NEWBURY PARK (1903-1947)
(On Same Site)

1947

1903-1947 (1956)

LINK FROM NEWBURY PARK TO ILFORD / SEVEN KINGS CLOSED TO PASSENGERS IN 1947 AND FREIGHT IN 1956

GRAVEL PIT

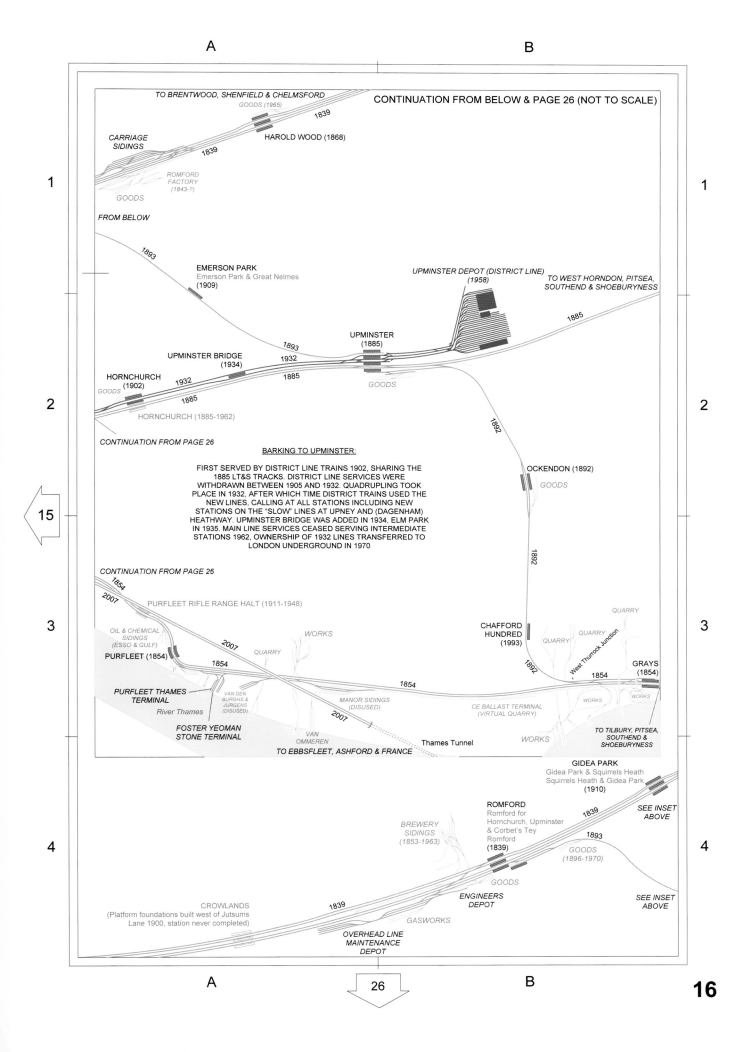

CONTINUATION FROM BELOW & PAGE 26 (NOT TO SCALE)

TO BRENTWOOD, SHENFIELD & CHELMSFORD
GOODS (1965)
1839

CARRIAGE
SIDINGS
1839
HAROLD WOOD (1868)

ROMFORD
FACTORY
(1843-?)
GOODS

FROM BELOW

1893

EMERSON PARK
Emerson Park & Great Nelmes
(1909)

UPMINSTER DEPOT (DISTRICT LINE)
(1958)

TO WEST HORNDON, PITSEA,
SOUTHEND & SHOEBURYNESS

1885

UPMINSTER
(1885)

1893

UPMINSTER BRIDGE
(1934)
1932

1932

HORNCHURCH
(1902)
GOODS

1932

1885
GOODS

1885

HORNCHURCH (1885-1962)

1892

CONTINUATION FROM PAGE 26

OCKENDON (1892)
GOODS

BARKING TO UPMINSTER:

FIRST SERVED BY DISTRICT LINE TRAINS 1902, SHARING THE
1885 LT&S TRACKS. DISTRICT LINE SERVICES WERE
WITHDRAWN BETWEEN 1905 AND 1932. QUADRUPLING TOOK
PLACE IN 1932, AFTER WHICH TIME DISTRICT TRAINS USED THE
NEW LINES, CALLING AT ALL STATIONS INCLUDING NEW
STATIONS ON THE "SLOW" LINES AT UPNEY AND (DAGENHAM)
HEATHWAY. UPMINSTER BRIDGE WAS ADDED IN 1934, ELM PARK
IN 1935. MAIN LINE SERVICES CEASED SERVING INTERMEDIATE
STATIONS 1962, OWNERSHIP OF 1932 LINES TRANSFERRED TO
LONDON UNDERGROUND IN 1970

1892

CONTINUATION FROM PAGE 26

1854
2007

PURFLEET RIFLE RANGE HALT (1911-1948)

QUARRY

OIL & CHEMICAL
SIDINGS
(ESSO & GULF)
PURFLEET (1854)

WORKS

2007

QUARRY

CHAFFORD
HUNDRED
(1993)

QUARRY

QUARRY

West Thurrock Junction

1854

GRAYS
(1854)

1854
QUARRY

1892

1854

PURFLEET THAMES
TERMINAL

River Thames

VAN DEN
BURGHS &
JURGENS
(DISUSED)

MANOR SIDINGS
(DISUSED)

CE BALLAST TERMINAL
(VIRTUAL QUARRY)

WORKS

WORKS

FOSTER YEOMAN
STONE TERMINAL

VAN
OMMEREN

2007

Thames Tunnel

TO TILBURY, PITSEA,
SOUTHEND &
SHOEBURYNESS

WORKS

TO EBBSFLEET, ASHFORD & FRANCE

GIDEA PARK
Gidea Park & Squirrels Heath
Squirrels Heath & Gidea Park
(1910)

ROMFORD
Romford for
Hornchurch, Upminster
& Corbet's Tey
Romford
(1839)

BREWERY
SIDINGS
(1853-1963)

1839

SEE INSET
ABOVE

1893

GOODS
(1896-1970)

SEE INSET
ABOVE

GOODS

ENGINEERS
DEPOT

CROWLANDS
(Platform foundations built west of Jutsums
Lane 1900, station never completed)

1839

GASWORKS

OVERHEAD LINE
MAINTENANCE
DEPOT

15

26

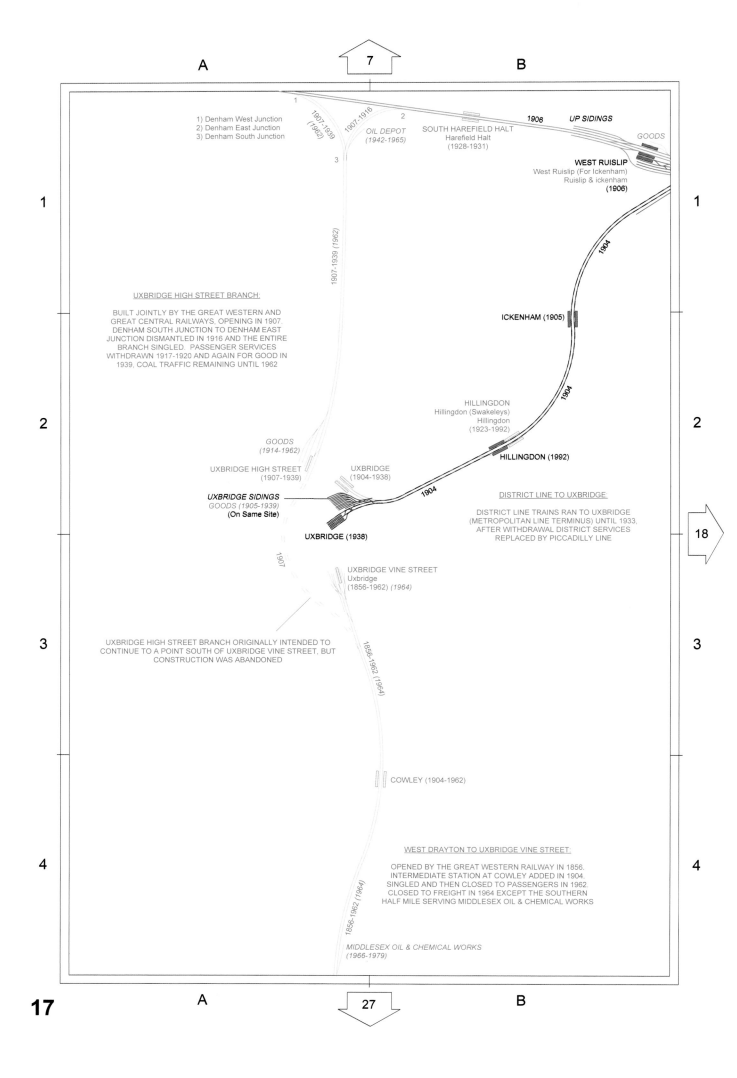

1

1) Denham West Junction
2) Denham East Junction
3) Denham South Junction

1

OIL DEPOT
(1942-1965)

1907-1916

2

1907-1939 (1962)

SOUTH HAREFIELD HALT
Harefield Halt
(1928-1931)

1906   UP SIDINGS

GOODS

WEST RUISLIP
West Ruislip (For Ickenham)
Ruislip & ickenham
(1906)

1904

ICKENHAM (1905)

1

UXBRIDGE HIGH STREET BRANCH:

BUILT JOINTLY BY THE GREAT WESTERN AND
GREAT CENTRAL RAILWAYS, OPENING IN 1907.
DENHAM SOUTH JUNCTION TO DENHAM EAST
JUNCTION DISMANTLED IN 1916 AND THE ENTIRE
BRANCH SINGLED. PASSENGER SERVICES
WITHDRAWN 1917-1920 AND AGAIN FOR GOOD IN
1939, COAL TRAFFIC REMAINING UNTIL 1962

1904

HILLINGDON
Hillingdon (Swakeleys)
Hillingdon
(1923-1992)

HILLINGDON (1992)

GOODS
(1914-1962)

UXBRIDGE HIGH STREET
(1907-1939)

UXBRIDGE
(1904-1938)

1904

DISTRICT LINE TO UXBRIDGE:

DISTRICT LINE TRAINS RAN TO UXBRIDGE
(METROPOLITAN LINE TERMINUS) UNTIL 1933,
AFTER WITHDRAWAL DISTRICT SERVICES
REPLACED BY PICCADILLY LINE

UXBRIDGE SIDINGS
GOODS (1905-1939)
(On Same Site)

UXBRIDGE (1938)

2

18

1907

UXBRIDGE VINE STREET
Uxbridge
(1856-1962) (1964)

UXBRIDGE HIGH STREET BRANCH ORIGINALLY INTENDED TO
CONTINUE TO A POINT SOUTH OF UXBRIDGE VINE STREET, BUT
CONSTRUCTION WAS ABANDONED

3

1856-1962 (1964)

COWLEY (1904-1962)

WEST DRAYTON TO UXBRIDGE VINE STREET:

OPENED BY THE GREAT WESTERN RAILWAY IN 1856.
INTERMEDIATE STATION AT COWLEY ADDED IN 1904.
SINGLED AND THEN CLOSED TO PASSENGERS IN 1962.
CLOSED TO FREIGHT IN 1964 EXCEPT THE SOUTHERN
HALF MILE SERVING MIDDLESEX OIL & CHEMICAL WORKS

4

1856-1962 (1964)

MIDDLESEX OIL & CHEMICAL WORKS
(1966-1979)

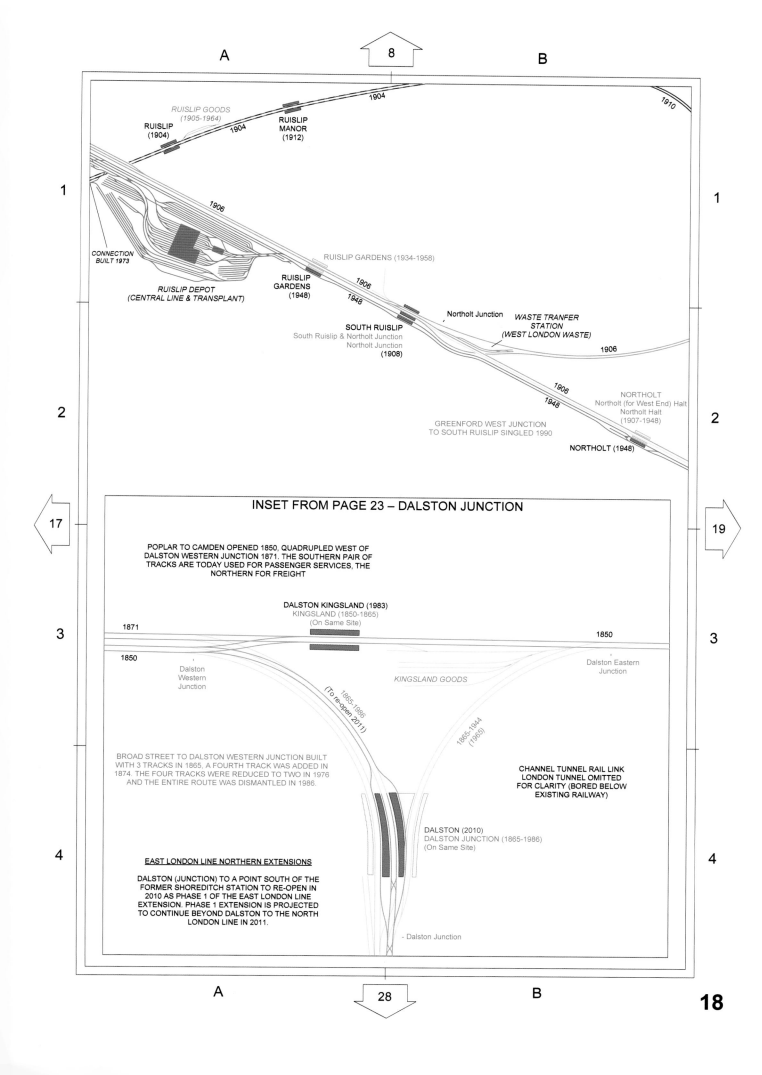

1   1

RUISLIP GOODS
(1905-1964)
RUISLIP
(1904)
1904
RUISLIP
MANOR
(1912)
1904
1910

1906

*CONNECTION
BUILT 1973*

RUISLIP GARDENS (1934-1958)

*RUISLIP DEPOT
(CENTRAL LINE & TRANSPLANT)*

RUISLIP
GARDENS
(1948)
1906
1948

SOUTH RUISLIP
South Ruislip & Northolt Junction
Northolt Junction
(1908)

Northolt Junction

*WASTE TRANFER
STATION
(WEST LONDON WASTE)*

1906

1906
1948

2   2

GREENFORD WEST JUNCTION
TO SOUTH RUISLIP SINGLED 1990

NORTHOLT
Northolt (for West End) Halt
Northolt Halt
(1907-1948)

NORTHOLT (1948)

17   19

INSET FROM PAGE 23 – DALSTON JUNCTION

POPLAR TO CAMDEN OPENED 1850, QUADRUPLED WEST OF
DALSTON WESTERN JUNCTION 1871. THE SOUTHERN PAIR OF
TRACKS ARE TODAY USED FOR PASSENGER SERVICES, THE
NORTHERN FOR FREIGHT

DALSTON KINGSLAND (1983)
KINGSLAND (1850-1865)
(On Same Site)

3   1871   1850   3
         1850

Dalston
Western
Junction

KINGSLAND GOODS

Dalston Eastern
Junction

1865-1986
(To re-open 2011)

1865-1944
(1965)

BROAD STREET TO DALSTON WESTERN JUNCTION BUILT
WITH 3 TRACKS IN 1865, A FOURTH TRACK WAS ADDED IN
1874. THE FOUR TRACKS WERE REDUCED TO TWO IN 1976
AND THE ENTIRE ROUTE WAS DISMANTLED IN 1986.

CHANNEL TUNNEL RAIL LINK
LONDON TUNNEL OMITTED
FOR CLARITY (BORED BELOW
EXISTING RAILWAY)

4   4

DALSTON (2010)
DALSTON JUNCTION (1865-1986)
(On Same Site)

EAST LONDON LINE NORTHERN EXTENSIONS

DALSTON (JUNCTION) TO A POINT SOUTH OF THE
FORMER SHOREDITCH STATION TO RE-OPEN IN
2010 AS PHASE 1 OF THE EAST LONDON LINE
EXTENSION. PHASE 1 EXTENSION IS PROJECTED
TO CONTINUE BEYOND DALSTON TO THE NORTH
LONDON LINE IN 2011.

- Dalston Junction

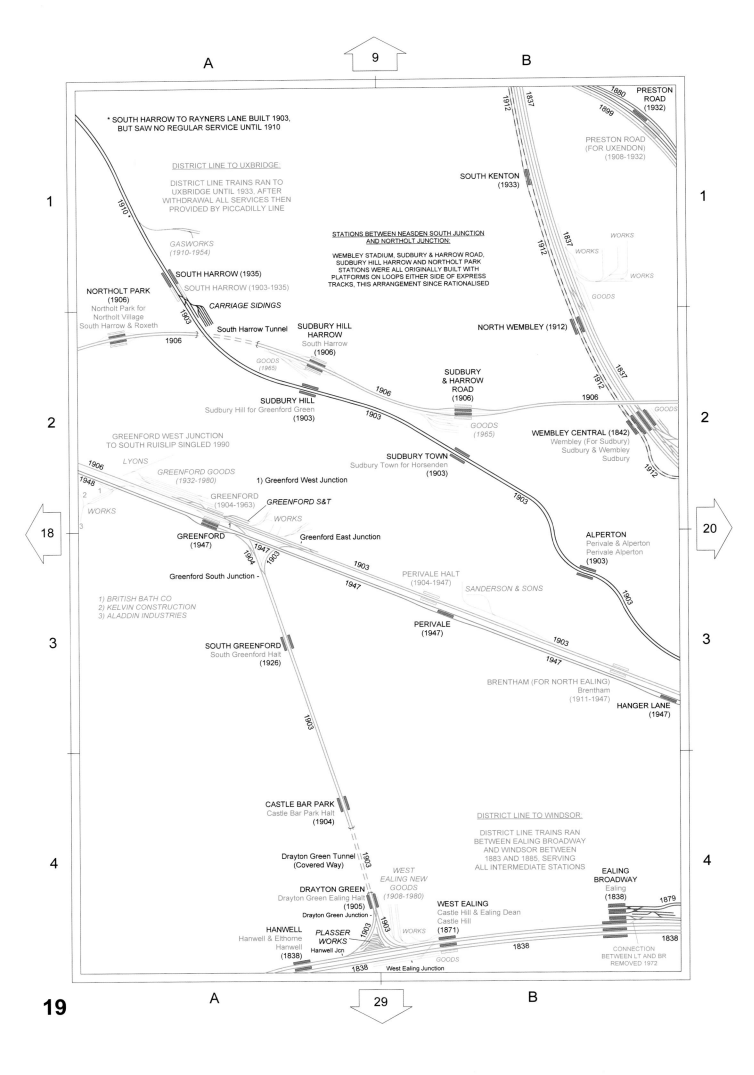

* SOUTH HARROW TO RAYNERS LANE BUILT 1903,
BUT SAW NO REGULAR SERVICE UNTIL 1910

DISTRICT LINE TO UXBRIDGE:

DISTRICT LINE TRAINS RAN TO
UXBRIDGE UNTIL 1933, AFTER
WITHDRAWAL ALL SERVICES THEN
PROVIDED BY PICCADILLY LINE

STATIONS BETWEEN NEASDEN SOUTH JUNCTION
AND NORTHOLT JUNCTION:

WEMBLEY STADIUM, SUDBURY & HARROW ROAD,
SUDBURY HILL HARROW AND NORTHOLT PARK
STATIONS WERE ALL ORIGINALLY BUILT WITH
PLATFORMS ON LOOPS EITHER SIDE OF EXPRESS
TRACKS, THIS ARRANGEMENT SINCE RATIONALISED

PRESTON ROAD (1932)

PRESTON ROAD
(FOR UXENDON)
(1908-1932)

SOUTH KENTON (1933)

WORKS
WORKS
WORKS
GOODS

NORTH WEMBLEY (1912)

SUDBURY & HARROW ROAD (1906)

GASWORKS (1910-1954)

SOUTH HARROW (1935)
SOUTH HARROW (1903-1935)

CARRIAGE SIDINGS

NORTHOLT PARK (1906)
Northolt Park for
Northolt Village
South Harrow & Roxeth

South Harrow Tunnel

SUDBURY HILL HARROW
South Harrow (1906)

GOODS (1965)

SUDBURY HILL
Sudbury Hill for Greenford Green (1903)

WEMBLEY CENTRAL (1842)
Wembley (For Sudbury)
Sudbury & Wembley
Sudbury

GOODS

GOODS (1965)

GREENFORD WEST JUNCTION
TO SOUTH RUISLIP SINGLED 1990

LYONS

GREENFORD GOODS (1932-1980)

SUDBURY TOWN
Sudbury Town for Horsenden (1903)

GREENFORD (1904-1963)

1) Greenford West Junction

GREENFORD S&T

WORKS

GREENFORD (1947)

Greenford East Junction

ALPERTON
Perivale & Alperton
Perivale Alperton (1903)

Greenford South Junction -

1) BRITISH BATH CO
2) KELVIN CONSTRUCTION
3) ALADDIN INDUSTRIES

PERIVALE HALT (1904-1947)

SANDERSON & SONS

SOUTH GREENFORD
South Greenford Halt (1926)

PERIVALE (1947)

BRENTHAM (FOR NORTH EALING)
Brentham (1911-1947)

HANGER LANE (1947)

CASTLE BAR PARK
Castle Bar Park Halt (1904)

DISTRICT LINE TO WINDSOR:

DISTRICT LINE TRAINS RAN
BETWEEN EALING BROADWAY
AND WINDSOR BETWEEN
1883 AND 1885, SERVING
ALL INTERMEDIATE STATIONS

Drayton Green Tunnel
(Covered Way)

WEST EALING NEW GOODS (1908-1980)

EALING BROADWAY
Ealing (1838)

DRAYTON GREEN
Drayton Green Ealing Halt (1905)
Drayton Green Junction -

WEST EALING
Castle Hill & Ealing Dean
Castle Hill (1871)

Drayton Green Junction -

HANWELL
Hanwell & Elthorne
Hanwell (1838)

PLASSER WORKS

Hanwell Jcn

WORKS

GOODS

CONNECTION
BETWEEN LT AND BR
REMOVED 1972

West Ealing Junction

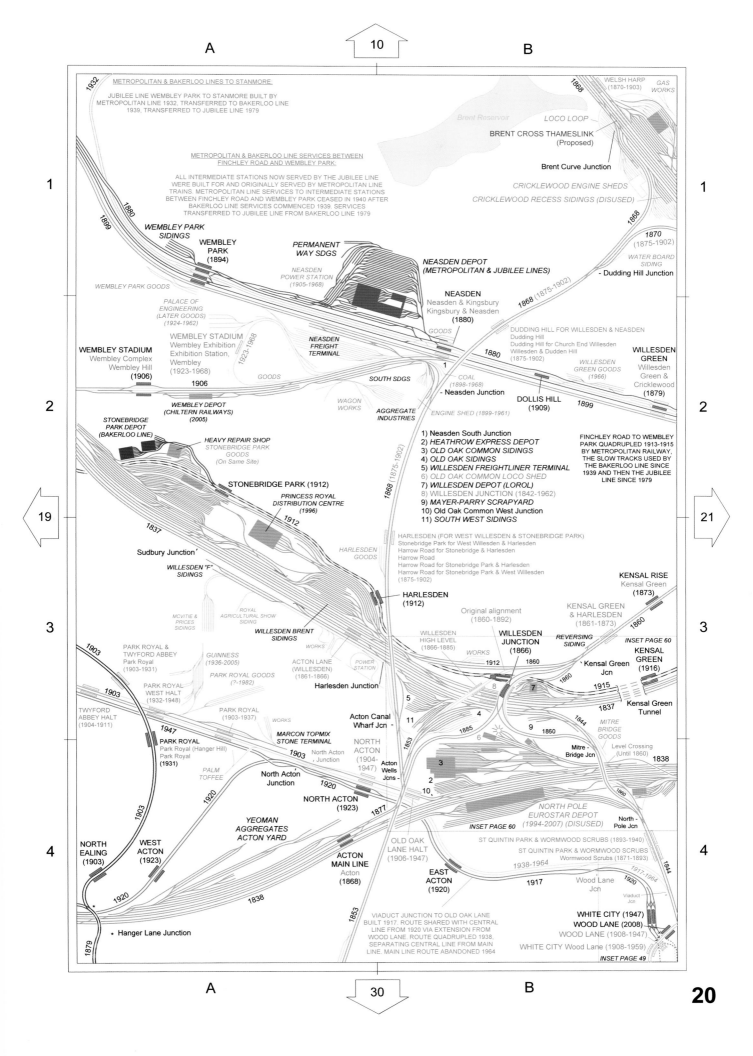

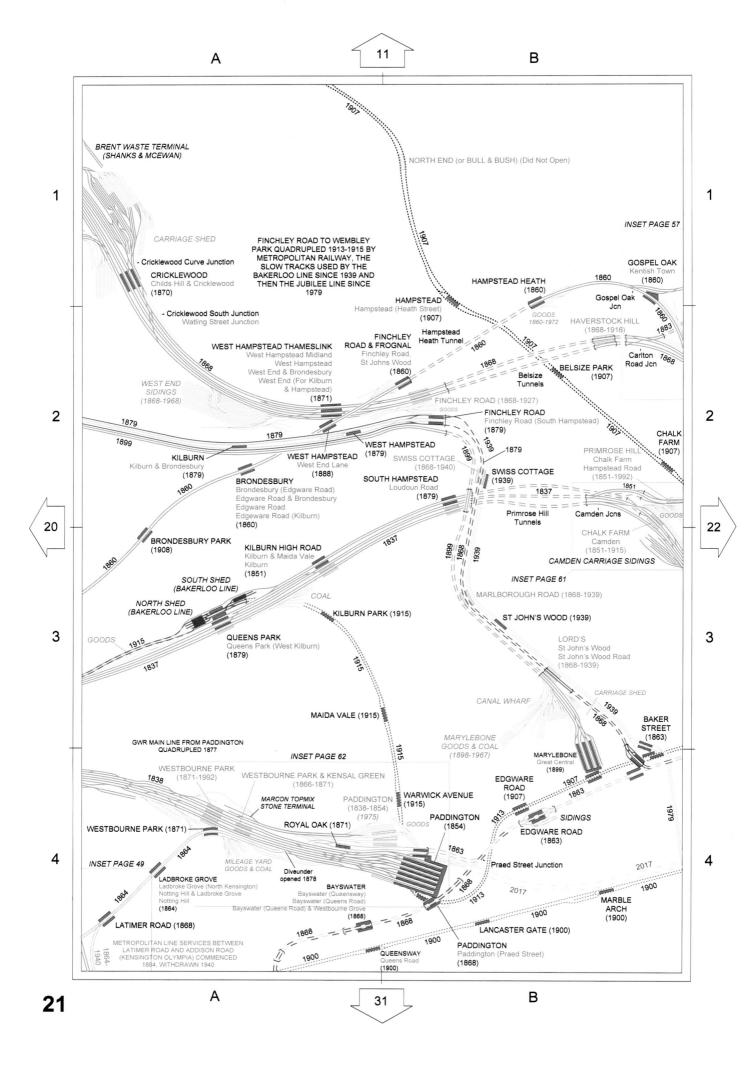

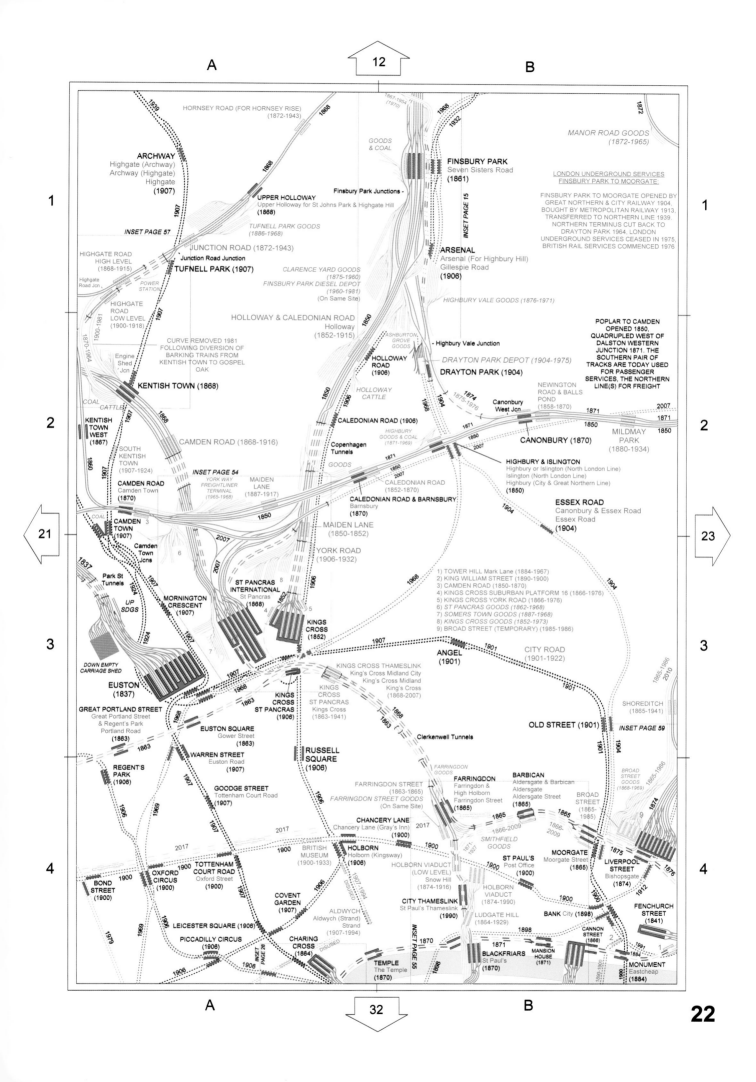

HORNSEY ROAD (FOR HORNSEY RISE)
(1872-1943)

GOODS & COAL

MANOR ROAD GOODS
(1872-1965)

ARCHWAY
Highgate (Archway)
Archway (Highgate)
Highgate
(1907)

FINSBURY PARK
Seven Sisters Road
(1861)

UPPER HOLLOWAY
Upper Holloway for St Johns Park & Highgate Hill
(1868)

Finsbury Park Junctions -

INSET PAGE 57

TUFNELL PARK GOODS
(1886-1968)

ARSENAL
Arsenal (For Highbury Hill)
Gillespie Road
(1906)

LONDON UNDERGROUND SERVICES
FINSBURY PARK TO MOORGATE:

FINSBURY PARK TO MOORGATE OPENED BY
GREAT NORTHERN & CITY RAILWAY 1904,
BOUGHT BY METROPOLITAN RAILWAY 1913,
TRANSFERRED TO NORTHERN LINE 1939.
NORTHERN TERMINUS CUT BACK TO
DRAYTON PARK 1964, LONDON
UNDERGROUND SERVICES CEASED IN 1975,
BRITISH RAIL SERVICES COMMENCED 1976

JUNCTION ROAD (1872-1943)

HIGHGATE ROAD
HIGH LEVEL
(1868-1915)

Junction Road Junction

TUFNELL PARK (1907)

Highgate
Road Jcn

POWER
STATION

CLARENCE YARD GOODS
(1875-1960)
FINSBURY PARK DIESEL DEPOT
(1960-1981)
(On Same Site)

HIGHBURY VALE GOODS (1876-1971)

POPLAR TO CAMDEN
OPENED 1850,
QUADRUPLED WEST OF
DALSTON WESTERN
JUNCTION 1871. THE
SOUTHERN PAIR OF
TRACKS ARE TODAY USED
FOR PASSENGER
SERVICES, THE NORTHERN
LINE(S) FOR FREIGHT

HIGHGATE
ROAD
LOW LEVEL
(1900-1918)

HOLLOWAY & CALEDONIAN ROAD
Holloway
(1852-1915)

ASHBURTON
GROVE
GOODS

- Highbury Vale Junction

DRAYTON PARK DEPOT (1904-1975)

NEWINGTON
ROAD & BALLS
POND
(1858-1870)

CURVE REMOVED 1981
FOLLOWING DIVERSION OF
BARKING TRAINS FROM
KENTISH TOWN TO GOSPEL
OAK

Engine
Shed
Jcn

HOLLOWAY
ROAD
(1906)

DRAYTON PARK (1904)

Canonbury
West Jcn

2007

1871
1850

MILDMAY
PARK
(1880-1934)

KENTISH TOWN (1868)

COAL CATTLE

HOLLOWAY
CATTLE

CALEDONIAN ROAD (1906)

CANONBURY (1870)

KENTISH
TOWN
WEST
(1867)

SOUTH
KENTISH
TOWN
(1907-1924)

CAMDEN ROAD (1868-1916)

HIGHBURY
GOODS & COAL
(1871-1969)

GOODS

HIGHBURY & ISLINGTON
Highbury or Islington (North London Line)
Islington (North London Line)
Highbury (City & Great Northern Line)
(1850)

CAMDEN ROAD
Camden Town
(1870)

INSET PAGE 54

YORK WAY
FREIGHTLINER
TERMINAL
(1965-1968)

MAIDEN
LANE
(1887-1917)

CALEDONIAN ROAD
(1852-1870)

CALEDONIAN ROAD & BARNSBURY
Barnsbury
(1870)

ESSEX ROAD
Canonbury & Essex Road
Essex Road
(1904)

COAL

CAMDEN
TOWN
(1907)

Copenhagen
Tunnels

MAIDEN LANE
(1850-1852)

Camden
Town
Jcns

YORK ROAD
(1906-1932)

1) TOWER HILL Mark Lane (1884-1967)
2) KING WILLIAM STREET (1890-1900)
3) CAMDEN ROAD (1850-1870)
4) KINGS CROSS SUBURBAN PLATFORM 16 (1866-1976)
5) KINGS CROSS YORK ROAD (1866-1976)
6) ST PANCRAS GOODS (1862-1968)
7) SOMERS TOWN GOODS (1887-1968)
8) KINGS CROSS GOODS (1852-1973)
9) BROAD STREET (TEMPORARY) (1985-1986)

Park St
Tunnels

UP
SDGS

MORNINGTON
CRESCENT
(1907)

ST PANCRAS
INTERNATIONAL
St Pancras
(1868)

KINGS
CROSS
(1852)

ANGEL
(1901)

CITY ROAD
(1901-1922)

SHOREDITCH
(1865-1941)

DOWN EMPTY
CARRIAGE SHED

EUSTON
(1837)

KINGS
CROSS
THAMESLINK
King's Cross Midland City
King's Cross Midland
King's Cross
(1868-2007)

OLD STREET (1901)

INSET PAGE 59

GREAT PORTLAND STREET
Great Portland Street
& Regent's Park
Portland Road
(1863)

KINGS
CROSS
ST PANCRAS
(1906)

KINGS
CROSS
ST PANCRAS
Kings Cross
(1863-1941)

BROAD
STREET
GOODS
(1868-1969)

EUSTON SQUARE
Gower Street
(1863)

Clerkenwell Tunnels

WARREN STREET
Euston Road
(1907)

RUSSELL
SQUARE
(1906)

FARRINGDON
GOODS

BARBICAN
Aldersgate & Barbican
Aldersgate
Aldersgate Street
(1865)

BROAD
STREET
(1865-1985)

REGENT'S
PARK
(1906)

GOODGE STREET
Tottenham Court Road
(1907)

FARRINGDON STREET
(1863-1865)
FARRINGDON STREET GOODS
(On Same Site)

FARRINGDON
Farringdon &
High Holborn
Farringdon Street
(1865)

CHANCERY LANE
Chancery Lane (Gray's Inn)
(1900)

SMITHFIELD
GOODS

MOORGATE
Moorgate Street
(1865)

LIVERPOOL
STREET
Bishopsgate
(1874)

BOND
STREET
(1900)

OXFORD
CIRCUS
(1900)

TOTTENHAM
COURT ROAD
Oxford Street
(1900)

BRITISH
MUSEUM
(1900-1933)

HOLBORN
Holborn (Kingsway)
(1906)

HOLBORN VIADUCT
(LOW LEVEL)
Snow Hill
(1874-1916)

ST PAUL'S
Post Office
(1900)

HOLBORN
VIADUCT
(1874-1990)

BANK City (1898)

FENCHURCH
STREET
(1841)

COVENT
GARDEN
(1907)

CITY THAMESLINK
St Paul's Thameslink
(1990)

LUDGATE HILL
(1864-1929)

CANNON
STREET
(1866)

LEICESTER SQUARE (1906)

ALDWYCH
Aldwych (Strand)
Strand
(1907-1994)

BLACKFRIARS
St Paul's
(1870)

MANSION
HOUSE
(1871)

MONUMENT
Eastcheap
(1884)

PICCADILLY CIRCUS
(1906)

CHARING
CROSS
(1864)

TEMPLE
The Temple
(1870)

INSET PAGE 55

DISUSED

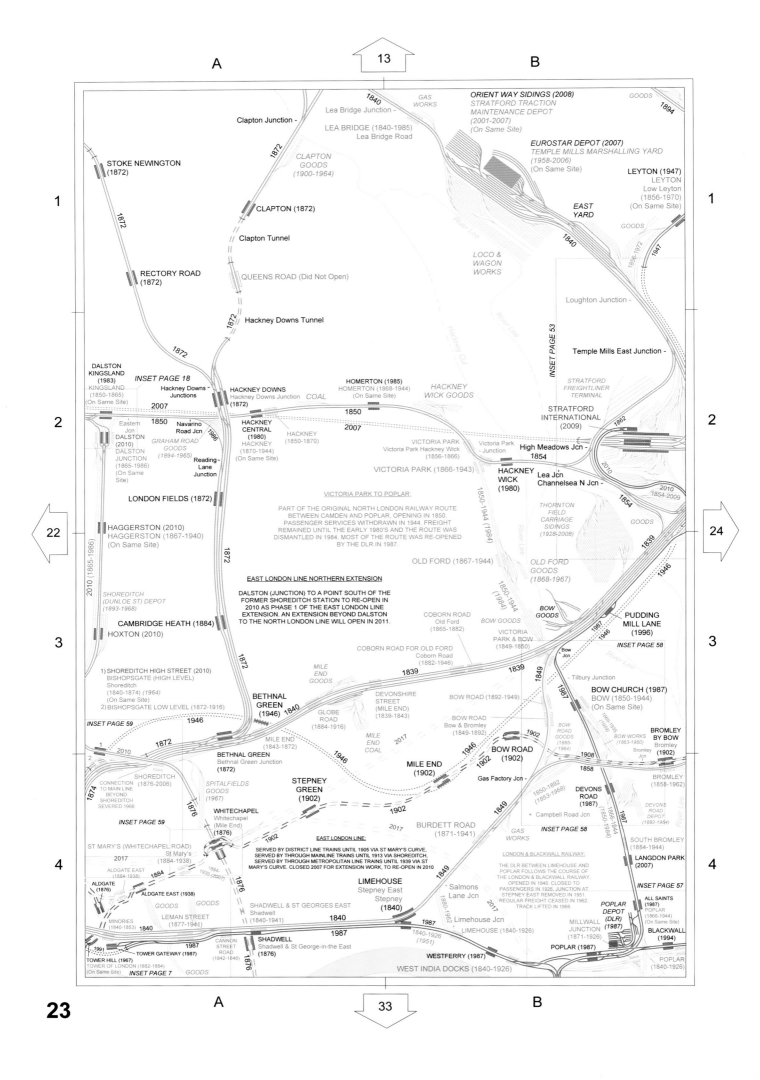

1

STOKE NEWINGTON
(1872)

Clapton Junction -

Lea Bridge Jcn
1840

LEA BRIDGE (1840-1985)
Lea Bridge Road

GAS
WORKS

ORIENT WAY SIDINGS (2008)
STRATFORD TRACTION
MAINTENANCE DEPOT
(2001-2007)
(On Same Site)

GOODS
1894

EUROSTAR DEPOT (2007)
TEMPLE MILLS MARSHALLING YARD
(1958-2006)
(On Same Site)

1872

CLAPTON
GOODS
(1900-1964)

LEYTON (1947)
LEYTON
Low Leyton
(1856-1970)
(On Same Site)

CLAPTON (1872)

EAST
YARD

1

1840

Clapton Tunnel

QUEENS ROAD (Did Not Open)

RECTORY ROAD
(1872)

LOCO &
WAGON
WORKS

GOODS

1872

1856-1972

1947

Loughton Junction -

1872

Hackney Downs Tunnel

INSET PAGE 53

Temple Mills East Junction -

1872

DALSTON
KINGSLAND
(1983)
KINGSLAND
(1850-1865)
(On Same Site)

INSET PAGE 18

Hackney Downs
Junctions
2007

HACKNEY DOWNS
Hackney Downs Junction
(1872)

COAL

HOMERTON (1985)
HOMERTON (1868-1944)
(On Same Site)

HACKNEY
WICK GOODS

STRATFORD
FREIGHTLINER
TERMINAL

STRATFORD
INTERNATIONAL
(2009)

1862

2

Eastern
Jcn
DALSTON
(2010)
DALSTON
JUNCTION
(1865-1986)
(On Same Site)

1850

1886

Navarino
Road Jcn

Reading -
Lane
Junction

GRAHAM ROAD
GOODS
(1894-1965)

HACKNEY
CENTRAL
(1980)
HACKNEY
(1870-1944)
(On Same Site)

1850

HACKNEY
(1850-1870)

2007

VICTORIA PARK
Victoria Park Hackney Wick
(1856-1866)

VICTORIA PARK (1866-1943)

Victoria Park
- Junction

HACKNEY
WICK
(1980)

High Meadows Jcn -
1854

Lea Jcn
Channelsea N Jcn -

2

1854

2010
1854-2009

THORNTON
FIELD
CARRIAGE
SIDINGS
(1928-2008)

GOODS

1839

LONDON FIELDS (1872)

VICTORIA PARK TO POPLAR:

PART OF THE ORIGINAL NORTH LONDON RAILWAY ROUTE
BETWEEN CAMDEN AND POPLAR, OPENING IN 1850.
PASSENGER SERVICES WITHDRAWN IN 1944. FREIGHT
REMAINED UNTIL THE EARLY 1980'S AND THE ROUTE WAS
DISMANTLED IN 1984. MOST OF THE ROUTE WAS RE-OPENED
BY THE DLR IN 1987.

1850-1944 (1984)

OLD FORD (1867-1944)

OLD FORD
GOODS
(1868-1967)

1946

22

HAGGERSTON (2010)
HAGGERSTON (1867-1940)
(On Same Site)

2010 (1865-1986)

SHOREDITCH
(DUNLOE ST) DEPOT
(1893-1968)

EAST LONDON LINE NORTHERN EXTENSION

DALSTON (JUNCTION) TO A POINT SOUTH OF THE
FORMER SHOREDITCH STATION TO RE-OPEN IN
2010 AS PHASE 1 OF THE EAST LONDON LINE
EXTENSION. AN EXTENSION BEYOND DALSTON
TO THE NORTH LONDON LINE WILL OPEN IN 2011.

1850-1944 (1984)

BOW
GOODS

VICTORIA
PARK & BOW
(1849-1850)

COBORN ROAD
Old Ford
(1865-1882)

BOW GOODS

1839

1987

1946

PUDDING
MILL LANE
(1996)

INSET PAGE 58

24

3

CAMBRIDGE HEATH (1884)
HOXTON (2010)

1872

1) SHOREDITCH HIGH STREET (2010)
BISHOPSGATE (HIGH LEVEL)
Shoreditch
(1840-1874) (1964)
(On Same Site)
2) BISHOPSGATE LOW LEVEL (1872-1916)

MILE
END
GOODS

COBORN ROAD FOR OLD FORD
Coborn Road
(1882-1946)

1839

1839

1849

Bow
Jcn

1987

Tilbury Junction -

BOW CHURCH (1987)
BOW (1850-1944)
(On Same Site)

3

INSET PAGE 59

1946

DEVONSHIRE
STREET
(MILE END)
(1839-1843)

BOW ROAD (1892-1949)

1988-1935
(1949)

BOW
ROAD
GOODS
(1885-
1964)

BOW WORKS
(1863-1960)

BROMLEY
BY BOW
Bromley
(1902)

BETHNAL
GREEN
(1946)

1840

GLOBE
ROAD
(1884-1916)

MILE END
(1843-1872)

MILE
END
COAL

2017

BOW ROAD
Bow & Bromley
(1849-1892)

1946

1902

BOW ROAD
(1902)

1902

1908

Bromley
Jcn

1858

BROMLEY
(1858-1962)

1872

BETHNAL GREEN
Bethnal Green Junction
(1872)

STEPNEY
GREEN
(1902)

MILE END
(1902)

Gas Factory Jcn -

DEVONS
ROAD
(1987)

1850-1892
(1853-1968)

DEVONS
ROAD
DEPOT
(1882-1964)

1

2

2010

1872

SHOREDITCH
(1876-2006)

SPITALFIELDS
GOODS
(1967)

WHITECHAPEL
Whitechapel
(Mile End)
(1876)

1876

1902

1902

2017

BURDETT ROAD
(1871-1941)

1849

1987

SOUTH BROMLEY
(1884-1944)

LANGDON PARK
(2007)

4

1874

CONNECTION
TO MAIN LINE
BEYOND
SHOREDITCH
SEVERED 1966

INSET PAGE 59

ST MARY'S (WHITECHAPEL ROAD)
St Mary's
(1884-1938)

2017

1884

ALDGATE EAST
(1884-1938)

ALDGATE
(1876)

1876

1884-
1939 (2007)

ALDGATE EAST (1938)

EAST LONDON LINE:

SERVED BY DISTRICT LINE TRAINS UNTIL 1905 VIA ST MARY'S CURVE,
SERVED BY THROUGH MAINLINE TRAINS UNTIL 1913 VIA SHOREDITCH,
SERVED BY THROUGH METROPOLITAN LINE TRAINS UNTIL 1939 VIA ST
MARY'S CURVE. CLOSED 2007 FOR EXTENSION WORK, TO RE-OPEN IN 2010.

1849

GAS
WORKS

LONDON & BLACKWALL RAILWAY:

THE DLR BETWEEN LIMEHOUSE AND
POPLAR FOLLOWS THE COURSE OF
THE LONDON & BLACKWALL RAILWAY,
OPENED IN 1840. CLOSED TO
PASSENGERS IN 1926. JUNCTION AT
STEPNEY EAST REMOVED IN 1951.
REGULAR FREIGHT CEASED IN 1962.
TRACK LIFTED IN 1966.

INSET PAGE 58

INSET PAGE 57

ALL SAINTS
(1987)
POPLAR
(1866-1944)
(On Same Site)

4

GOODS

GOODS

LEMAN STREET
(1877-1944)

MINORIES
(1840-1853)

1840

1884

CANNON
STREET
ROAD
(1842-1848)

SHADWELL & ST GEORGES EAST
Shadwell
(1840-1941)

LIMEHOUSE
Stepney East
Stepney
(1840)

Salmons
Lane Jcn

1840

POPLAR
DEPOT
(DLR)
(1987)

MILLWALL
JUNCTION
(1987)

BLACKWALL
(1994)

1991

1840

TOWER GATEWAY (1987)

1987

SHADWELL
Shadwell & St George-in-the-East
(1876)

1840

1987

1840-1962

1987

LIMEHOUSE (1840-1926)

1840-1926
(1951)

POPLAR (1987)

POPLAR
(1840-1926)

TOWER HILL (1967)
TOWER OF LONDON (1882-1884)
(On Same Site)

INSET PAGE 7

GOODS

1876

Limehouse Jcn

WESTFERRY (1987)

WEST INDIA DOCKS (1840-1926)

23

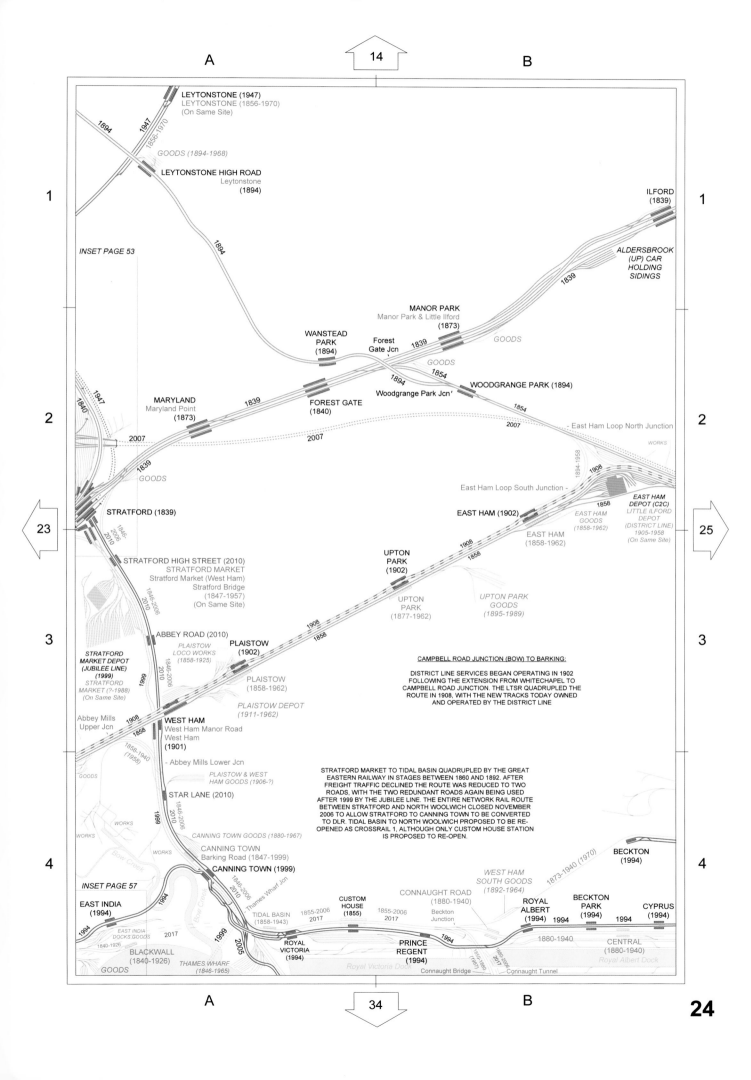

LEYTONSTONE (1947)
LEYTONSTONE (1856-1970)
(On Same Site)

1894

1947

1856-1970

GOODS (1894-1968)

LEYTONSTONE HIGH ROAD
Leytonstone
(1894)

1894

ILFORD
(1839)

1

ALDERSBROOK
(UP) CAR
HOLDING
SIDINGS

INSET PAGE 53

1894

1839

MANOR PARK
Manor Park & Little Ilford
(1873)

WANSTEAD
PARK
(1894)

Forest
Gate Jcn

1839

GOODS

1947

1840

GOODS
1854

WOODGRANGE PARK (1894)

MARYLAND
Maryland Point
(1873)

1839

FOREST GATE
(1840)

1894

Woodgrange Park Jcn'

1854

2

2007

2007

- East Ham Loop North Junction

WORKS

2007

1839

GOODS

1894-1958

1908

East Ham Loop South Junction -

1858

EAST HAM
DEPOT (C2C)
LITTLE ILFORD
DEPOT
(DISTRICT LINE)
1905-1958
(On Same Site)

STRATFORD (1839)

1846-
2006
2010

EAST HAM (1902)

EAST HAM
GOODS
(1858-1962)

23

UPTON
PARK
(1902)

1908

EAST HAM
(1858-1962)

25

STRATFORD HIGH STREET (2010)
STRATFORD MARKET
Stratford Market (West Ham)
Stratford Bridge
(1847-1957)
(On Same Site)

1846-2006
2010

1908

1858

UPTON
PARK
(1877-1962)

UPTON PARK
GOODS
(1895-1989)

ABBEY ROAD (2010)

PLAISTOW
(1902)

1908

1858

STRATFORD
MARKET DEPOT
(JUBILEE LINE)
(1999)
STRATFORD
MARKET (?-1988)
(On Same Site)

PLAISTOW LOCO WORKS
(1858-1925)

1846-2006
2010

1999

PLAISTOW
(1858-1962)

PLAISTOW DEPOT
(1911-1962)

3

CAMPBELL ROAD JUNCTION (BOW) TO BARKING:

DISTRICT LINE SERVICES BEGAN OPERATING IN 1902
FOLLOWING THE EXTENSION FROM WHITECHAPEL TO
CAMPBELL ROAD JUNCTION. THE LTSR QUADRUPLED THE
ROUTE IN 1908, WITH THE NEW TRACKS TODAY OWNED
AND OPERATED BY THE DISTRICT LINE

Abbey Mills
Upper Jcn

1908

1858

WEST HAM
West Ham Manor Road
West Ham
(1901)

1858-1940
(1958)

- Abbey Mills Lower Jcn

PLAISTOW & WEST
HAM GOODS (1906-?)

GOODS

STAR LANE (2010)

1858-2006
2010

STRATFORD MARKET TO TIDAL BASIN QUADRUPLED BY THE GREAT
EASTERN RAILWAY IN STAGES BETWEEN 1860 AND 1892. AFTER
FREIGHT TRAFFIC DECLINED THE ROUTE WAS REDUCED TO TWO
ROADS, WITH THE TWO REDUNDANT ROADS AGAIN BEING USED
AFTER 1999 BY THE JUBILEE LINE. THE ENTIRE NETWORK RAIL ROUTE
BETWEEN STRATFORD AND NORTH WOOLWICH CLOSED NOVEMBER
2006 TO ALLOW STRATFORD TO CANNING TOWN TO BE CONVERTED
TO DLR. TIDAL BASIN TO NORTH WOOLWICH PROPOSED TO BE RE-
OPENED AS CROSSRAIL 1, ALTHOUGH ONLY CUSTOM HOUSE STATION
IS PROPOSED TO RE-OPEN.

WORKS

WORKS

1999

CANNING TOWN GOODS (1880-1967)

CANNING TOWN
Barking Road (1847-1999)

CANNING TOWN (1999)

BECKTON
(1994)

4

INSET PAGE 57

Bow Creek

1846-2006
2010

Thames Wharf Jcn

1873-1940 (1970)

WEST HAM
SOUTH GOODS
(1892-1964)

EAST INDIA
(1994)

1994

Bow Creek

CONNAUGHT ROAD
(1880-1940)

Beckton
Junction

ROYAL
ALBERT
(1994)

BECKTON
PARK
(1994)

CYPRUS
(1994)

1994
EAST INDIA
DOCKS GOODS

2017

1999

2005

TIDAL BASIN
(1858-1943)

1855-2006
2017

CUSTOM
HOUSE
(1855)

1855-2006
2017

1994

1994

CENTRAL
(1880-1940)

1840-1926

BLACKWALL
(1840-1926)

GOODS

THAMES WHARF
(1846-1965)

ROYAL
VICTORIA
(1994)

PRINCE
REGENT
(1994)

Royal Victoria Dock

Connaught Bridge

Connaught Tunnel

1880-1940

1855-1860
(1861)

1880-2006
2017

Royal Albert Dock

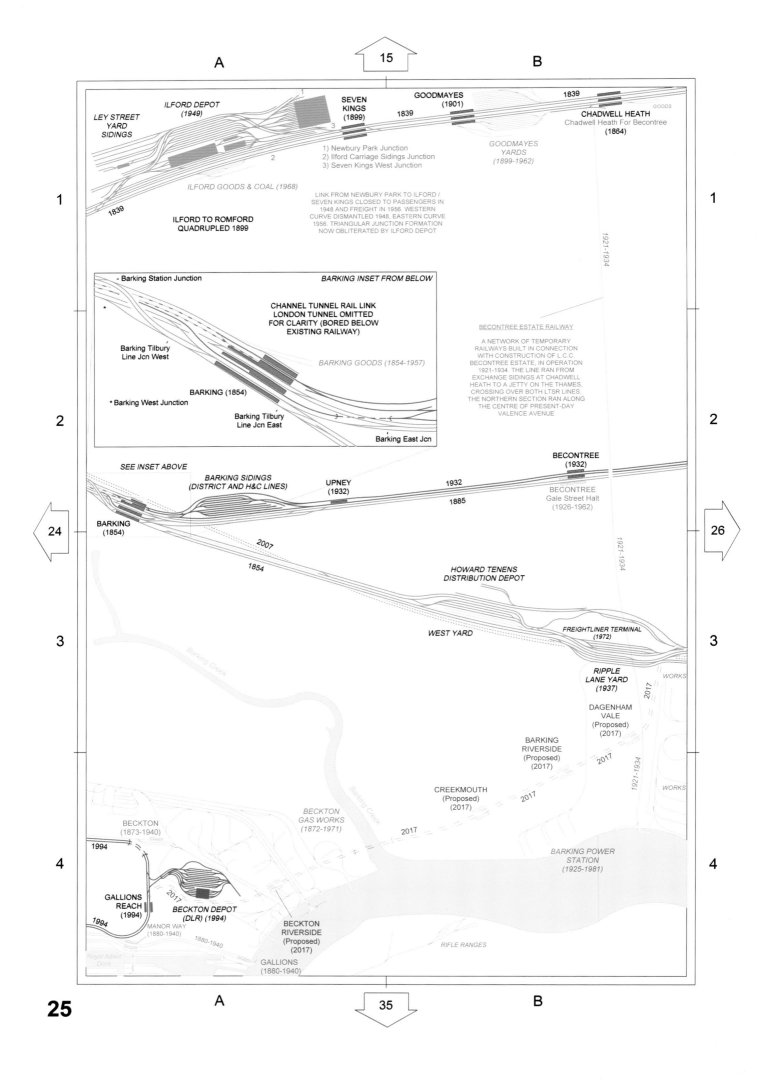

LEY STREET
YARD
SIDINGS

ILFORD DEPOT
(1949)

SEVEN
KINGS
(1899)

GOODMAYES
(1901)

1839

1839

CHADWELL HEATH
Chadwell Heath For Becontree
(1864)

GOODS

1) Newbury Park Junction
2) Ilford Carriage Sidings Junction
3) Seven Kings West Junction

GOODMAYES
YARDS
(1899-1962)

ILFORD GOODS & COAL (1968)

1839

ILFORD TO ROMFORD
QUADRUPLED 1899

LINK FROM NEWBURY PARK TO ILFORD /
SEVEN KINGS CLOSED TO PASSENGERS IN
1948 AND FREIGHT IN 1956. WESTERN
CURVE DISMANTLED 1948, EASTERN CURVE
1956. TRIANGULAR JUNCTION FORMATION
NOW OBLITERATED BY ILFORD DEPOT

1921-1934

- Barking Station Junction

BARKING INSET FROM BELOW

CHANNEL TUNNEL RAIL LINK
LONDON TUNNEL OMITTED
FOR CLARITY (BORED BELOW
EXISTING RAILWAY)

Barking Tilbury
Line Jcn West

BARKING GOODS (1854-1957)

BARKING (1854)

* Barking West Junction

Barking Tilbury
Line Jcn East

Barking East Jcn

BECONTREE ESTATE RAILWAY

A NETWORK OF TEMPORARY
RAILWAYS BUILT IN CONNECTION
WITH CONSTRUCTION OF L.C.C.
BECONTREE ESTATE, IN OPERATION
1921-1934. THE LINE RAN FROM
EXCHANGE SIDINGS AT CHADWELL
HEATH TO A JETTY ON THE THAMES,
CROSSING OVER BOTH LTSR LINES.
THE NORTHERN SECTION RAN ALONG
THE CENTRE OF PRESENT-DAY
VALENCE AVENUE

BECONTREE
(1932)

SEE INSET ABOVE

BARKING SIDINGS
(DISTRICT AND H&C LINES)

UPNEY
(1932)

1932

1885

BECONTREE
Gale Street Halt
(1926-1962)

BARKING
(1854)

2007

1854

HOWARD TENENS
DISTRIBUTION DEPOT

1921-1934

WEST YARD

FREIGHTLINER TERMINAL
(1972)

RIPPLE
LANE YARD
(1937)

WORKS

2017

DAGENHAM
VALE
(Proposed)
(2017)

BARKING
RIVERSIDE
(Proposed)
(2017)

2017

1921-1934

WORKS

CREEKMOUTH
(Proposed)
(2017)

2017

Barking Creek

BECKTON
GAS WORKS
(1872-1971)

2017

BARKING POWER
STATION
(1925-1981)

BECKTON
(1873-1940)

1994

GALLIONS
REACH
(1994)

2017

BECKTON DEPOT
(DLR) (1994)

1994

MANOR WAY
(1880-1940)

1880-1940

BECKTON
RIVERSIDE
(Proposed)
(2017)

GALLIONS
(1880-1940)

RIFLE RANGES

Royal Albert
Dock

Barking Creek

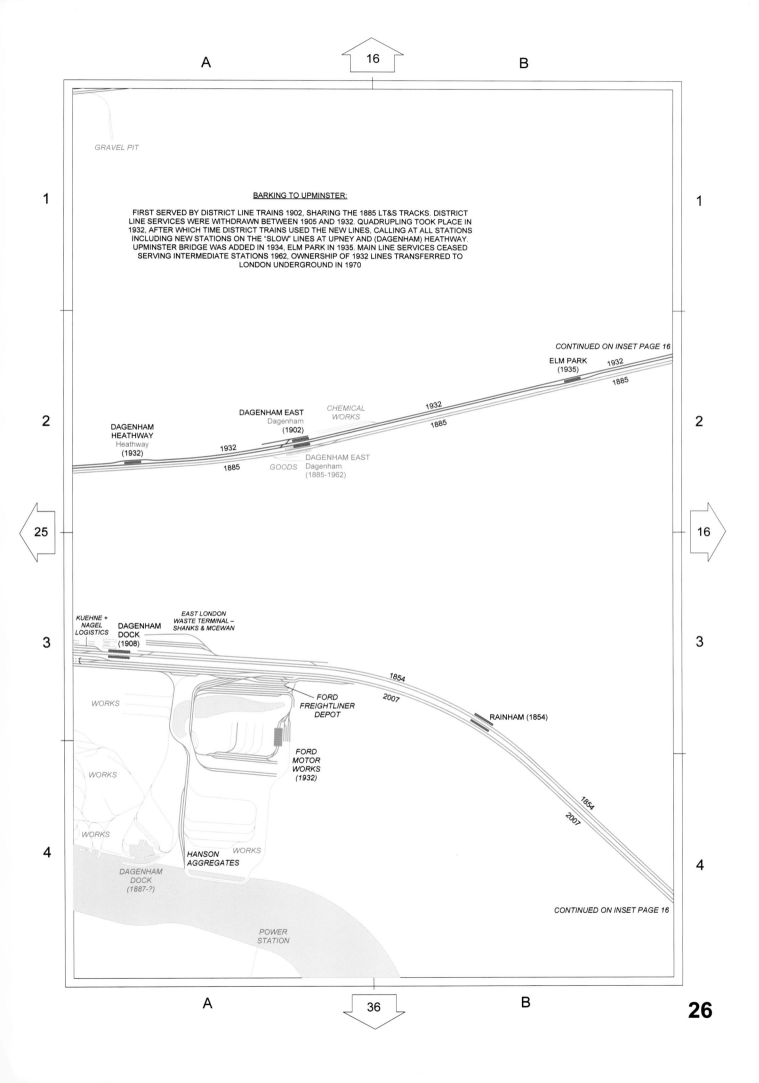

GRAVEL PIT

BARKING TO UPMINSTER:

FIRST SERVED BY DISTRICT LINE TRAINS 1902, SHARING THE 1885 LT&S TRACKS. DISTRICT LINE SERVICES WERE WITHDRAWN BETWEEN 1905 AND 1932. QUADRUPLING TOOK PLACE IN 1932, AFTER WHICH TIME DISTRICT TRAINS USED THE NEW LINES, CALLING AT ALL STATIONS INCLUDING NEW STATIONS ON THE "SLOW" LINES AT UPNEY AND (DAGENHAM) HEATHWAY. UPMINSTER BRIDGE WAS ADDED IN 1934, ELM PARK IN 1935. MAIN LINE SERVICES CEASED SERVING INTERMEDIATE STATIONS 1962, OWNERSHIP OF 1932 LINES TRANSFERRED TO LONDON UNDERGROUND IN 1970

CONTINUED ON INSET PAGE 16

ELM PARK
(1935)

1932

1885

CHEMICAL
WORKS

DAGENHAM EAST
Dagenham
(1902)

1932

1885

DAGENHAM
HEATHWAY
Heathway
(1932)

1932

1885

DAGENHAM EAST
Dagenham
(1885-1962)

GOODS

KUEHNE +
NAGEL
LOGISTICS

EAST LONDON
WASTE TERMINAL –
SHANKS & MCEWAN

DAGENHAM
DOCK
(1908)

1854

2007

FORD
FREIGHTLINER
DEPOT

RAINHAM (1854)

WORKS

WORKS

FORD
MOTOR
WORKS
(1932)

1854

2007

WORKS

WORKS

HANSON
AGGREGATES

DAGENHAM
DOCK
(1887-?)

CONTINUED ON INSET PAGE 16

POWER
STATION

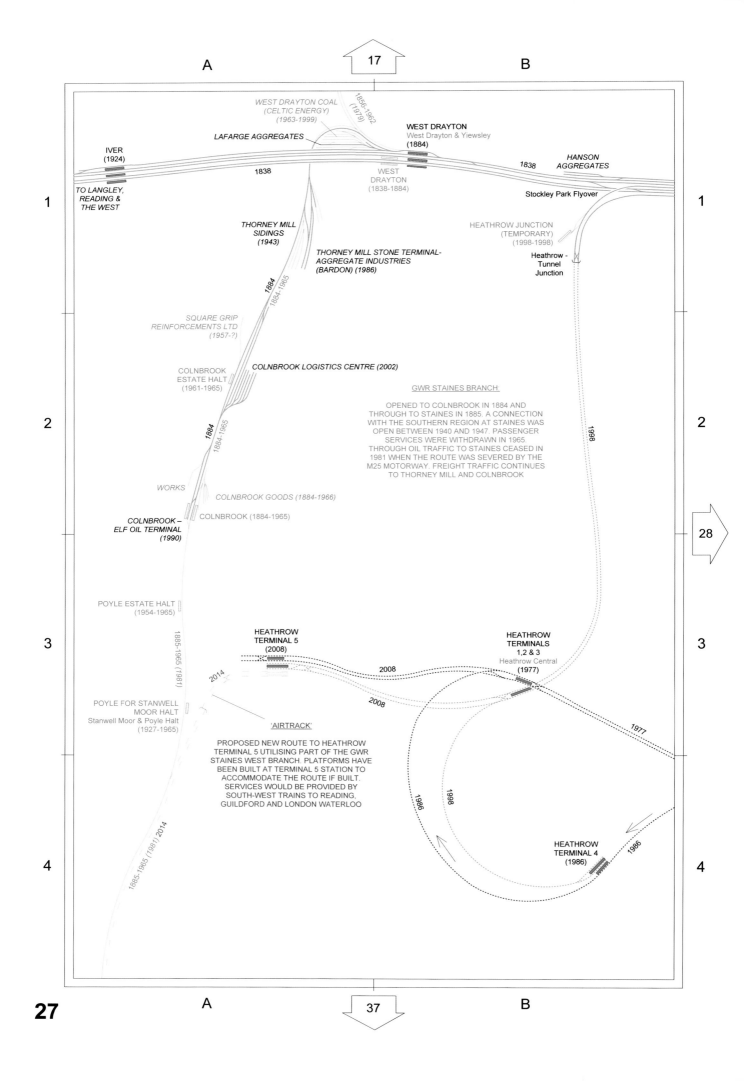

WEST DRAYTON COAL
(CELTIC ENERGY)
(1963-1999)

LAFARGE AGGREGATES

1856-1962
(1979)

WEST DRAYTON
West Drayton & Yiewsley
(1884)

HANSON
AGGREGATES

IVER
(1924)

1838

WEST
DRAYTON
(1838-1884)

1838

Stockley Park Flyover

TO LANGLEY,
READING &
THE WEST

HEATHROW JUNCTION
(TEMPORARY)
(1998-1998)

Heathrow -
Tunnel
Junction

THORNEY MILL
SIDINGS
(1943)

THORNEY MILL STONE TERMINAL-
AGGREGATE INDUSTRIES
(BARDON) (1986)

1884
1884-1965

SQUARE GRIP
REINFORCEMENTS LTD
(1957-?)

COLNBROOK
ESTATE HALT
(1961-1965)

COLNBROOK LOGISTICS CENTRE (2002)

GWR STAINES BRANCH:

OPENED TO COLNBROOK IN 1884 AND
THROUGH TO STAINES IN 1885. A CONNECTION
WITH THE SOUTHERN REGION AT STAINES WAS
OPEN BETWEEN 1940 AND 1947. PASSENGER
SERVICES WERE WITHDRAWN IN 1965.
THROUGH OIL TRAFFIC TO STAINES CEASED IN
1981 WHEN THE ROUTE WAS SEVERED BY THE
M25 MOTORWAY. FREIGHT TRAFFIC CONTINUES
TO THORNEY MILL AND COLNBROOK

1884
1884-1965

1998

WORKS

COLNBROOK GOODS (1884-1966)

COLNBROOK (1884-1965)

COLNBROOK –
ELF OIL TERMINAL
(1990)

28

POYLE ESTATE HALT
(1954-1965)

1885-1965 (1981)

HEATHROW
TERMINAL 5
(2008)

HEATHROW
TERMINALS
1,2 & 3
Heathrow Central
(1977)

2008

2014

2008

POYLE FOR STANWELL
MOOR HALT
Stanwell Moor & Poyle Halt
(1927-1965)

1977

'AIRTRACK'

PROPOSED NEW ROUTE TO HEATHROW
TERMINAL 5 UTILISING PART OF THE GWR
STAINES WEST BRANCH. PLATFORMS HAVE
BEEN BUILT AT TERMINAL 5 STATION TO
ACCOMMODATE THE ROUTE IF BUILT.
SERVICES WOULD BE PROVIDED BY
SOUTH-WEST TRAINS TO READING,
GUILDFORD AND LONDON WATERLOO

1986

1998

1885-1965 (1981) 2014

HEATHROW
TERMINAL 4
(1986)

1986

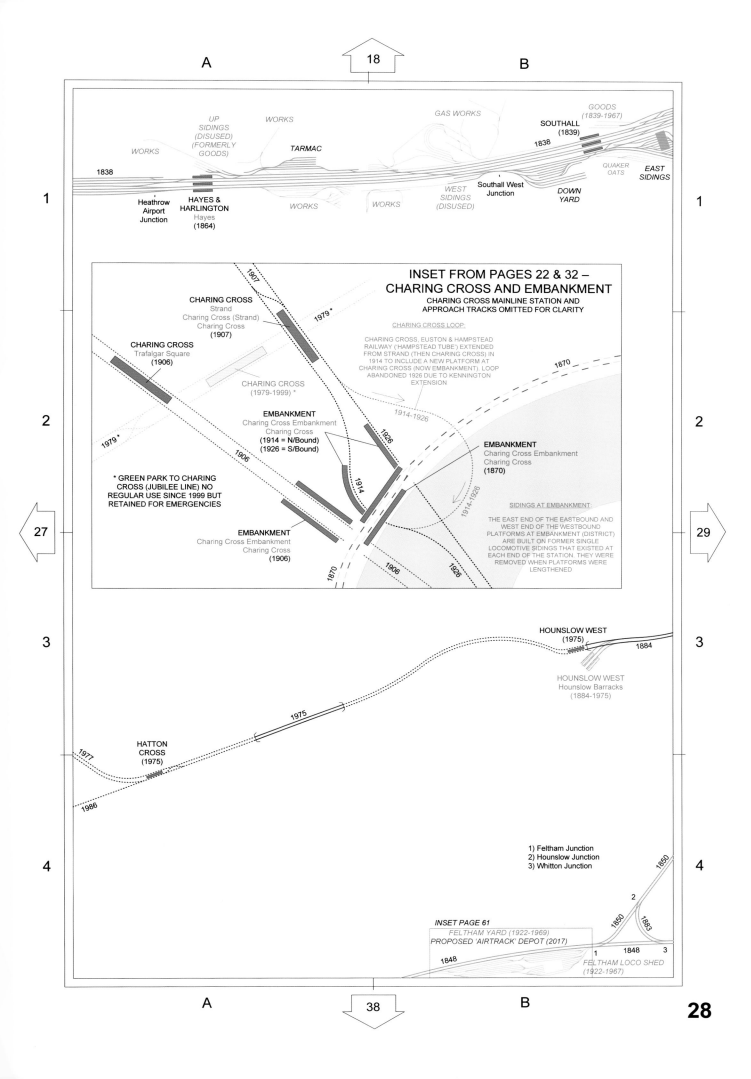

1   1

WORKS

1838

UP SIDINGS (DISUSED) (FORMERLY GOODS)

WORKS

TARMAC

GAS WORKS

GOODS (1839-1967)

SOUTHALL (1839)

1838

QUAKER OATS

EAST SIDINGS

Heathrow Airport Junction

HAYES & HARLINGTON
Hayes (1864)

WORKS

WORKS

WEST SIDINGS (DISUSED)

Southall West Junction

DOWN YARD

INSET FROM PAGES 22 & 32 – CHARING CROSS AND EMBANKMENT
CHARING CROSS MAINLINE STATION AND APPROACH TRACKS OMITTED FOR CLARITY

1907

CHARING CROSS
Strand
Charing Cross (Strand)
Charing Cross
(1907)

1979 *

CHARING CROSS LOOP:

CHARING CROSS, EUSTON & HAMPSTEAD RAILWAY ('HAMPSTEAD TUBE') EXTENDED FROM STRAND (THEN CHARING CROSS) IN 1914 TO INCLUDE A NEW PLATFORM AT CHARING CROSS (NOW EMBANKMENT). LOOP ABANDONED 1926 DUE TO KENNINGTON EXTENSION

CHARING CROSS
Trafalgar Square
(1906)

1870

CHARING CROSS
(1979-1999) *

1914-1926

EMBANKMENT
Charing Cross Embankment
Charing Cross
(1914 = N/Bound)
(1926 = S/Bound)

1926

EMBANKMENT
Charing Cross Embankment
Charing Cross
(1870)

1979 *

1906

1914

1914-1926

* GREEN PARK TO CHARING CROSS (JUBILEE LINE) NO REGULAR USE SINCE 1999 BUT RETAINED FOR EMERGENCIES

SIDINGS AT EMBANKMENT:

THE EAST END OF THE EASTBOUND AND WEST END OF THE WESTBOUND PLATFORMS AT EMBANKMENT (DISTRICT) ARE BUILT ON FORMER SINGLE LOCOMOTIVE SIDINGS THAT EXISTED AT EACH END OF THE STATION. THEY WERE REMOVED WHEN PLATFORMS WERE LENGTHENED

EMBANKMENT
Charing Cross Embankment
Charing Cross
(1906)

1870

1906

1926

2   2

27   29

HOUNSLOW WEST
(1975)

1884

HOUNSLOW WEST
Hounslow Barracks
(1884-1975)

3   3

1975

HATTON CROSS
(1975)

1977

1986

1) Feltham Junction
2) Hounslow Junction
3) Whitton Junction

1850

4   4

2

1850

1883

INSET PAGE 61
FELTHAM YARD (1922-1969)
PROPOSED 'AIRTRACK' DEPOT (2017)

1

1848

3

1848

FELTHAM LOCO SHED (1922-1967)

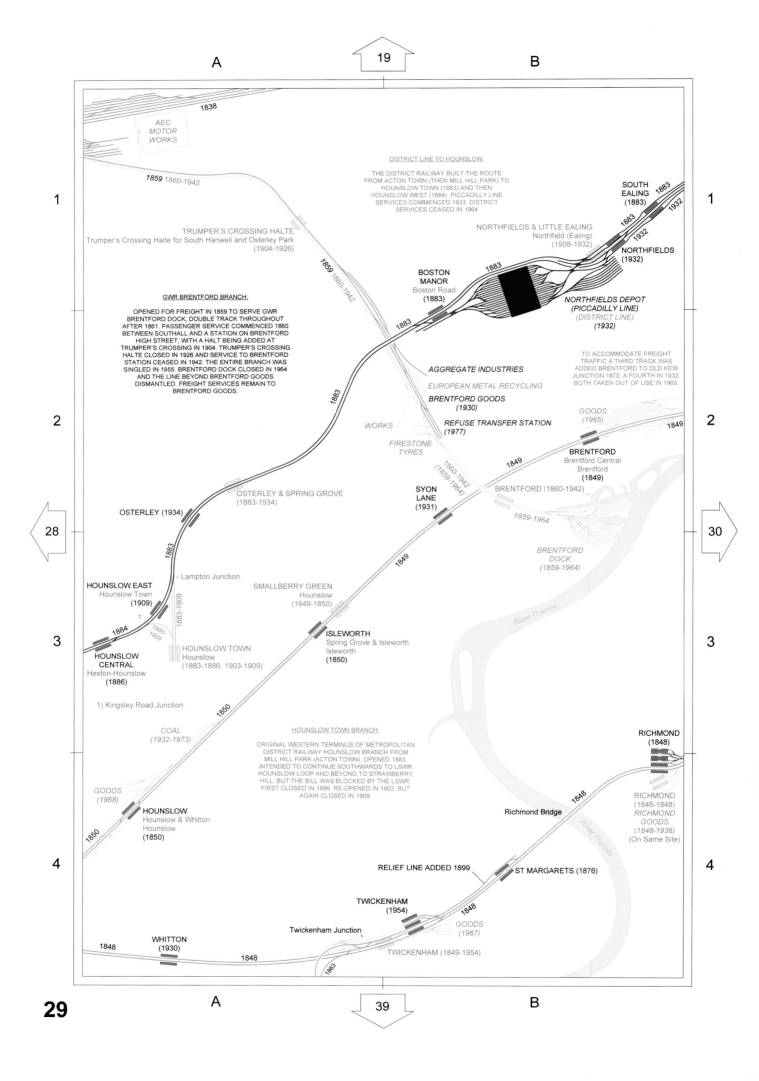

1838

AEC MOTOR WORKS

1859 1860-1942

TRUMPER'S CROSSING HALTE
Trumper's Crossing Halte for South Hanwell and Osterley Park
(1904-1926)

DISTRICT LINE TO HOUNSLOW:

THE DISTRICT RAILWAY BUILT THE ROUTE
FROM ACTON TOWN (THEN MILL HILL PARK) TO
HOUNSLOW TOWN (1883) AND THEN
HOUNSLOW WEST (1884). PICCADILLY LINE
SERVICES COMMENCED 1933, DISTRICT
SERVICES CEASED IN 1964

SOUTH
EALING
(1883)

1883
1883
1932

NORTHFIELDS & LITTLE EALING
Northfield (Ealing)
(1908-1932)

1883
1932

NORTHFIELDS
(1932)

GWR BRENTFORD BRANCH:

OPENED FOR FREIGHT IN 1859 TO SERVE GWR
BRENTFORD DOCK, DOUBLE TRACK THROUGHOUT
AFTER 1861. PASSENGER SERVICE COMMENCED 1860
BETWEEN SOUTHALL AND A STATION ON BRENTFORD
HIGH STREET, WITH A HALT BEING ADDED AT
TRUMPER'S CROSSING IN 1904. TRUMPER'S CROSSING
HALTE CLOSED IN 1926 AND SERVICE TO BRENTFORD
STATION CEASED IN 1942. THE ENTIRE BRANCH WAS
SINGLED IN 1955. BRENTFORD DOCK CLOSED IN 1964
AND THE LINE BEYOND BRENTFORD GOODS
DISMANTLED. FREIGHT SERVICES REMAIN TO
BRENTFORD GOODS.

1859 1860-1942

BOSTON
MANOR
Boston Road
(1883)

1883

1883

*NORTHFIELDS DEPOT
(PICCADILLY LINE)
(DISTRICT LINE)
(1932)*

TO ACCOMMODATE FREIGHT
TRAFFIC A THIRD TRACK WAS
ADDED BRENTFORD TO OLD KEW
JUNCTION 1870, A FOURTH IN 1932.
BOTH TAKEN OUT OF USE IN 1965.

AGGREGATE INDUSTRIES

EUROPEAN METAL RECYCLING

*BRENTFORD GOODS
(1930)*

*GOODS
(1965)*

1849

1883

*REFUSE TRANSFER STATION
(1977)*

WORKS

*FIRESTONE
TYRES*

1860-1942
(1859-1964)

1849

BRENTFORD
Brentford Central
Brentford
(1849)

OSTERLEY & SPRING GROVE
(1883-1934)

SYON
LANE
(1931)

BRENTFORD (1860-1942)

OSTERLEY (1934)

1859-1964

1883

*BRENTFORD
DOCK
(1859-1964)*

1849

- Lampton Junction

HOUNSLOW EAST
Hounslow Town
(1909)

1883-1909

SMALLBERRY GREEN
Hounslow
(1849-1850)

River Thames

1884

1905-
1909

1

ISLEWORTH
Spring Grove & Isleworth
Isleworth
(1850)

HOUNSLOW
CENTRAL
Heston-Hounslow
(1886)

HOUNSLOW TOWN
Hounslow
(1883-1886, 1903-1909)

1) Kingsley Road Junction

1850

RICHMOND
(1848)

*COAL
(1932-1973)*

HOUNSLOW TOWN BRANCH:

ORIGINAL WESTERN TERMINUS OF METROPOLITAN
DISTRICT RAILWAY HOUNSLOW BRANCH FROM
MILL HILL PARK (ACTON TOWN), OPENED 1883.
INTENDED TO CONTINUE SOUTHWARDS TO LSWR
HOUNSLOW LOOP AND BEYOND TO STRAWBERRY
HILL, BUT THE BILL WAS BLOCKED BY THE LSWR.
FIRST CLOSED IN 1886. RE-OPENED IN 1903, BUT
AGAIN CLOSED IN 1909.

*RICHMOND
(1846-1848)
RICHMOND
GOODS
(1848-1936)
(On Same Site)*

*GOODS
(1968)*

HOUNSLOW
Hounslow & Whitton
Hounslow
(1850)

1850

1848

Richmond Bridge

River Thames

RELIEF LINE ADDED 1899

ST MARGARETS (1876)

TWICKENHAM
(1954)

1848

*GOODS
(1967)*

WHITTON
(1930)

Twickenham Junction

1848

1848

1883

TWICKENHAM (1849-1954)

1848

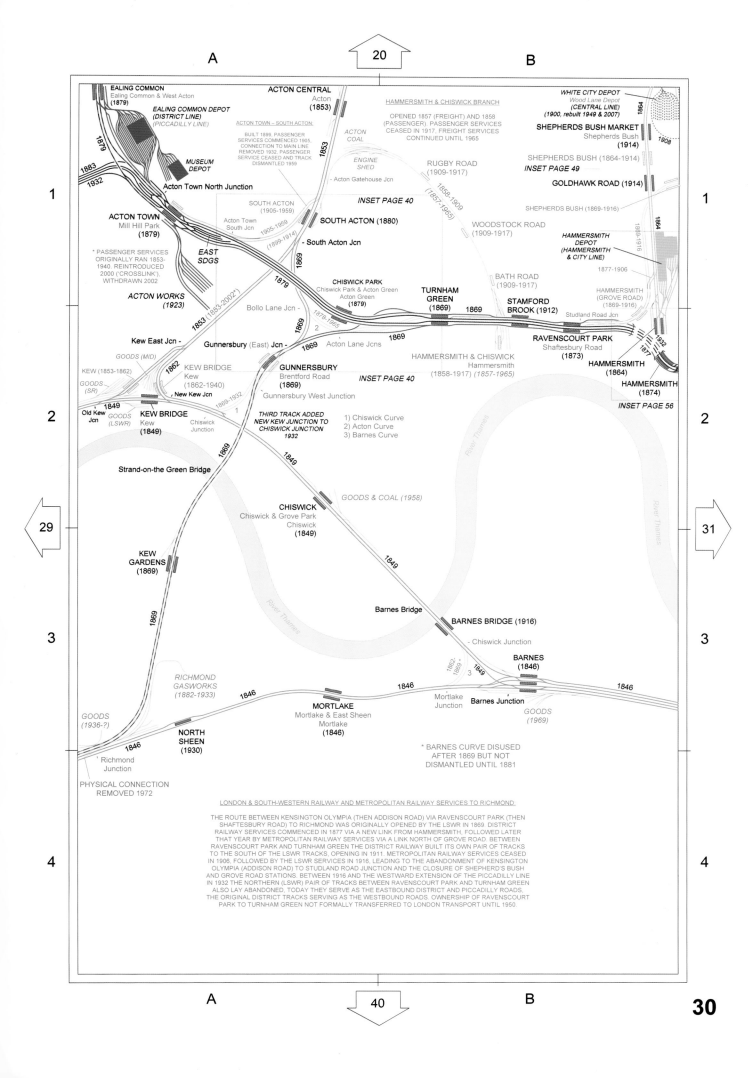

EALING COMMON
Ealing Common & West Acton
(1879)

EALING COMMON DEPOT
(DISTRICT LINE)
(PICCADILLY LINE)

MUSEUM
DEPOT

ACTON CENTRAL
Acton
(1853)

HAMMERSMITH & CHISWICK BRANCH

OPENED 1857 (FREIGHT) AND 1858
(PASSENGER). PASSENGER SERVICES
CEASED IN 1917, FREIGHT SERVICES
CONTINUED UNTIL 1965

WHITE CITY DEPOT
Wood Lane Depot
(CENTRAL LINE)
(1900, rebuilt 1949 & 2007)

SHEPHERDS BUSH MARKET
Shepherds Bush
(1914)

SHEPHERDS BUSH (1864-1914)

INSET PAGE 49

GOLDHAWK ROAD (1914)

SHEPHERDS BUSH (1869-1916)

ACTON
COAL

ENGINE
SHED

RUGBY ROAD
(1909-1917)

ACTON TOWN – SOUTH ACTON:

BUILT 1899, PASSENGER
SERVICES COMMENCED 1905,
CONNECTION TO MAIN LINE
REMOVED 1932, PASSENGER
SERVICE CEASED AND TRACK
DISMANTLED 1959

- Acton Gatehouse Jcn

INSET PAGE 40

WOODSTOCK ROAD
(1909-1917)

HAMMERSMITH
DEPOT
(HAMMERSMITH
& CITY LINE)

1877-1906

Acton Town North Junction

SOUTH ACTON
(1905-1959)

SOUTH ACTON (1880)

- South Acton Jcn

BATH ROAD
(1909-1917)

HAMMERSMITH
(GROVE ROAD)
(1869-1916)

ACTON TOWN
Mill Hill Park
(1879)

Acton Town
South Jcn
1905-1959

TURNHAM
GREEN
(1869)

STAMFORD
BROOK (1912)

CHISWICK PARK
Chiswick Park & Acton Green
Acton Green
(1879)

1869

Studland Road Jcn

RAVENSCOURT PARK
Shaftesbury Road
(1873)

EAST
SDGS

1899-1914

* PASSENGER SERVICES
ORIGINALLY RAN 1853-
1940. REINTRODUCED
2000 ('CROSSLINK'),
WITHDRAWN 2002

ACTON WORKS
(1923)

Bollo Lane Jcn -

1869

HAMMERSMITH
(1864)

Kew East Jcn -

1853 (1853-2002*)

Gunnersbury (East) Jcn -

Acton Lane Jcns

HAMMERSMITH & CHISWICK
Hammersmith
(1858-1917) (1857-1965)

HAMMERSMITH
(1874)

GOODS (MID)

1862

KEW BRIDGE
Kew
(1862-1940)

GUNNERSBURY
Brentford Road
(1869)

INSET PAGE 40

INSET PAGE 56

KEW (1853-1862)

- New Kew Jcn

Gunnersbury West Junction

GOODS
(SR)

1869-1932

Chiswick
Junction

1

1849
Old Kew
Jcn

GOODS
(LSWR)

KEW BRIDGE
Kew
(1849)

THIRD TRACK ADDED
NEW KEW JUNCTION TO
CHISWICK JUNCTION
1932

1) Chiswick Curve
2) Acton Curve
3) Barnes Curve

Strand-on-the Green Bridge

1869

1849

GOODS & COAL (1958)

CHISWICK
Chiswick & Grove Park
Chiswick
(1849)

KEW
GARDENS
(1869)

1849

River Thames

1869

Barnes Bridge

BARNES BRIDGE (1916)

- Chiswick Junction

RICHMOND
GASWORKS
(1882-1933)

1846

1862-
1869 *

1849

BARNES
(1846)

3

1846

MORTLAKE
Mortlake & East Sheen
Mortlake
(1846)

Mortlake
Junction

Barnes Junction

GOODS
(1969)

GOODS
(1936-?)

NORTH
SHEEN
(1930)

Richmond
Junction

* BARNES CURVE DISUSED
AFTER 1869 BUT NOT
DISMANTLED UNTIL 1881

PHYSICAL CONNECTION
REMOVED 1972

LONDON & SOUTH-WESTERN RAILWAY AND METROPOLITAN RAILWAY SERVICES TO RICHMOND:

THE ROUTE BETWEEN KENSINGTON OLYMPIA (THEN ADDISON ROAD) VIA RAVENSCOURT PARK (THEN
SHAFTESBURY ROAD) TO RICHMOND WAS ORIGINALLY OPENED BY THE LSWR IN 1869. DISTRICT
RAILWAY SERVICES COMMENCED IN 1877 VIA A NEW LINK FROM HAMMERSMITH, FOLLOWED LATER
THAT YEAR BY METROPOLITAN RAILWAY SERVICES VIA A LINK NORTH OF GROVE ROAD. BETWEEN
RAVENSCOURT PARK AND TURNHAM GREEN THE DISTRICT RAILWAY BUILT ITS OWN PAIR OF TRACKS
TO THE SOUTH OF THE LSWR TRACKS, OPENING IN 1911. METROPOLITAN RAILWAY SERVICES CEASED
IN 1906, FOLLOWED BY THE LSWR SERVICES IN 1916, LEADING TO THE ABANDONMENT OF KENSINGTON
OLYMPIA (ADDISON ROAD) TO STUDLAND ROAD JUNCTION AND THE CLOSURE OF SHEPHERD'S BUSH
AND GROVE ROAD STATIONS. BETWEEN 1916 AND THE WESTWARD EXTENSION OF THE PICCADILLY LINE
IN 1932 THE NORTHERN (LSWR) PAIR OF TRACKS BETWEEN RAVENSCOURT PARK AND TURNHAM GREEN
ALSO LAY ABANDONED, TODAY THEY SERVE AS THE EASTBOUND DISTRICT AND PICCADILLY ROADS,
THE ORIGINAL DISTRICT TRACKS SERVING AS THE WESTBOUND ROADS. OWNERSHIP OF RAVENSCOURT
PARK TO TURNHAM GREEN NOT FORMALLY TRANSFERRED TO LONDON TRANSPORT UNTIL 1950.

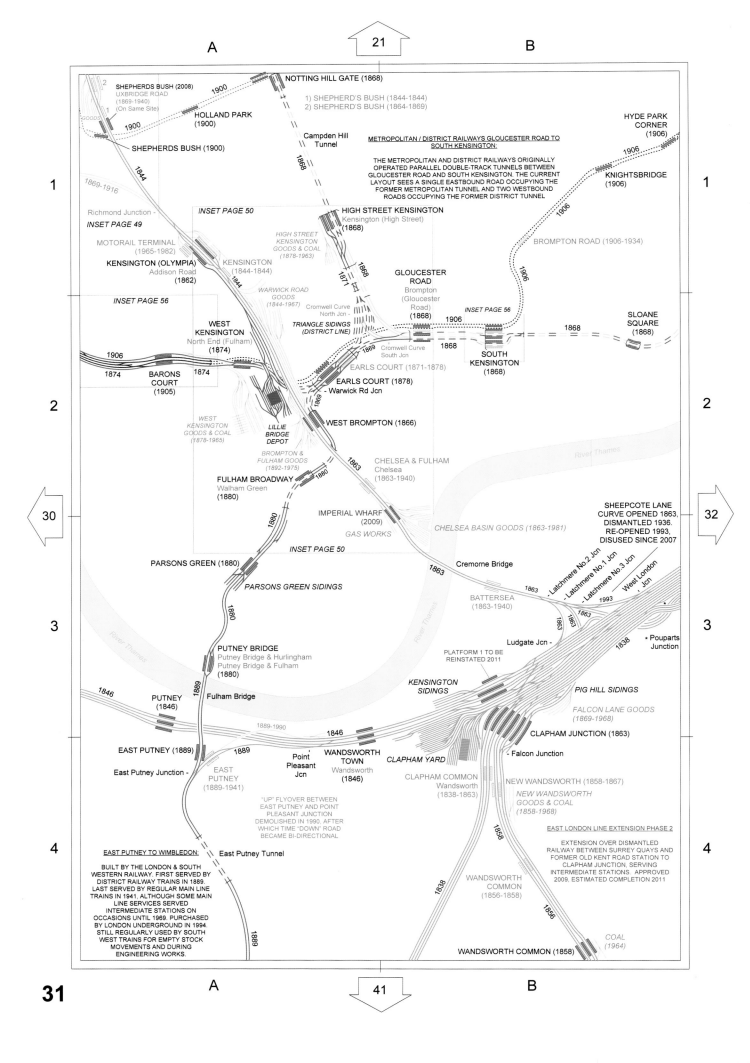

SHEPHERDS BUSH (2008)
UXBRIDGE ROAD (1869-1940) (On Same Site)
GOODS
1900
NOTTING HILL GATE (1868)
1) SHEPHERD'S BUSH (1844-1844)
2) SHEPHERD'S BUSH (1864-1869)

HOLLAND PARK (1900)
1900

HYDE PARK CORNER (1906)
1906

Campden Hill Tunnel

SHEPHERDS BUSH (1900)

1844

1868

KNIGHTSBRIDGE (1906)
1906

METROPOLITAN / DISTRICT RAILWAYS GLOUCESTER ROAD TO SOUTH KENSINGTON:

THE METROPOLITAN AND DISTRICT RAILWAYS ORIGINALLY OPERATED PARALLEL DOUBLE-TRACK TUNNELS BETWEEN GLOUCESTER ROAD AND SOUTH KENSINGTON. THE CURRENT LAYOUT SEES A SINGLE EASTBOUND ROAD OCCUPYING THE FORMER METROPOLITAN TUNNEL AND TWO WESTBOUND ROADS OCCUPYING THE FORMER DISTRICT TUNNEL

1869-1916

Richmond Junction -
INSET PAGE 49

INSET PAGE 50

HIGH STREET KENSINGTON (1868)
Kensington (High Street)

BROMPTON ROAD (1906-1934)

MOTORAIL TERMINAL (1965-1982)

KENSINGTON (1844-1844)

HIGH STREET KENSINGTON GOODS & COAL (1878-1963)

GLOUCESTER ROAD
Brompton (Gloucester Road) (1868)

1906

KENSINGTON (OLYMPIA)
Addison Road (1862)

1844

WARWICK ROAD GOODS (1844-1967)

1868

1871

Cromwell Curve North Jcn -

INSET PAGE 56

SLOANE SQUARE (1868)

INSET PAGE 56

TRIANGLE SIDINGS (DISTRICT LINE)

1906

1868

WEST KENSINGTON
North End (Fulham) (1874)

Cromwell Curve South Jcn -

1868

SOUTH KENSINGTON (1868)

1906

1874

1869

1868

BARONS COURT (1905)

1874

1874

EARLS COURT (1871-1878)

EARLS COURT (1878)
- Warwick Rd Jcn

WEST KENSINGTON GOODS & COAL (1878-1965)

LILLIE BRIDGE DEPOT

1869

WEST BROMPTON (1866)

River Thames

BROMPTON & FULHAM GOODS (1892-1975)

1863

CHELSEA & FULHAM
Chelsea (1863-1940)

FULHAM BROADWAY
Walham Green (1880)

1880

SHEEPCOTE LANE CURVE OPENED 1863, DISMANTLED 1936. RE-OPENED 1993, DISUSED SINCE 2007

30

IMPERIAL WHARF (2009)

CHELSEA BASIN GOODS (1863-1981)

32

GAS WORKS

1880

INSET PAGE 50

Cremorne Bridge

PARSONS GREEN (1880)

1863

BATTERSEA (1863-1940)

- Latchmere No.2 Jcn
- Latchmere No.1 Jcn
- Latchmere No.3 Jcn

West London Jcn

PARSONS GREEN SIDINGS

1863

1993

1880

Pouparts Junction

3

River Thames

1863

1863

1863

1838

3

Ludgate Jcn -

PLATFORM 1 TO BE REINSTATED 2011

PUTNEY BRIDGE
Putney Bridge & Hurlingham
Putney Bridge & Fulham (1880)

KENSINGTON SIDINGS

PIG HILL SIDINGS

1846

PUTNEY (1846)

1889

Fulham Bridge

FALCON LANE GOODS (1869-1968)

1889-1990

1846

CLAPHAM JUNCTION (1863)

EAST PUTNEY (1889)

1889

WANDSWORTH TOWN
Wandsworth (1846)

CLAPHAM YARD

- Falcon Junction

East Putney Junction -

EAST PUTNEY (1889-1941)

Point Pleasant Jcn

CLAPHAM COMMON
Wandsworth (1838-1863)

NEW WANDSWORTH (1858-1867)

NEW WANDSWORTH GOODS & COAL (1858-1968)

"UP" FLYOVER BETWEEN EAST PUTNEY AND POINT PLEASANT JUNCTION DEMOLISHED IN 1990, AFTER WHICH TIME "DOWN" ROAD BECAME BI-DIRECTIONAL

1858

EAST LONDON LINE EXTENSION PHASE 2

4

EAST PUTNEY TO WIMBLEDON:

BUILT BY THE LONDON & SOUTH WESTERN RAILWAY. FIRST SERVED BY DISTRICT RAILWAY TRAINS IN 1889. LAST SERVED BY REGULAR MAIN LINE TRAINS IN 1941, ALTHOUGH SOME MAIN LINE SERVICES SERVED INTERMEDIATE STATIONS ON OCCASIONS UNTIL 1969. PURCHASED BY LONDON UNDERGROUND IN 1994. STILL REGULARLY USED BY SOUTH WEST TRAINS FOR EMPTY STOCK MOVEMENTS AND DURING ENGINEERING WORKS.

East Putney Tunnel

1838

WANDSWORTH COMMON (1856-1858)

EXTENSION OVER DISMANTLED RAILWAY BETWEEN SURREY QUAYS AND FORMER OLD KENT ROAD STATION TO CLAPHAM JUNCTION, SERVING INTERMEDIATE STATIONS. APPROVED 2009, ESTIMATED COMPLETION 2011

1856

4

1889

COAL (1964)

WANDSWORTH COMMON (1858)

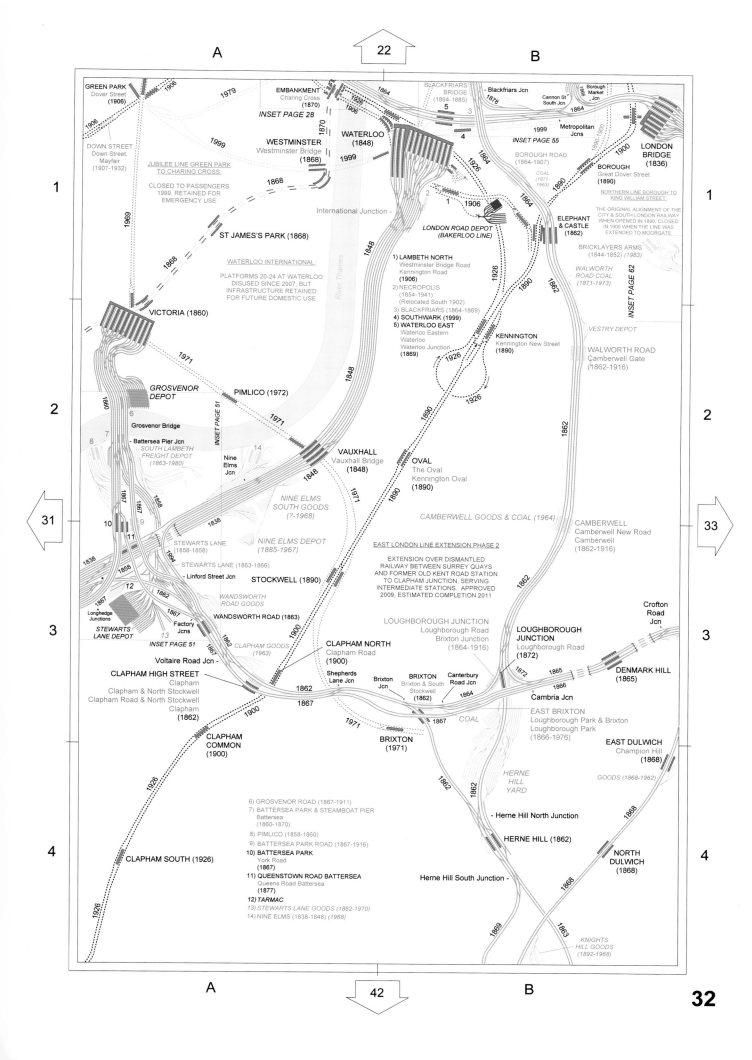

GREEN PARK
Dover Street
(1906)
1906
1979
1906
1906
1999

DOWN STREET
Down Street,
Mayfair
(1907-1932)

1868

1969

JUBILEE LINE GREEN PARK
TO CHARING CROSS:

CLOSED TO PASSENGERS
1999, RETAINED FOR
EMERGENCY USE

ST JAMES'S PARK (1868)

WATERLOO INTERNATIONAL:

PLATFORMS 20-24 AT WATERLOO
DISUSED SINCE 2007, BUT
INFRASTRUCTURE RETAINED
FOR FUTURE DOMESTIC USE

EMBANKMENT
Charing Cross
(1870)
1926
1906
1864

INSET PAGE 28

WESTMINSTER
Westminster Bridge
(1868)
1870
1999

WATERLOO
(1848)

BLACKFRIARS
BRIDGE
(1864-1885)
5
3
1878
4

Borough
Market
Jcn

Cannon St
South Jcn
1864

1999
Metropolitan
Jcns
1890-1900

LONDON
BRIDGE
(1836)

- Blackfriars Jcn

1906

1926

1864

International Junction -

River Thames

1848

1) LAMBETH NORTH
Westminster Bridge Road
Kennington Road
(1906)
2) NECROPOLIS
(1854-1941)
(Relocated South 1902)
3) BLACKFRIARS (1864-1869)
4) SOUTHWARK (1999)
5) WATERLOO EAST
Waterloo Eastern
Waterloo
Waterloo Junction
(1869)

LONDON ROAD DEPOT
(BAKERLOO LINE)

1926

1
1906

1864

1926

1890

1926

KENNINGTON
Kennington New Street
(1890)

1926

BOROUGH ROAD
(1864-1907)

COAL
(1871-
1963)

BOROUGH
Great Dover Street
(1890)

ELEPHANT
& CASTLE
(1862)

NORTHERN LINE BOROUGH TO
KING WILLIAM STREET

THE ORIGINAL ALIGNMENT OF THE
CITY & SOUTH LONDON RAILWAY
WHEN OPENED IN 1890, CLOSED
IN 1900 WHEN THE LINE WAS
EXTENDED TO MOORGATE

BRICKLAYERS ARMS
(1844-1852) (1983)

WALWORTH
ROAD COAL
(1871-1973)

VESTRY DEPOT

WALWORTH ROAD
Camberwell Gate
(1862-1916)

1890

1862

VICTORIA (1860)

1971

GROSVENOR
DEPOT

1880

6

8 7

Grosvenor Bridge

- Battersea Pier Jcn

SOUTH LAMBETH
FREIGHT DEPOT
(1863-1980)

Nine
Elms
Jcn

PIMLICO (1972)

1971

14

VAUXHALL
Vauxhall Bridge
(1848)

1848

1971

OVAL
The Oval
Kennington Oval
(1890)

1890

1862

CAMBERWELL GOODS & COAL (1964)

CAMBERWELL
Camberwell New Road
Camberwell
(1862-1916)

1867
1867
1858

1838

NINE ELMS
SOUTH GOODS
(?-1968)

NINE ELMS DEPOT
(1885-1967)

EAST LONDON LINE EXTENSION PHASE 2

EXTENSION OVER DISMANTLED
RAILWAY BETWEEN SURREY QUAYS
AND FORMER OLD KENT ROAD STATION
TO CLAPHAM JUNCTION, SERVING
INTERMEDIATE STATIONS. APPROVED
2009, ESTIMATED COMPLETION 2011

10
9
11

1954

STEWARTS LANE
(1858-1858)

STEWARTS LANE (1863-1866)

- Linford Street Jcn

STOCKWELL (1890)

WANDSWORTH
ROAD GOODS

1862

1838

1858

12

1867

Longhedge
Junctions

STEWARTS
LANE DEPOT

13

INSET PAGE 51

1867

1862

1867

Factory
Jcns

WANDSWORTH ROAD (1863)

CLAPHAM GOODS
(1963)

1900

1862

1862

LOUGHBOROUGH JUNCTION
Loughborough Road
Brixton Junction
(1864-1916)

CLAPHAM NORTH
Clapham Road
(1900)

Shepherds
Lane Jcn

LOUGHBOROUGH
JUNCTION
Loughborough Road
(1872)

Crofton
Road
Jcn

1872

1865

1866

DENMARK HILL
(1865)

Voltaire Road Jcn -

CLAPHAM HIGH STREET
Clapham
Clapham & North Stockwell
Clapham Road & North Stockwell
Clapham
(1862)

1862

1867

Brixton
Jcn

BRIXTON
Brixton & South
Stockwell
(1862)

Canterbury
Road Jcn

1864

Cambria Jcn

EAST BRIXTON
Loughborough Park & Brixton
Loughborough Park
(1866-1976)

EAST DULWICH
Champion Hill
(1868)

1900

1971

1867

COAL

GOODS (1868-1962)

CLAPHAM
COMMON
(1900)

BRIXTON
(1971)

1862

1862

HERNE
HILL
YARD

1868

1868

- Herne Hill North Junction

6) GROSVENOR ROAD (1867-1911)
7) BATTERSEA PARK & STEAMBOAT PIER
Battersea
(1860-1870)
8) PIMLICO (1858-1860)
9) BATTERSEA PARK ROAD (1867-1916)
10) BATTERSEA PARK
York Road
(1867)
11) QUEENSTOWN ROAD BATTERSEA
Queens Road Battersea
(1877)
12) TARMAC
13) STEWARTS LANE GOODS (1862-1970)
14) NINE ELMS (1838-1848) (1968)

CLAPHAM SOUTH (1926)

1926

1926

HERNE HILL (1862)

Herne Hill South Junction -

NORTH
DULWICH
(1868)

1868

1869

1863

KNIGHTS
HILL GOODS
(1892-1968)

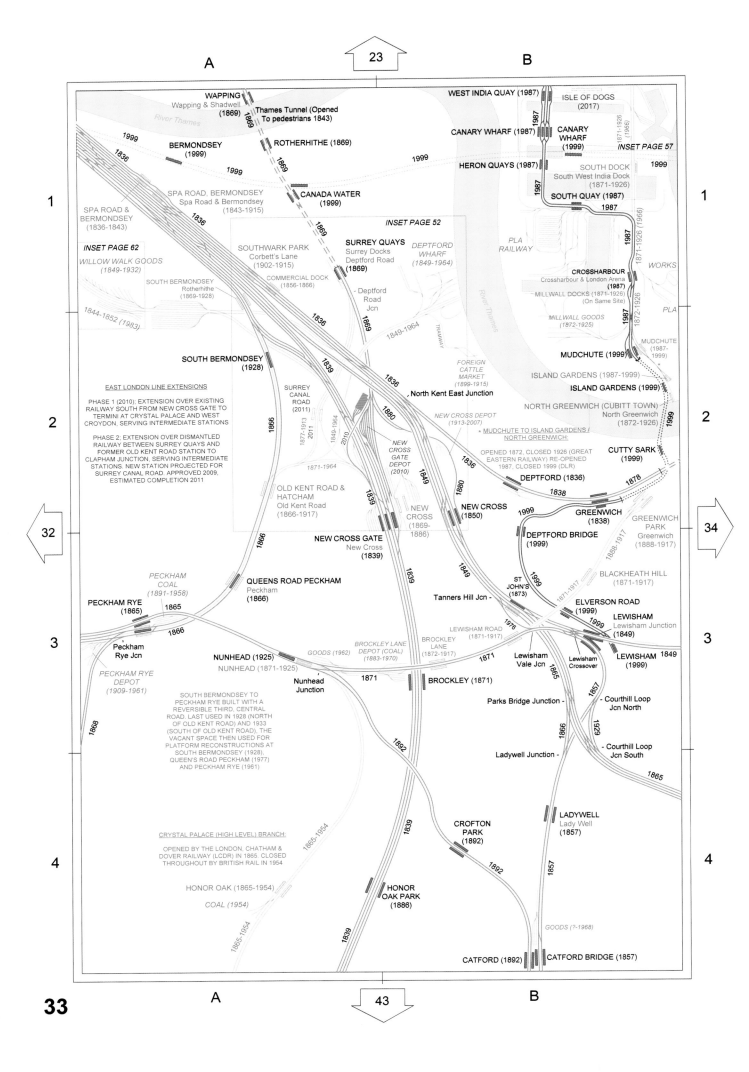

WAPPING
Wapping & Shadwell
(1869)
Thames Tunnel (Opened
To pedestrians 1843)

River Thames

1999

1999

1836

BERMONDSEY
(1999)

ROTHERHITHE (1869)

1869

1999

WEST INDIA QUAY (1987)

ISLE OF DOGS
(2017)

1987

CANARY WHARF (1987)

CANARY
WHARF
(1999)

1987

1871-1926
(1966)

INSET PAGE 57

HERON QUAYS (1987)

1999

SOUTH DOCK
South West India Dock
(1871-1926)

1999

1

SPA ROAD &
BERMONDSEY
(1836-1843)

SPA ROAD, BERMONDSEY
Spa Road & Bermondsey
(1843-1915)

CANADA WATER
(1999)

1836

1869

1987

SOUTH QUAY (1987)

1987

*PLA
RAILWAY*

1987

WORKS

1

INSET PAGE 62

*WILLOW WALK GOODS
(1849-1932)*

1844-1852 (1983)

SOUTHWARK PARK
Corbett's Lane
(1902-1915)

COMMERCIAL DOCK
(1856-1866)

INSET PAGE 52

SURREY QUAYS
Surrey Docks
Deptford Road
(1869)

*DEPTFORD
WHARF
(1849-1964)*

1869

- Deptford
Road
Jcn

1849-1964

TRAMWAY

CROSSHARBOUR
Crossharbour & London Arena
(1987)

MILLWALL DOCKS (1871-1926)
(On Same Site)

*MILLWALL GOODS
(1872-1925)*

1987

1872-1926

PLA

SOUTH BERMONDSEY
Rotherhithe
(1869-1928)

SOUTH BERMONDSEY
(1928)

SURREY
CANAL
ROAD
(2011)

1836

1839

1836

River Thames

*FOREIGN
CATTLE
MARKET
(1899-1915)*

North Kent East Junction

MUDCHUTE (1999)

MUDCHUTE
(1987-
1999)

ISLAND GARDENS (1987-1999)

ISLAND GARDENS (1999)

2

EAST LONDON LINE EXTENSIONS

PHASE 1 (2010): EXTENSION OVER EXISTING
RAILWAY SOUTH FROM NEW CROSS GATE TO
TERMINI AT CRYSTAL PALACE AND WEST
CROYDON, SERVING INTERMEDIATE STATIONS

PHASE 2: EXTENSION OVER DISMANTLED
RAILWAY BETWEEN SURREY QUAYS AND
FORMER OLD KENT ROAD STATION TO
CLAPHAM JUNCTION, SERVING INTERMEDIATE
STATIONS. NEW STATION PROJECTED FOR
SURREY CANAL ROAD. APPROVED 2009,
ESTIMATED COMPLETION 2011

1866

1877-1913
2011

1849-1964

2010

1871-1964

1880

1836

*NEW CROSS DEPOT
(1913-2007)*

*MUDCHUTE TO ISLAND GARDENS /
NORTH GREENWICH:*

NORTH GREENWICH (CUBITT TOWN)
North Greenwich
(1872-1926)

*OPENED 1872, CLOSED 1926 (GREAT
EASTERN RAILWAY) RE-OPENED
1987, CLOSED 1999 (DLR)*

1999

2

*NEW
CROSS
GATE
DEPOT
(2010)*

1849

1880

DEPTFORD (1836)

CUTTY SARK
(1999)

1878

1838

OLD KENT ROAD &
HATCHAM
Old Kent Road
(1866-1917)

NEW CROSS
(1850)

1999

GREENWICH
(1838)

*GREENWICH
PARK
Greenwich
(1888-1917)*

NEW CROSS GATE
New Cross
(1839)

1839

NEW
CROSS
(1869-
1886)

DEPTFORD BRIDGE
(1999)

1888-1917

3

*PECKHAM
COAL
(1891-1958)*

QUEENS ROAD PECKHAM
Peckham
(1866)

Tanners Hill Jcn -

1849

ST
JOHN'S
(1873)

1999

1871-1917

*BLACKHEATH HILL
(1871-1917)*

ELVERSON ROAD
(1999)

LEWISHAM
Lewisham Junction
(1849)

PECKHAM RYE
(1865)

1865

1866

Peckham
Rye Jcn

1976

*LEWISHAM ROAD
(1871-1917)*

BROCKLEY
LANE
(1872-1917)

Lewisham
Vale Jcn

Lewisham
Crossover

LEWISHAM
(1999)

1849

3

*PECKHAM RYE
DEPOT
(1909-1961)*

NUNHEAD (1925)
NUNHEAD (1871-1925)

GOODS (1962)

*BROCKLEY LANE
DEPOT (COAL)
(1883-1970)*

1871

1865

1857

- Courthill Loop
Jcn North

Nunhead
Junction

BROCKLEY (1871)

Parks Bridge Junction -

1868

SOUTH BERMONDSEY TO
PECKHAM RYE BUILT WITH A
REVERSIBLE THIRD, CENTRAL
ROAD. LAST USED IN 1928 (NORTH
OF OLD KENT ROAD) AND 1933
(SOUTH OF OLD KENT ROAD), THE
VACANT SPACE THEN USED FOR
PLATFORM RECONSTRUCTIONS AT
SOUTH BERMONDSEY (1928),
QUEEN'S ROAD PECKHAM (1977)
AND PECKHAM RYE (1961)

1892

1866

1929

Ladywell Junction -

- Courthill Loop
Jcn South

1865

4

CRYSTAL PALACE (HIGH LEVEL) BRANCH:

OPENED BY THE LONDON, CHATHAM &
DOVER RAILWAY (LCDR) IN 1865. CLOSED
THROUGHOUT BY BRITISH RAIL IN 1954

HONOR OAK (1865-1954)

COAL (1954)

1865-1954

CROFTON
PARK
(1892)

HONOR
OAK PARK
(1886)

1892

1839

LADYWELL
Lady Well
(1857)

1857

GOODS (?-1968)

4

1865-1954

1839

CATFORD (1892)

CATFORD BRIDGE (1857)

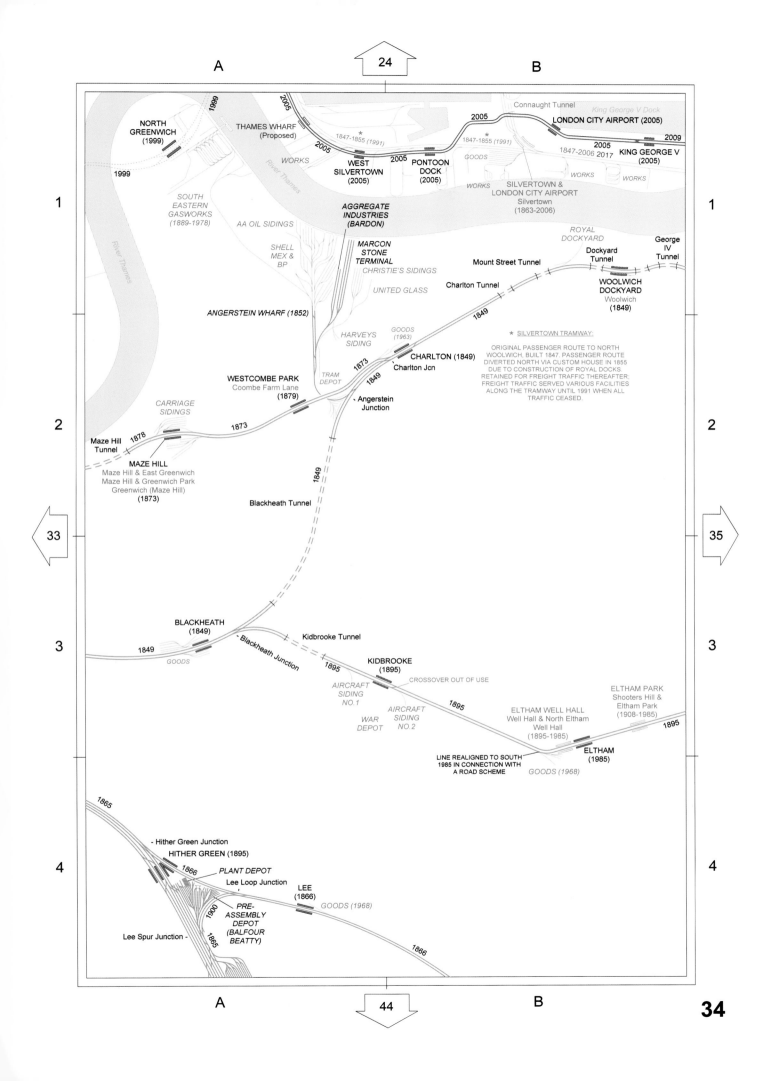

NORTH
GREENWICH
(1999)

1999

2005

THAMES WHARF
(Proposed)

2005

1847-1855 (1991)

WEST
SILVERTOWN
(2005)

2005

PONTOON
DOCK
(2005)

Connaught Tunnel

King George V Dock

LONDON CITY AIRPORT (2005)

2005

2009

2005

KING GEORGE V
(2005)

1847-2006 2017

1847-1855 (1991)

GOODS

SOUTH
EASTERN
GASWORKS
(1889-1978)

River Thames

AA OIL SIDINGS

SHELL
MEX &
BP

River Thames

WORKS

WORKS

SILVERTOWN &
LONDON CITY AIRPORT
Silvertown
(1863-2006)

WORKS

WORKS

*AGGREGATE
INDUSTRIES
(BARDON)*

*MARCON
STONE
TERMINAL*

CHRISTIE'S SIDINGS

UNITED GLASS

Mount Street Tunnel

Charlton Tunnel

1849

*ROYAL
DOCKYARD*

Dockyard
Tunnel

George
IV
Tunnel

WOOLWICH
DOCKYARD
Woolwich
(1849)

ANGERSTEIN WHARF (1852)

*HARVEYS
SIDING*

*GOODS
(1963)*

1873

1849

CHARLTON (1849)

Charlton Jcn

* SILVERTOWN TRAMWAY:

ORIGINAL PASSENGER ROUTE TO NORTH
WOOLWICH, BUILT 1847. PASSENGER ROUTE
DIVERTED NORTH VIA CUSTOM HOUSE IN 1855
DUE TO CONSTRUCTION OF ROYAL DOCKS.
RETAINED FOR FREIGHT TRAFFIC THEREAFTER;
FREIGHT TRAFFIC SERVED VARIOUS FACILITIES
ALONG THE TRAMWAY UNTIL 1991 WHEN ALL
TRAFFIC CEASED.

WESTCOMBE PARK
Coombe Farm Lane
(1879)

*TRAM
DEPOT*

Angerstein
Junction

*CARRIAGE
SIDINGS*

1873

1878

Maze Hill
Tunnel

MAZE HILL
Maze Hill & East Greenwich
Maze Hill & Greenwich Park
Greenwich (Maze Hill)
(1873)

1849

Blackheath Tunnel

BLACKHEATH
(1849)

1849

GOODS

Blackheath Junction

Kidbrooke Tunnel

1895

KIDBROOKE
(1895)

CROSSOVER OUT OF USE

*AIRCRAFT
SIDING
NO.1*

*AIRCRAFT
SIDING
NO.2*

*WAR
DEPOT*

1895

ELTHAM WELL HALL
Well Hall & North Eltham
Well Hall
(1895-1985)

ELTHAM PARK
Shooters Hill &
Eltham Park
(1908-1985)

1895

LINE REALIGNED TO SOUTH
1985 IN CONNECTION WITH
A ROAD SCHEME

ELTHAM
(1985)

GOODS (1968)

1865

- Hither Green Junction
HITHER GREEN (1895)

1866

PLANT DEPOT

Lee Loop Junction

LEE
(1866)

GOODS (1968)

1900

*PRE-
ASSEMBLY
DEPOT
(BALFOUR
BEATTY)*

Lee Spur Junction -

1865

1866

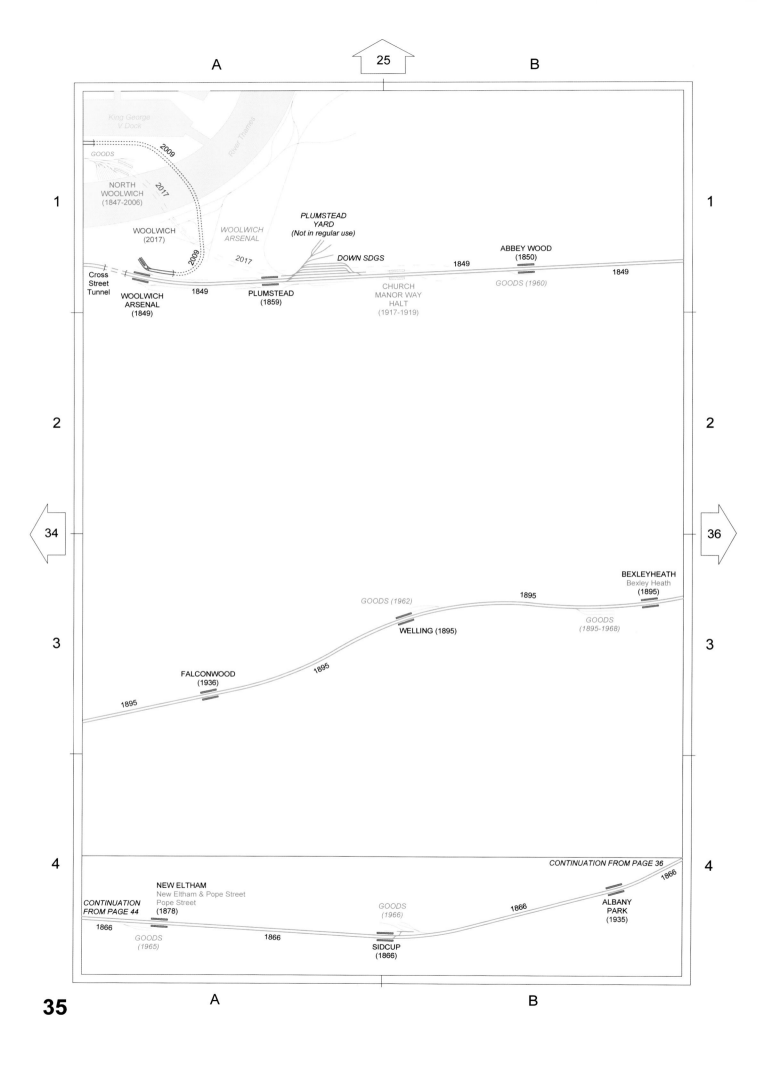

King George V Dock

GOODS

NORTH WOOLWICH
(1847-2006)

WOOLWICH
(2017)

2009

2017

2009

2017

Woolwich Arsenal

PLUMSTEAD YARD
(Not in regular use)

DOWN SDGS

ABBEY WOOD
(1850)

1849

1849

GOODS (1960)

Cross Street Tunnel

WOOLWICH ARSENAL
(1849)

1849

PLUMSTEAD
(1859)

CHURCH MANOR WAY HALT
(1917-1919)

1849

34

36

BEXLEYHEATH
Bexley Heath
(1895)

GOODS (1962)

1895

GOODS
(1895-1968)

WELLING (1895)

FALCONWOOD
(1936)

1895

1895

1895

CONTINUATION FROM PAGE 36

1866

NEW ELTHAM
New Eltham & Pope Street
Pope Street
(1878)

GOODS
(1966)

1866

ALBANY PARK
(1935)

CONTINUATION FROM PAGE 44

1866

GOODS
(1965)

1866

SIDCUP
(1866)

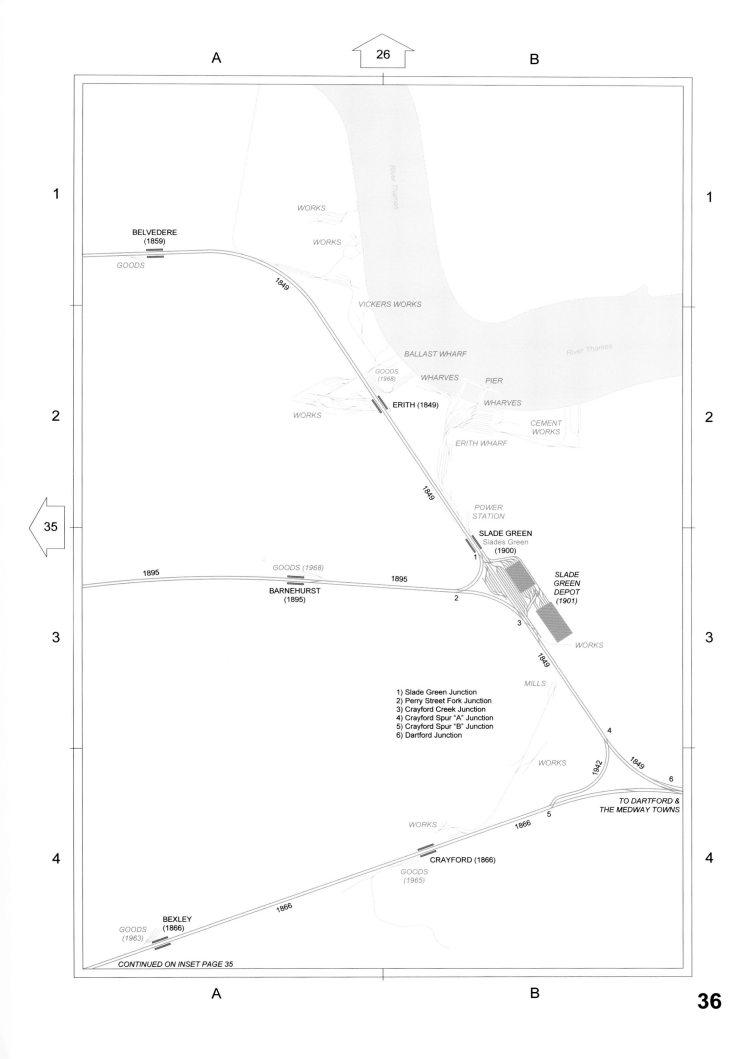

1   1

BELVEDERE
(1859)
GOODS

River Thames

WORKS

WORKS

1849

VICKERS WORKS

BALLAST WHARF
River Thames

WHARVES

GOODS
(1968)   *PIER*

2   ERITH (1849)   *WHARVES*   2

WORKS   *CEMENT*
WORKS

ERITH WHARF

1849

POWER
STATION

SLADE GREEN
Slades Green
(1900)
1

35   1895   *GOODS (1968)*   1895   *SLADE*
GREEN
BARNEHURST   2   *DEPOT*
(1895)   *(1901)*

3   3   *WORKS*   3

1849

MILLS

1) Slade Green Junction
2) Perry Street Fork Junction
3) Crayford Creek Junction
4) Crayford Spur "A" Junction   4
5) Crayford Spur "B" Junction   1942   1849
6) Dartford Junction   6

WORKS

TO DARTFORD &
THE MEDWAY TOWNS
5
WORKS   1866

4   CRAYFORD (1866)   4
GOODS
(1965)

1866

GOODS   BEXLEY
(1963)   (1866)

CONTINUED ON INSET PAGE 35

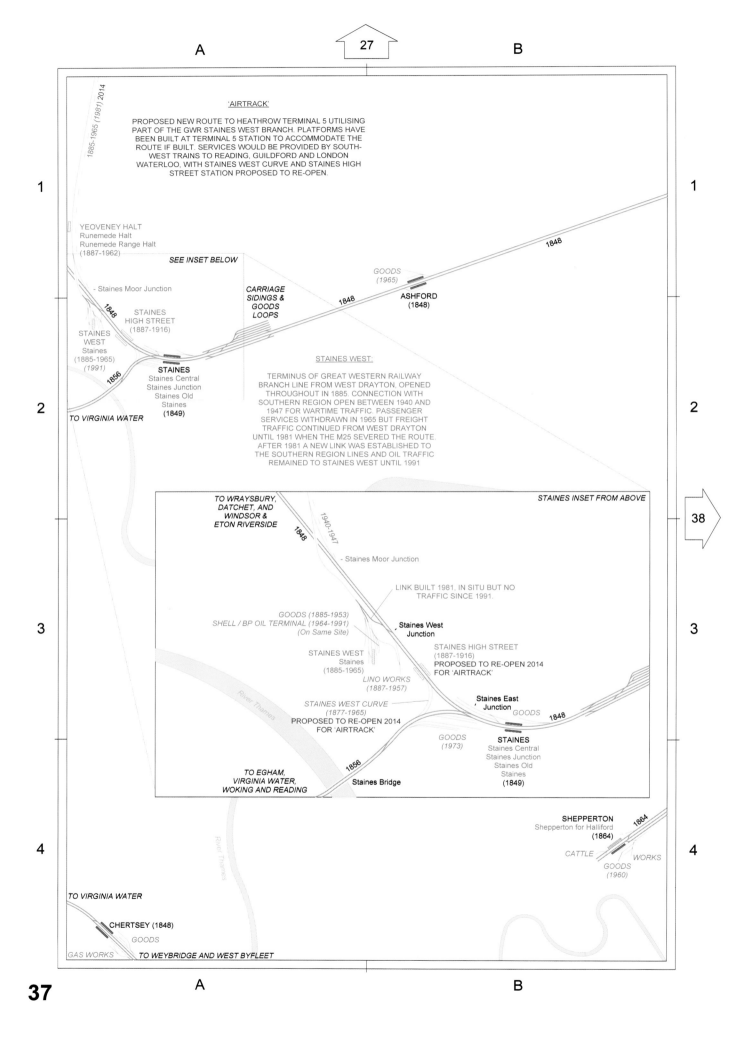

1885-1965 (1981) 2014

'AIRTRACK'

PROPOSED NEW ROUTE TO HEATHROW TERMINAL 5 UTILISING
PART OF THE GWR STAINES WEST BRANCH. PLATFORMS HAVE
BEEN BUILT AT TERMINAL 5 STATION TO ACCOMMODATE THE
ROUTE IF BUILT. SERVICES WOULD BE PROVIDED BY SOUTH-
WEST TRAINS TO READING, GUILDFORD AND LONDON
WATERLOO, WITH STAINES WEST CURVE AND STAINES HIGH
STREET STATION PROPOSED TO RE-OPEN.

YEOVENEY HALT
Runemede Halt
Runemede Range Halt
(1887-1962)

SEE INSET BELOW

1848

- Staines Moor Junction

*CARRIAGE
SIDINGS &
GOODS
LOOPS*

1848

*GOODS
(1965)*

1848

STAINES
HIGH STREET
(1887-1916)

ASHFORD
(1848)

STAINES
WEST
Staines
(1885-1965)
(1991)

1848

STAINES WEST:

TERMINUS OF GREAT WESTERN RAILWAY
BRANCH LINE FROM WEST DRAYTON, OPENED
THROUGHOUT IN 1885. CONNECTION WITH
SOUTHERN REGION OPEN BETWEEN 1940 AND
1947 FOR WARTIME TRAFFIC. PASSENGER
SERVICES WITHDRAWN IN 1965 BUT FREIGHT
TRAFFIC CONTINUED FROM WEST DRAYTON
UNTIL 1981 WHEN THE M25 SEVERED THE ROUTE.
AFTER 1981 A NEW LINK WAS ESTABLISHED TO
THE SOUTHERN REGION LINES AND OIL TRAFFIC
REMAINED TO STAINES WEST UNTIL 1991

1856

STAINES
Staines Central
Staines Junction
Staines Old
Staines
(1849)

TO VIRGINIA WATER

*TO WRAYSBURY,
DATCHET, AND
WINDSOR &
ETON RIVERSIDE*

STAINES INSET FROM ABOVE

38

1848

1940-1947

- Staines Moor Junction

LINK BUILT 1981, IN SITU BUT NO
TRAFFIC SINCE 1991.

GOODS (1885-1953)
SHELL / BP OIL TERMINAL (1964-1991)
(On Same Site)

Staines West
Junction

STAINES WEST
Staines
(1885-1965)

STAINES HIGH STREET
(1887-1916)
PROPOSED TO RE-OPEN 2014
FOR 'AIRTRACK'

*LINO WORKS
(1887-1957)*

River Thames

*STAINES WEST CURVE
(1877-1965)*
PROPOSED TO RE-OPEN 2014
FOR 'AIRTRACK'

Staines East
Junction

GOODS

1848

*GOODS
(1973)*

STAINES
Staines Central
Staines Junction
Staines Old
Staines
(1849)

1856

*TO EGHAM,
VIRGINIA WATER,
WOKING AND READING*

Staines Bridge

SHEPPERTON
Shepperton for Halliford
(1864)

1864

CATTLE

WORKS

*GOODS
(1960)*

River Thames

TO VIRGINIA WATER

CHERTSEY (1848)

GOODS

GAS WORKS   *TO WEYBRIDGE AND WEST BYFLEET*

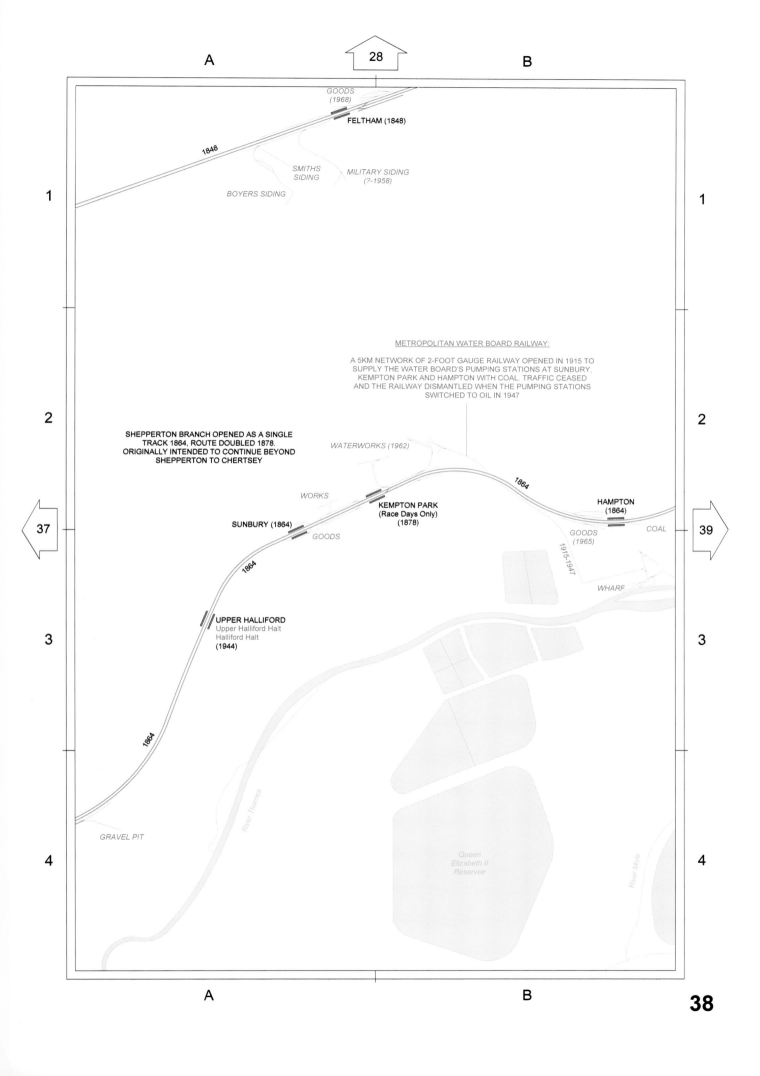

GOODS
(1968)

FELTHAM (1848)

1848

SMITHS
SIDING

MILITARY SIDING
(?-1958)

BOYERS SIDING

1

METROPOLITAN WATER BOARD RAILWAY:

A 5KM NETWORK OF 2-FOOT GAUGE RAILWAY OPENED IN 1915 TO
SUPPLY THE WATER BOARD'S PUMPING STATIONS AT SUNBURY,
KEMPTON PARK AND HAMPTON WITH COAL. TRAFFIC CEASED
AND THE RAILWAY DISMANTLED WHEN THE PUMPING STATIONS
SWITCHED TO OIL IN 1947

2

SHEPPERTON BRANCH OPENED AS A SINGLE
TRACK 1864, ROUTE DOUBLED 1878.
ORIGINALLY INTENDED TO CONTINUE BEYOND
SHEPPERTON TO CHERTSEY

WATERWORKS (1962)

1864

WORKS

KEMPTON PARK
(Race Days Only)
(1878)

HAMPTON
(1864)

SUNBURY (1864)

GOODS

COAL

37

GOODS
(1965)

39

1915-1947

1864

WHARF

UPPER HALLIFORD
Upper Halliford Halt
Halliford Halt
(1944)

3

1864

River Thames

GRAVEL PIT

Queen
Elizabeth II
Reservoir

River Mole

4

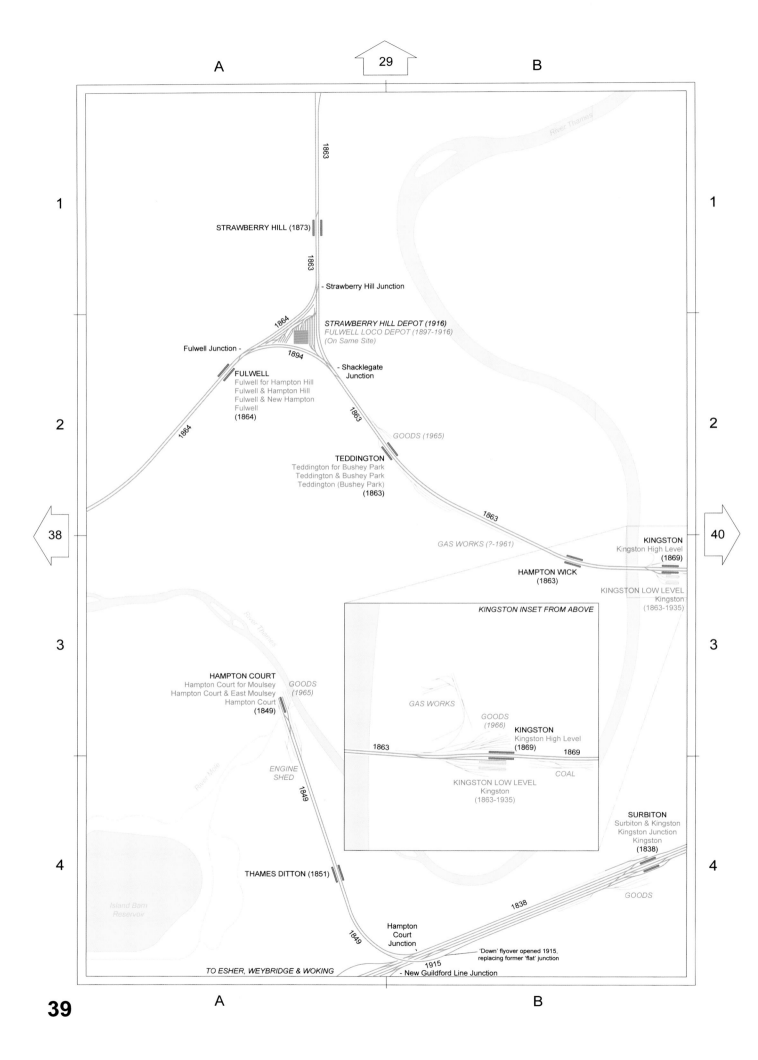

STRAWBERRY HILL (1873)

1863

1863

- Strawberry Hill Junction

1864

STRAWBERRY HILL DEPOT (1916)
FULWELL LOCO DEPOT (1897-1916)
(On Same Site)

Fulwell Junction -

1894

- Shacklegate Junction

FULWELL
Fulwell for Hampton Hill
Fulwell & Hampton Hill
Fulwell & New Hampton
Fulwell
(1864)

1864

1863

GOODS (1965)

TEDDINGTON
Teddington for Bushey Park
Teddington & Bushey Park
Teddington (Bushey Park)
(1863)

1863

GAS WORKS (?-1961)

KINGSTON
Kingston High Level
(1869)

HAMPTON WICK
(1863)

KINGSTON LOW LEVEL
Kingston
(1863-1935)

KINGSTON INSET FROM ABOVE

GAS WORKS

GOODS
(1966)

KINGSTON
Kingston High Level
(1869)

1863

1869

COAL

KINGSTON LOW LEVEL
Kingston
(1863-1935)

HAMPTON COURT
Hampton Court for Moulsey
Hampton Court & East Moulsey
Hampton Court
(1849)

GOODS
(1965)

ENGINE SHED

1849

River Thames

River Mole

Island Barn Reservoir

THAMES DITTON (1851)

1849

Hampton Court Junction

1849

SURBITON
Surbiton & Kingston
Kingston Junction
Kingston
(1838)

1838

GOODS

'Down' flyover opened 1915,
replacing former 'flat' junction

1915

TO ESHER, WEYBRIDGE & WOKING

- New Guildford Line Junction

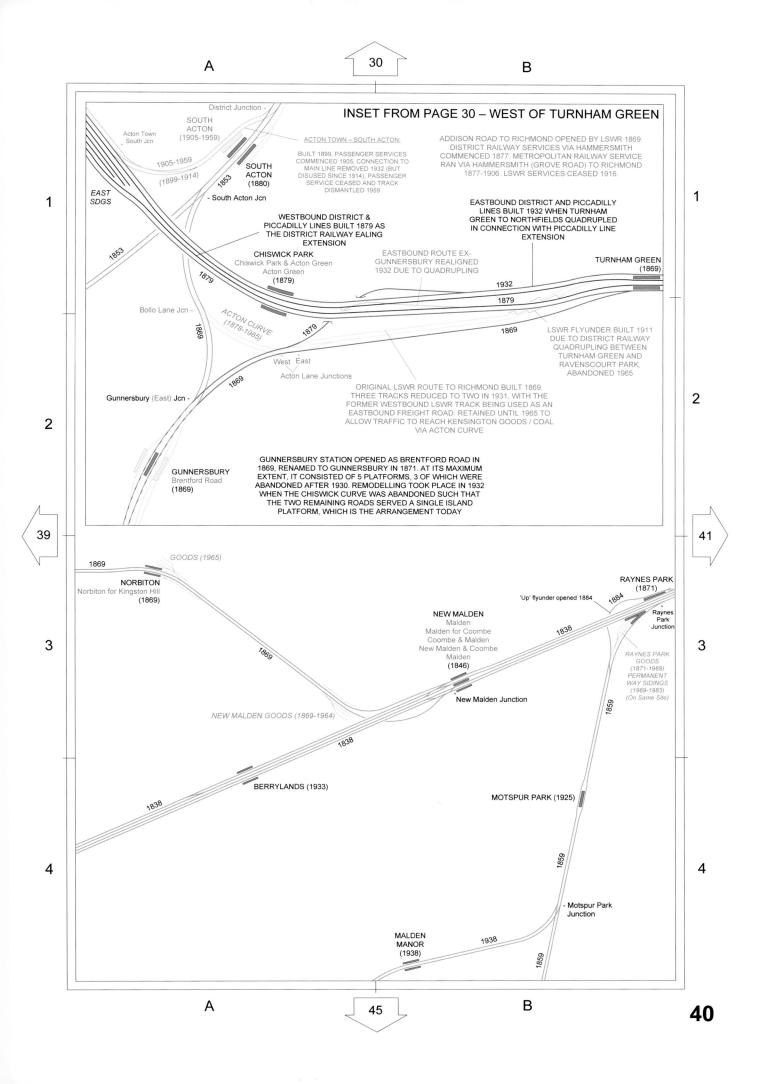

INSET FROM PAGE 30 – WEST OF TURNHAM GREEN

District Junction -

SOUTH ACTON
(1905-1959)

Acton Town - South Jcn

1905-1959

(1899-1914)

SOUTH ACTON
(1880)

EAST SDGS

1853

- South Acton Jcn

ACTON TOWN – SOUTH ACTON:

BUILT 1899, PASSENGER SERVICES COMMENCED 1905, CONNECTION TO MAIN LINE REMOVED 1932 (BUT DISUSED SINCE 1914), PASSENGER SERVICE CEASED AND TRACK DISMANTLED 1959

ADDISON ROAD TO RICHMOND OPENED BY LSWR 1869. DISTRICT RAILWAY SERVICES VIA HAMMERSMITH COMMENCED 1877. METROPOLITAN RAILWAY SERVICE RAN VIA HAMMERSMITH (GROVE ROAD) TO RICHMOND 1877-1906. LSWR SERVICES CEASED 1916.

WESTBOUND DISTRICT & PICCADILLY LINES BUILT 1879 AS THE DISTRICT RAILWAY EALING EXTENSION

EASTBOUND DISTRICT AND PICCADILLY LINES BUILT 1932 WHEN TURNHAM GREEN TO NORTHFIELDS QUADRUPLED IN CONNECTION WITH PICCADILLY LINE EXTENSION

1853

CHISWICK PARK
Chiswick Park & Acton Green
Acton Green
(1879)

EASTBOUND ROUTE EX-GUNNERSBURY REALIGNED 1932 DUE TO QUADRUPLING

TURNHAM GREEN
(1869)

1879

1932

Bollo Lane Jcn -

ACTON CURVE
(1878-1965)

1879

1879

1869

LSWR FLYUNDER BUILT 1911 DUE TO DISTRICT RAILWAY QUADRUPLING BETWEEN TURNHAM GREEN AND RAVENSCOURT PARK, ABANDONED 1965

West East
Acton Lane Junctions

Gunnersbury (East) Jcn -

1869

ORIGINAL LSWR ROUTE TO RICHMOND BUILT 1869. THREE TRACKS REDUCED TO TWO IN 1931, WITH THE FORMER WESTBOUND LSWR TRACK BEING USED AS AN EASTBOUND FREIGHT ROAD. RETAINED UNTIL 1965 TO ALLOW TRAFFIC TO REACH KENSINGTON GOODS / COAL VIA ACTON CURVE

GUNNERSBURY
Brentford Road
(1869)

GUNNERSBURY STATION OPENED AS BRENTFORD ROAD IN 1869, RENAMED TO GUNNERSBURY IN 1871. AT ITS MAXIMUM EXTENT, IT CONSISTED OF 5 PLATFORMS, 3 OF WHICH WERE ABANDONED AFTER 1930. REMODELLING TOOK PLACE IN 1932 WHEN THE CHISWICK CURVE WAS ABANDONED SUCH THAT THE TWO REMAINING ROADS SERVED A SINGLE ISLAND PLATFORM, WHICH IS THE ARRANGEMENT TODAY

1869

GOODS (1965)

NORBITON
Norbiton for Kingston Hill
(1869)

RAYNES PARK
(1871)

'Up' flyunder opened 1884

1884

1869

NEW MALDEN
Malden
Malden for Coombe
Coombe & Malden
New Malden & Coombe
Malden
(1846)

1838

Raynes Park Junction

RAYNES PARK GOODS (1871-1969) PERMANENT WAY SIDINGS (1969-1983) (On Same Site)

New Malden Junction

1859

NEW MALDEN GOODS (1869-1964)

1838

BERRYLANDS (1933)

MOTSPUR PARK (1925)

1838

1859

- Motspur Park Junction

MALDEN MANOR
(1938)

1938

1859

← 39
41 →

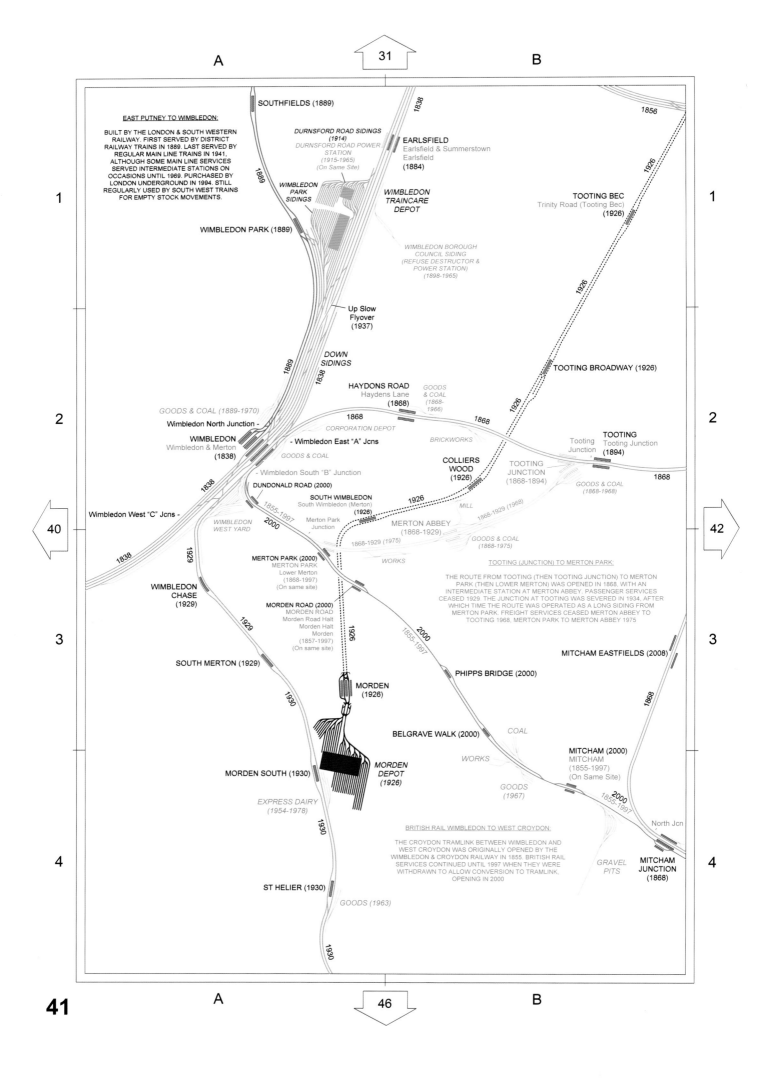

SOUTHFIELDS (1889)

1838

DURNSFORD ROAD SIDINGS
(1914)
*DURNSFORD ROAD POWER
STATION
(1915-1965)
(On Same Site)*

EARLSFIELD
Earlsfield & Summerstown
Earlsfield
(1884)

1889

*WIMBLEDON
PARK
SIDINGS*

WIMBLEDON
TRAINCARE
DEPOT

1926

TOOTING BEC
Trinity Road (Tooting Bec)
(1926)

EAST PUTNEY TO WIMBLEDON:

BUILT BY THE LONDON & SOUTH WESTERN
RAILWAY. FIRST SERVED BY DISTRICT
RAILWAY TRAINS IN 1889. LAST SERVED BY
REGULAR MAIN LINE TRAINS IN 1941,
ALTHOUGH SOME MAIN LINE SERVICES
SERVED INTERMEDIATE STATIONS ON
OCCASIONS UNTIL 1969. PURCHASED BY
LONDON UNDERGROUND IN 1994. STILL
REGULARLY USED BY SOUTH WEST TRAINS
FOR EMPTY STOCK MOVEMENTS.

WIMBLEDON PARK (1889)

1926

*WIMBLEDON BOROUGH
COUNCIL SIDING
(REFUSE DESTRUCTOR &
POWER STATION)
(1898-1965)*

Up Slow
Flyover
(1937)

*DOWN
SIDINGS*

1889

1838

HAYDONS ROAD
Haydens Lane
(1868)

*GOODS
& COAL
(1868-
1966)*

TOOTING BROADWAY (1926)

GOODS & COAL (1889-1970)

1868

1926

Wimbledon North Junction -

1868

TOOTING
Tooting Junction
(1894)

WIMBLEDON
Wimbledon & Merton
(1838)

- Wimbledon East "A" Jcns

CORPORATION DEPOT

BRICKWORKS

Tooting
Junction

COLLIERS
WOOD
(1926)

TOOTING
JUNCTION
(1868-1894)

1868

GOODS & COAL

- Wimbledon South "B" Junction

1838

DUNDONALD ROAD (2000)

1926

*GOODS & COAL
(1868-1968)*

Wimbledon West "C" Jcns -

SOUTH WIMBLEDON
South Wimbledon (Merton)
(1926)

MILL

1855-1997

1868-1929 (1968)

1929

*WIMBLEDON
WEST YARD*

2000

Merton Park
Junction

MERTON ABBEY
(1868-1929)

1838

1868-1929 (1975)

*GOODS & COAL
(1868-1975)*

MERTON PARK (2000)
MERTON PARK
Lower Merton
(1868-1997)
(On same site)

WORKS

TOOTING (JUNCTION) TO MERTON PARK:

THE ROUTE FROM TOOTING (THEN TOOTING JUNCTION) TO MERTON
PARK (THEN LOWER MERTON) WAS OPENED IN 1868, WITH AN
INTERMEDIATE STATION AT MERTON ABBEY. PASSENGER SERVICES
CEASED 1929. THE JUNCTION AT TOOTING WAS SEVERED IN 1934, AFTER
WHICH TIME THE ROUTE WAS OPERATED AS A LONG SIDING FROM
MERTON PARK. FREIGHT SERVICES CEASED MERTON ABBEY TO
TOOTING 1968, MERTON PARK TO MERTON ABBEY 1975

WIMBLEDON
CHASE
(1929)

MORDEN ROAD (2000)
MORDEN ROAD
Morden Road Halt
Morden Halt
Morden
(1857-1997)
(On same site)

1926

MITCHAM EASTFIELDS (2008)

1929

1868

PHIPPS BRIDGE (2000)

1855-1997

2000

SOUTH MERTON (1929)

1930

MORDEN
(1926)

COAL

BELGRAVE WALK (2000)

WORKS

MITCHAM (2000)
MITCHAM
(1855-1997)
(On Same Site)

MORDEN SOUTH (1930)

*MORDEN
DEPOT
(1926)*

*GOODS
(1967)*

2000

1855-1997

*EXPRESS DAIRY
(1954-1978)*

North Jcn

1930

BRITISH RAIL WIMBLEDON TO WEST CROYDON:

THE CROYDON TRAMLINK BETWEEN WIMBLEDON AND
WEST CROYDON WAS ORIGINALLY OPENED BY THE
WIMBLEDON & CROYDON RAILWAY IN 1855. BRITISH RAIL
SERVICES CONTINUED UNTIL 1997 WHEN THEY WERE
WITHDRAWN TO ALLOW CONVERSION TO TRAMLINK,
OPENING IN 2000

*GRAVEL
PITS*

MITCHAM
JUNCTION
(1868)

ST HELIER (1930)

GOODS (1963)

1930

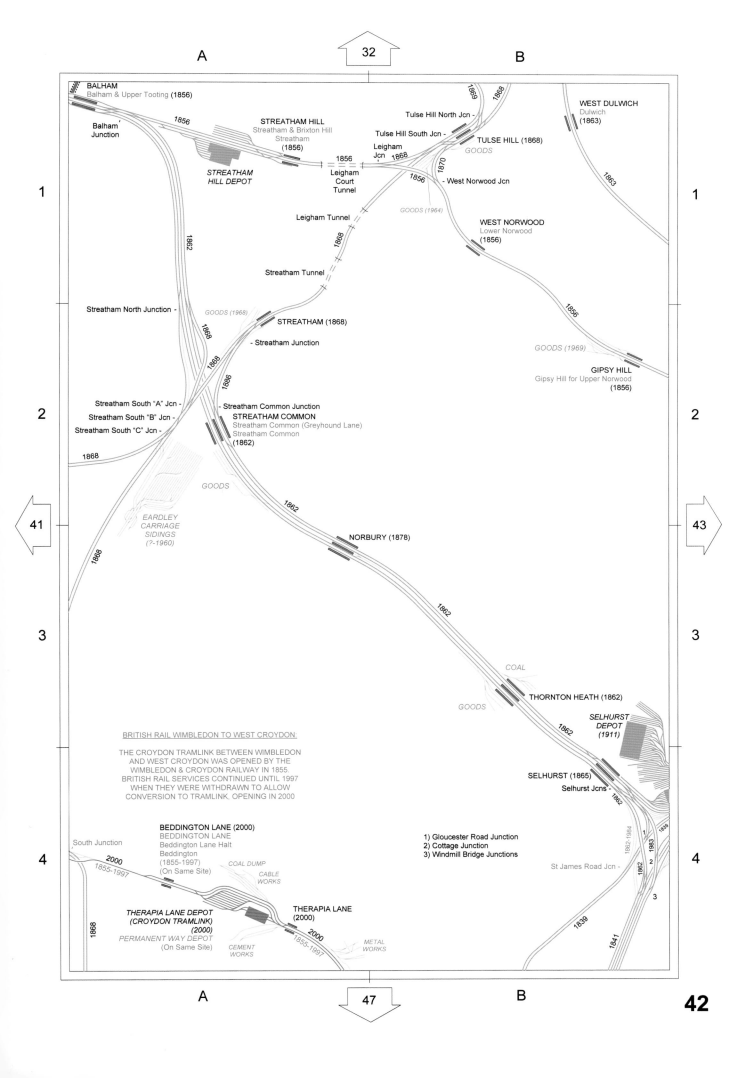

BALHAM
Balham & Upper Tooting (1856)

Balham Junction

1856

STREATHAM HILL
Streatham & Brixton Hill
Streatham
(1856)

Tulse Hill North Jcn -

Tulse Hill South Jcn -

TULSE HILL (1868)
GOODS

WEST DULWICH
Dulwich
(1863)

1869
1868

Leigham
Jcn

1856
1868

1856

1870

- West Norwood Jcn

1863

1

1862

1856
Leigham
Court
Tunnel

GOODS (1964)

WEST NORWOOD
Lower Norwood
(1856)

1

Leigham Tunnel

1868

Streatham Tunnel

1856

Streatham North Junction -

GOODS (1968)

STREATHAM (1868)

GOODS (1969)

GIPSY HILL
Gipsy Hill for Upper Norwood
(1856)

1868

- Streatham Junction

1868

1886

Streatham South "A" Jcn -
Streatham South "B" Jcn -
Streatham South "C" Jcn -

- Streatham Common Junction
STREATHAM COMMON
Streatham Common (Greyhound Lane)
Streatham Common
(1862)

2

2

1868

GOODS

41

EARDLEY
CARRIAGE
SIDINGS
(?-1960)

1862

NORBURY (1878)

43

1868

3

1862

3

COAL

GOODS

THORNTON HEATH (1862)

1862

SELHURST
DEPOT
(1911)

BRITISH RAIL WIMBLEDON TO WEST CROYDON:

THE CROYDON TRAMLINK BETWEEN WIMBLEDON
AND WEST CROYDON WAS OPENED BY THE
WIMBLEDON & CROYDON RAILWAY IN 1855.
BRITISH RAIL SERVICES CONTINUED UNTIL 1997
WHEN THEY WERE WITHDRAWN TO ALLOW
CONVERSION TO TRAMLINK, OPENING IN 2000

SELHURST (1865)

Selhurst Jcns -

1862

BEDDINGTON LANE (2000)
BEDDINGTON LANE
Beddington Lane Halt
Beddington
(1855-1997)
(On Same Site)

1) Gloucester Road Junction
2) Cottage Junction
3) Windmill Bridge Junctions

1862-1984

1
1983
1859

South Junction

2000
1855-1997

COAL DUMP

CABLE
WORKS

2

1862

4

St James Road Jcn -

4

THERAPIA LANE DEPOT
(CROYDON TRAMLINK)
(2000)

PERMANENT WAY DEPOT
(On Same Site)

THERAPIA LANE
(2000)

1868

2000
1855-1997

CEMENT
WORKS

METAL
WORKS

3

1839

1841

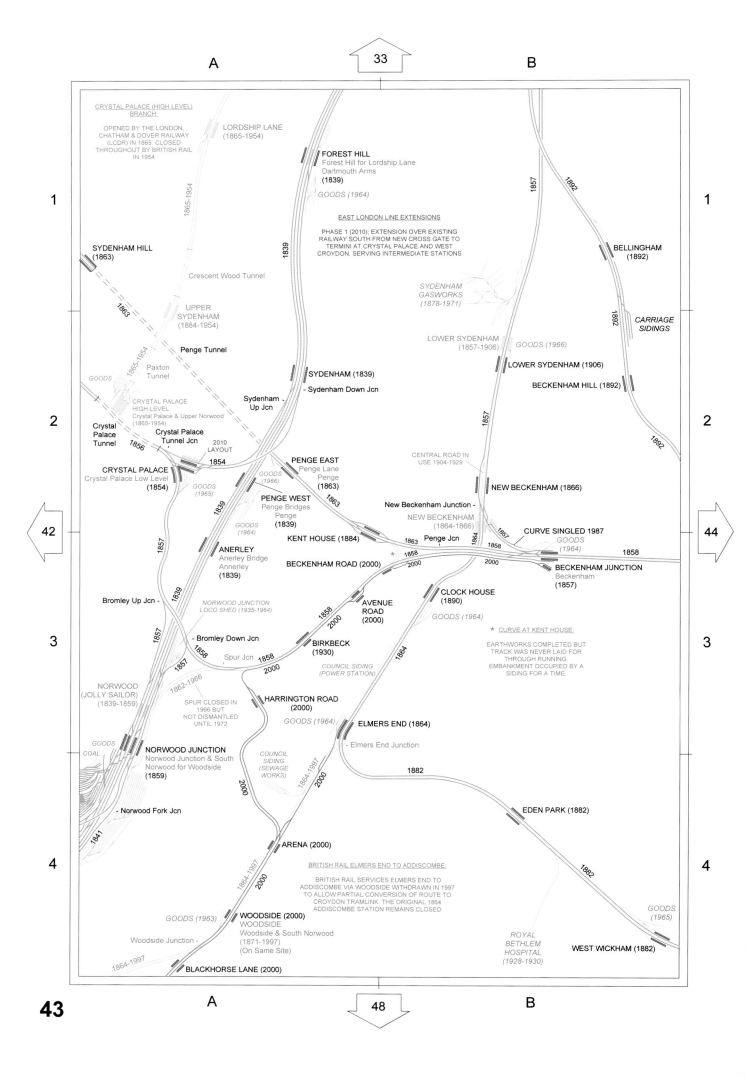

CRYSTAL PALACE (HIGH LEVEL) BRANCH:

OPENED BY THE LONDON, CHATHAM & DOVER RAILWAY (LCDR) IN 1865. CLOSED THROUGHOUT BY BRITISH RAIL IN 1954

LORDSHIP LANE (1865-1954)

FOREST HILL
Forest Hill for Lordship Lane
Dartmouth Arms
(1839)

GOODS (1964)

EAST LONDON LINE EXTENSIONS

PHASE 1 (2010); EXTENSION OVER EXISTING RAILWAY SOUTH FROM NEW CROSS GATE TO TERMINI AT CRYSTAL PALACE AND WEST CROYDON, SERVING INTERMEDIATE STATIONS

SYDENHAM HILL
(1863)

SYDENHAM GASWORKS (1878-1971)

BELLINGHAM
(1892)

Crescent Wood Tunnel

1863

1857

1892

UPPER SYDENHAM
(1884-1954)

1892

CARRIAGE SIDINGS

Penge Tunnel

Paxton Tunnel

GOODS

1865-1954

LOWER SYDENHAM
(1857-1906)

GOODS (1966)

LOWER SYDENHAM (1906)

BECKENHAM HILL (1892)

SYDENHAM (1839)

- Sydenham Down Jcn

Sydenham Up Jcn

CRYSTAL PALACE HIGH LEVEL
Crystal Palace & Upper Norwood
(1865-1954)

Crystal Palace Tunnel

Crystal Palace Tunnel Jcn

1857

1892

1856

2010 LAYOUT

CENTRAL ROAD IN USE 1904-1929

PENGE EAST
Penge Lane
Penge
(1863)

1854

1854

NEW BECKENHAM (1866)

CRYSTAL PALACE
Crystal Palace Low Level
(1854)

GOODS (1966)

GOODS (1965)

1839

PENGE WEST
Penge Bridges
Penge
(1839)

1863

New Beckenham Junction -

NEW BECKENHAM
(1864-1866)

GOODS (1964)

KENT HOUSE (1884)

1863

Penge Jcn

CURVE SINGLED 1987

GOODS (1964)

1857

ANERLEY
Anerley Bridge
Annerley
(1839)

BECKENHAM ROAD (2000)

*

1858

1864

1858

1858

2000

2000

1858

BECKENHAM JUNCTION
Beckenham
(1857)

Bromley Up Jcn -

NORWOOD JUNCTION LOCO SHED (1935-1964)

AVENUE ROAD
(2000)

CLOCK HOUSE
(1890)

1839

1858

2000

GOODS (1964)

* CURVE AT KENT HOUSE:

EARTHWORKS COMPLETED BUT TRACK WAS NEVER LAID FOR THROUGH RUNNING. EMBANKMENT OCCUPIED BY A SIDING FOR A TIME.

1857

- Bromley Down Jcn

Spur Jcn

1858

1858

BIRKBECK
(1930)

1864

1857

2000

COUNCIL SIDING (POWER STATION)

NORWOOD (JOLLY SAILOR)
(1839-1859)

1862-1966

SPUR CLOSED IN 1966 BUT NOT DISMANTLED UNTIL 1972

HARRINGTON ROAD
(2000)

GOODS (1964)

ELMERS END (1864)

GOODS COAL

NORWOOD JUNCTION
Norwood Junction & South Norwood for Woodside
(1859)

COUNCIL SIDING (SEWAGE WORKS)

1864-1997

- Elmers End Junction

2000

2000

1882

- Norwood Fork Jcn

EDEN PARK (1882)

1841

2000

ARENA (2000)

1882

BRITISH RAIL ELMERS END TO ADDISCOMBE:

BRITISH RAIL SERVICES ELMERS END TO ADDISCOMBE VIA WOODSIDE WITHDRAWN IN 1997 TO ALLOW PARTIAL CONVERSION OF ROUTE TO CROYDON TRAMLINK. THE ORIGINAL 1864 ADDISCOMBE STATION REMAINS CLOSED

1864-1997

2000

GOODS (1963)

WOODSIDE (2000)
WOODSIDE
Woodside & South Norwood
(1871-1997)
(On Same Site)

ROYAL BETHLEM HOSPITAL (1928-1930)

GOODS (1965)

Woodside Junction -

WEST WICKHAM (1882)

1864-1997

BLACKHORSE LANE (2000)

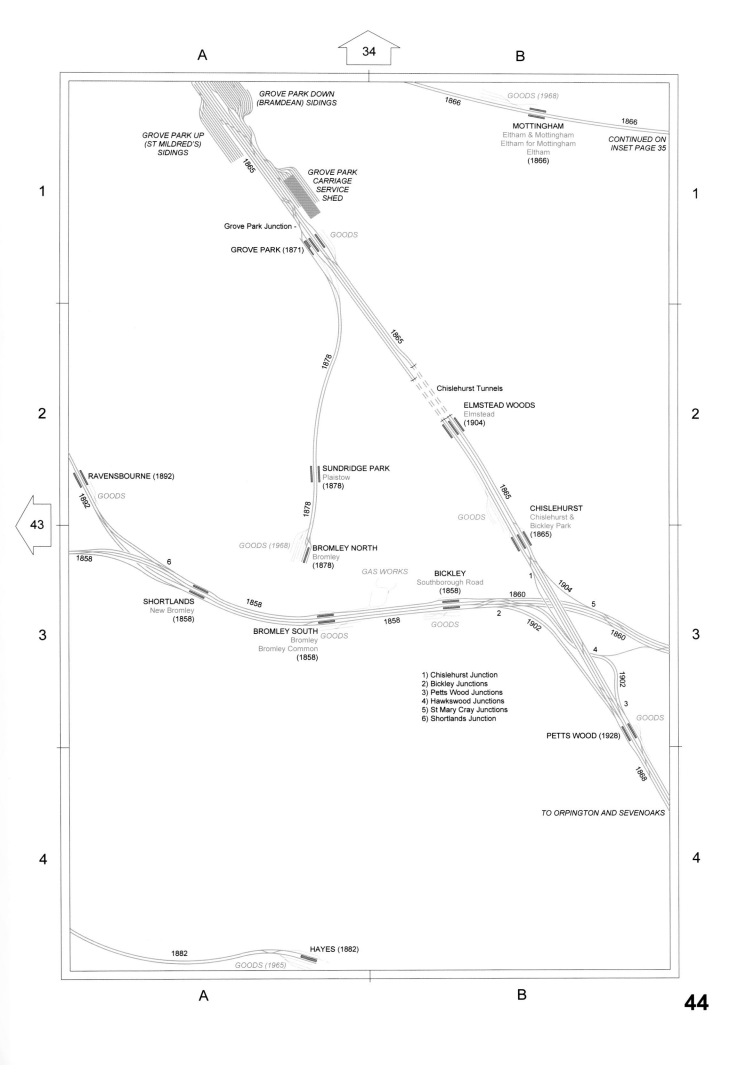

GROVE PARK DOWN
(BRAMDEAN) SIDINGS

GOODS (1968)

1866

1866

MOTTINGHAM
Eltham & Mottingham
Eltham for Mottingham
Eltham
(1866)

CONTINUED ON INSET PAGE 35

GROVE PARK UP
(ST MILDRED'S)
SIDINGS

1865

1

GROVE PARK
CARRIAGE
SERVICE
SHED

Grove Park Junction -

GOODS

GROVE PARK (1871)

1865

1878

1865

Chislehurst Tunnels

ELMSTEAD WOODS
Elmstead
(1904)

2

RAVENSBOURNE (1892)

GOODS

SUNDRIDGE PARK
Plaistow
(1878)

1865

1892

1878

GOODS

CHISLEHURST
Chislehurst &
Bickley Park
(1865)

1858

6

GOODS (1968)

BROMLEY NORTH
Bromley
(1878)

GAS WORKS

BICKLEY
Southborough Road
(1858)

1

1904

5

SHORTLANDS
New Bromley
(1858)

1858

1858

1860

1860

2

1902

4

1868

3

BROMLEY SOUTH
Bromley
Bromley Common
(1858)

GOODS

1858

GOODS

1902

3

GOODS

1) Chislehurst Junction
2) Bickley Junctions
3) Petts Wood Junctions
4) Hawkswood Junctions
5) St Mary Cray Junctions
6) Shortlands Junction

PETTS WOOD (1928)

1868

TO ORPINGTON AND SEVENOAKS

4

1882

HAYES (1882)

GOODS (1965)

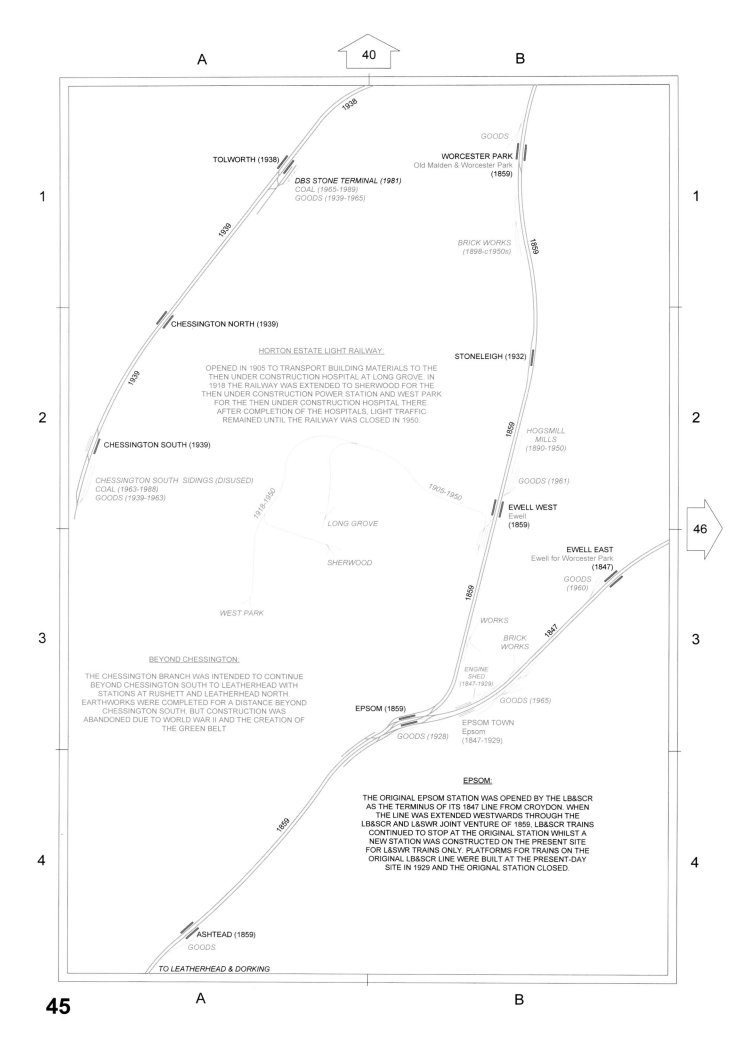

TOLWORTH (1938)

DBS STONE TERMINAL (1981)
COAL (1965-1989)
GOODS (1939-1965)

GOODS

WORCESTER PARK
Old Malden & Worcester Park
(1859)

BRICK WORKS
(1898-c1950s)

CHESSINGTON NORTH (1939)

STONELEIGH (1932)

HORTON ESTATE LIGHT RAILWAY:

OPENED IN 1905 TO TRANSPORT BUILDING MATERIALS TO THE
THEN UNDER CONSTRUCTION HOSPITAL AT LONG GROVE. IN
1918 THE RAILWAY WAS EXTENDED TO SHERWOOD FOR THE
THEN UNDER CONSTRUCTION POWER STATION AND WEST PARK
FOR THE THEN UNDER CONSTRUCTION HOSPITAL THERE.
AFTER COMPLETION OF THE HOSPITALS, LIGHT TRAFFIC
REMAINED UNTIL THE RAILWAY WAS CLOSED IN 1950.

HOGSMILL
MILLS
(1890-1950)

GOODS (1961)

CHESSINGTON SOUTH (1939)

CHESSINGTON SOUTH SIDINGS (DISUSED)
COAL (1963-1988)
GOODS (1939-1963)

1905-1950

EWELL WEST
Ewell
(1859)

LONG GROVE

EWELL EAST
Ewell for Worcester Park
(1847)

GOODS
(1960)

SHERWOOD

WEST PARK

WORKS

BRICK
WORKS

BEYOND CHESSINGTON:

THE CHESSINGTON BRANCH WAS INTENDED TO CONTINUE
BEYOND CHESSINGTON SOUTH TO LEATHERHEAD WITH
STATIONS AT RUSHETT AND LEATHERHEAD NORTH.
EARTHWORKS WERE COMPLETED FOR A DISTANCE BEYOND
CHESSINGTON SOUTH, BUT CONSTRUCTION WAS
ABANDONED DUE TO WORLD WAR II AND THE CREATION OF
THE GREEN BELT

ENGINE
SHED
(1847-1929)

GOODS (1965)

EPSOM (1859)

EPSOM TOWN
Epsom
(1847-1929)

GOODS (1928)

EPSOM:

THE ORIGINAL EPSOM STATION WAS OPENED BY THE LB&SCR
AS THE TERMINUS OF ITS 1847 LINE FROM CROYDON. WHEN
THE LINE WAS EXTENDED WESTWARDS THROUGH THE
LB&SCR AND L&SWR JOINT VENTURE OF 1859, LB&SCR TRAINS
CONTINUED TO STOP AT THE ORIGINAL STATION WHILST A
NEW STATION WAS CONSTRUCTED ON THE PRESENT SITE
FOR L&SWR TRAINS ONLY. PLATFORMS FOR TRAINS ON THE
ORIGINAL LB&SCR LINE WERE BUILT AT THE PRESENT-DAY
SITE IN 1929 AND THE ORIGNAL STATION CLOSED.

ASHTEAD (1859)

GOODS

TO LEATHERHEAD & DORKING

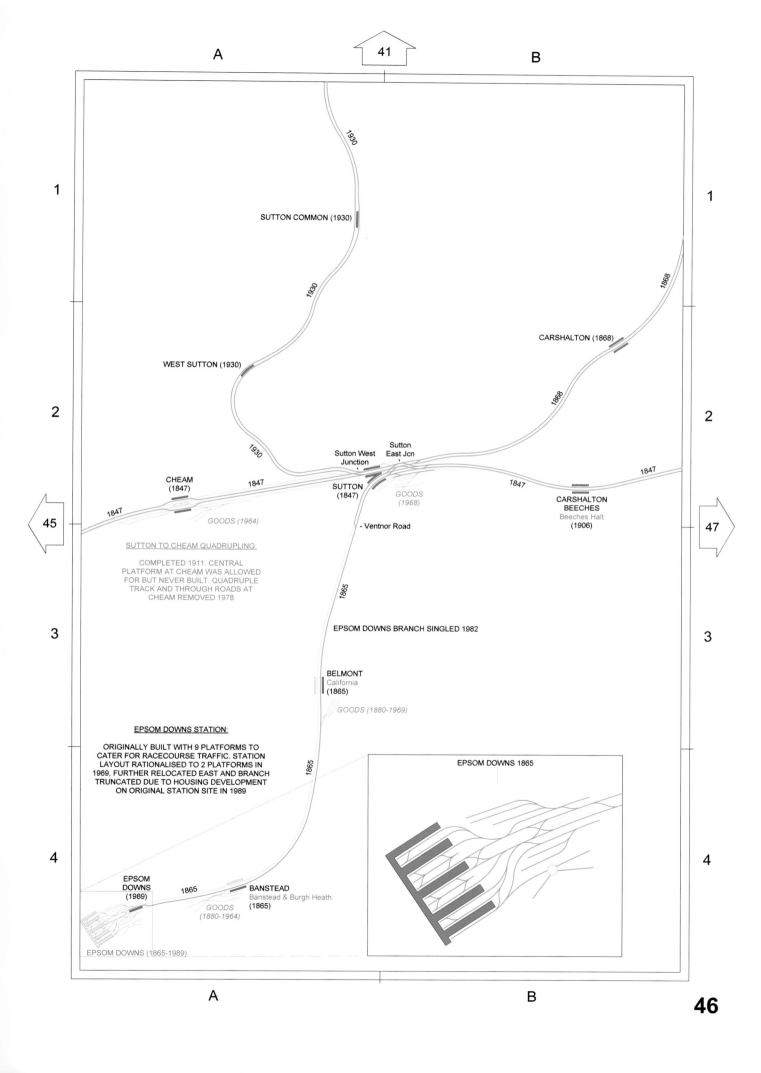

1

SUTTON COMMON (1930)

1930

1930

CARSHALTON (1868)

1868

WEST SUTTON (1930)

2

1868

2

1930

Sutton West Junction

Sutton East Jcn

CHEAM (1847)

1847

SUTTON (1847)

1847

1847

45

1847

GOODS (1964)

GOODS (1968)

CARSHALTON BEECHES
Beeches Halt (1906)

47

- Ventnor Road

SUTTON TO CHEAM QUADRUPLING:

COMPLETED 1911. CENTRAL PLATFORM AT CHEAM WAS ALLOWED FOR BUT NEVER BUILT. QUADRUPLE TRACK AND THROUGH ROADS AT CHEAM REMOVED 1978

1865

3

EPSOM DOWNS BRANCH SINGLED 1982

3

BELMONT
California (1865)

GOODS (1880-1969)

EPSOM DOWNS STATION:

ORIGINALLY BUILT WITH 9 PLATFORMS TO CATER FOR RACECOURSE TRAFFIC. STATION LAYOUT RATIONALISED TO 2 PLATFORMS IN 1969, FURTHER RELOCATED EAST AND BRANCH TRUNCATED DUE TO HOUSING DEVELOPMENT ON ORIGINAL STATION SITE IN 1989

1865

EPSOM DOWNS 1865

4

EPSOM DOWNS (1989)

1865

BANSTEAD
Banstead & Burgh Heath (1865)

GOODS (1880-1964)

4

EPSOM DOWNS (1865-1989)

46

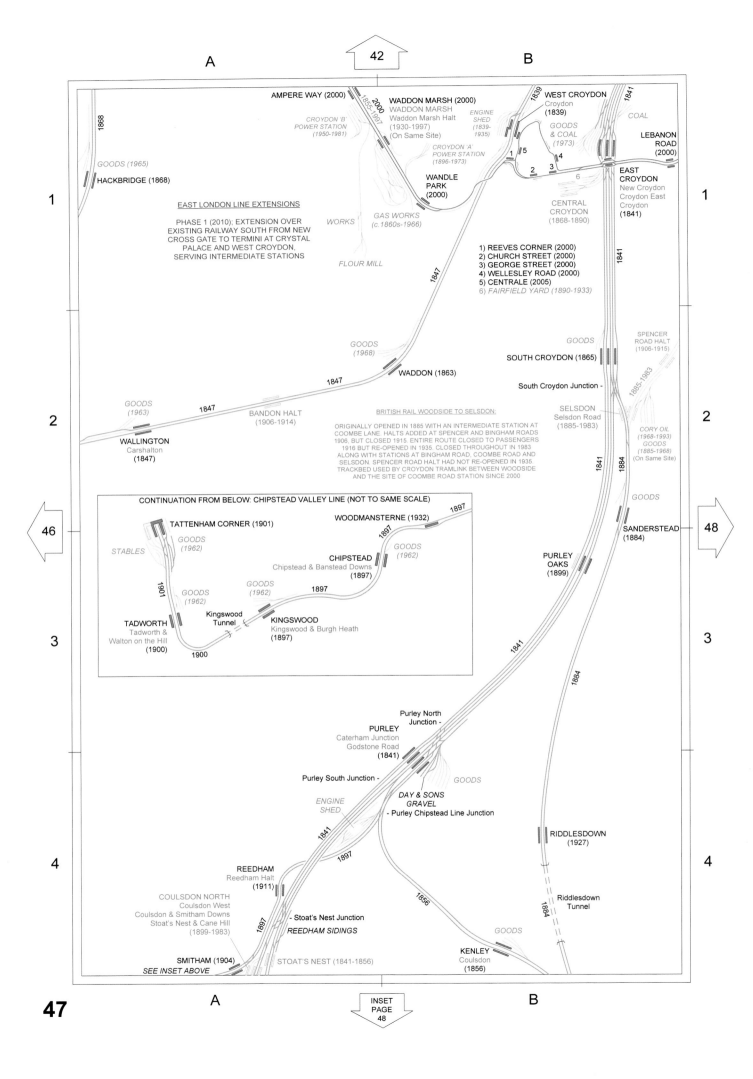

1855-1997
2000
1868

GOODS (1965)

HACKBRIDGE (1868)

AMPERE WAY (2000)

CROYDON 'B'
POWER STATION
(1950-1981)

WADDON MARSH (2000)
WADDON MARSH
Waddon Marsh Halt
(1930-1997)
(On Same Site)

CROYDON 'A'
POWER STATION
(1896-1973)

ENGINE
SHED
(1839-
1935)

1839 WEST CROYDON
Croydon
(1839)

1841

GOODS
& COAL
(1973)

COAL

1841

LEBANON
ROAD
(2000)

EAST
CROYDON
New Croydon
Croydon East
Croydon
(1841)

CENTRAL
CROYDON
(1868-1890)

1   5   4
2   3
6

WANDLE
PARK
(2000)

WORKS

GAS WORKS
(c.1860s-1966)

FLOUR MILL

EAST LONDON LINE EXTENSIONS

PHASE 1 (2010); EXTENSION OVER
EXISTING RAILWAY SOUTH FROM NEW
CROSS GATE TO TERMINI AT CRYSTAL
PALACE AND WEST CROYDON,
SERVING INTERMEDIATE STATIONS

1) REEVES CORNER (2000)
2) CHURCH STREET (2000)
3) GEORGE STREET (2000)
4) WELLESLEY ROAD (2000)
5) CENTRALE (2005)
6) *FAIRFIELD YARD (1890-1933)*

1847

1847

GOODS
(1968)

WADDON (1863)

GOODS
(1963)

BANDON HALT
(1906-1914)

WALLINGTON
Carshalton
(1847)

1847

GOODS

SOUTH CROYDON (1865)

South Croydon Junction -

SPENCER
ROAD HALT
(1906-1915)

1885-1983

SELSDON
Selsdon Road
(1885-1983)

CORY OIL
(1968-1993)
GOODS
(1885-1968)
(On Same Site)

GOODS

1841

1884

SANDERSTEAD
(1884)

BRITISH RAIL WOODSIDE TO SELSDON:

ORIGINALLY OPENED IN 1885 WITH AN INTERMEDIATE STATION AT
COOMBE LANE. HALTS ADDED AT SPENCER AND BINGHAM ROADS
1906, BUT CLOSED 1915. ENTIRE ROUTE CLOSED TO PASSENGERS
1916 BUT RE-OPENED IN 1935. CLOSED THROUGHOUT IN 1983
ALONG WITH STATIONS AT BINGHAM ROAD, COOMBE ROAD AND
SELSDON. SPENCER ROAD HALT HAD NOT RE-OPENED IN 1935.
TRACKBED USED BY CROYDON TRAMLINK BETWEEN WOODSIDE
AND THE SITE OF COOMBE ROAD STATION SINCE 2000

CONTINUATION FROM BELOW: CHIPSTEAD VALLEY LINE (NOT TO SAME SCALE)

1897

WOODMANSTERNE (1932)

TATTENHAM CORNER (1901)

GOODS
(1962)

STABLES

1901

1897

1897

CHIPSTEAD
Chipstead & Banstead Downs
(1897)

GOODS
(1962)

GOODS
(1962)

GOODS
(1962)

1897

PURLEY
OAKS
(1899)

TADWORTH
Tadworth &
Walton on the Hill
(1900)

1900

Kingswood
Tunnel

KINGSWOOD
Kingswood & Burgh Heath
(1897)

1841

1884

Purley North
Junction -

PURLEY
Caterham Junction
Godstone Road
(1841)

Purley South Junction -

GOODS

ENGINE
SHED

*DAY & SONS
GRAVEL*
- Purley Chipstead Line Junction

1841

1897

RIDDLESDOWN
(1927)

Riddlesdown
Tunnel

1884

REEDHAM
Reedham Halt
(1911)

COULSDON NORTH
Coulsdon West
Coulsdon & Smitham Downs
Stoat's Nest & Cane Hill
(1899-1983)

1897

1856

- Stoat's Nest Junction
REEDHAM SIDINGS

SMITHAM (1904)
SEE INSET ABOVE

STOAT'S NEST (1841-1856)

GOODS

KENLEY
Coulsdon
(1856)

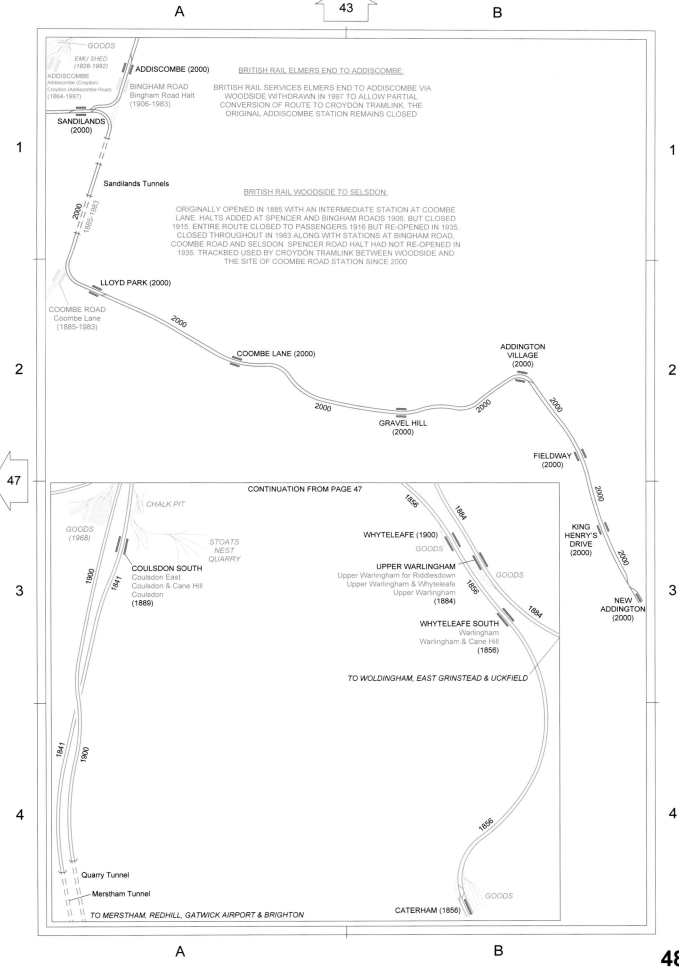

GOODS

EMU SHED
(1926-1992)

ADDISCOMBE
Addiscombe (Croydon)
Croydon (Addiscombe Road)
(1864-1997)

ADDISCOMBE (2000)

BINGHAM ROAD
Bingham Road Halt
(1906-1983)

SANDILANDS
(2000)

Sandilands Tunnels

2000

1885-1983

BRITISH RAIL ELMERS END TO ADDISCOMBE:

BRITISH RAIL SERVICES ELMERS END TO ADDISCOMBE VIA
WOODSIDE WITHDRAWN IN 1997 TO ALLOW PARTIAL
CONVERSION OF ROUTE TO CROYDON TRAMLINK. THE
ORIGINAL ADDISCOMBE STATION REMAINS CLOSED

BRITISH RAIL WOODSIDE TO SELSDON:

ORIGINALLY OPENED IN 1885 WITH AN INTERMEDIATE STATION AT COOMBE
LANE. HALTS ADDED AT SPENCER AND BINGHAM ROADS 1906, BUT CLOSED
1915. ENTIRE ROUTE CLOSED TO PASSENGERS 1916 BUT RE-OPENED IN 1935.
CLOSED THROUGHOUT IN 1983 ALONG WITH STATIONS AT BINGHAM ROAD,
COOMBE ROAD AND SELSDON. SPENCER ROAD HALT HAD NOT RE-OPENED IN
1935. TRACKBED USED BY CROYDON TRAMLINK BETWEEN WOODSIDE AND
THE SITE OF COOMBE ROAD STATION SINCE 2000

LLOYD PARK (2000)

COOMBE ROAD
Coombe Lane
(1885-1983)

2000

COOMBE LANE (2000)

ADDINGTON
VILLAGE
(2000)

2000

2000

GRAVEL HILL
(2000)

2000

2000

FIELDWAY
(2000)

2000

47

CONTINUATION FROM PAGE 47

CHALK PIT

GOODS
(1968)

STOATS
NEST
QUARRY

1900

1841

COULSDON SOUTH
Coulsdon East
Coulsdon & Cane Hill
Coulsdon
(1889)

1856

1884

WHYTELEAFE (1900)

GOODS

UPPER WARLINGHAM
Upper Warlingham for Riddlesdown
Upper Warlingham & Whyteleafe
Upper Warlingham
(1884)

GOODS

1856

1884

WHYTELEAFE SOUTH
Warlingham
Warlingham & Cane Hill
(1856)

KING
HENRY'S
DRIVE
(2000)

2000

NEW
ADDINGTON
(2000)

2000

TO WOLDINGHAM, EAST GRINSTEAD & UCKFIELD

1841

1900

1856

Quarry Tunnel

Merstham Tunnel

GOODS

TO MERSTHAM, REDHILL, GATWICK AIRPORT & BRIGHTON

CATERHAM (1856)

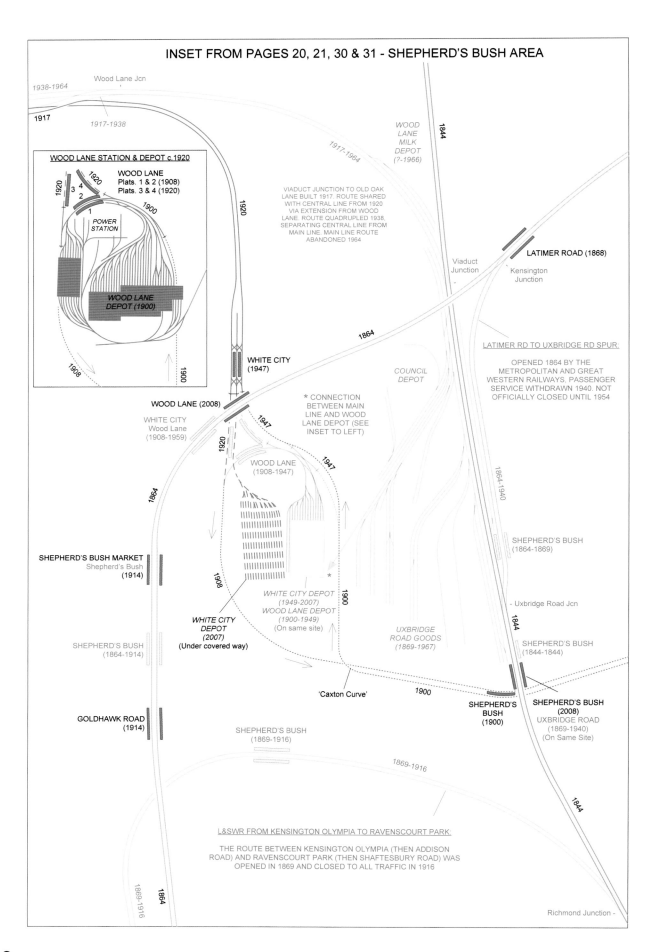

INSET FROM PAGES 20, 21, 30 & 31 - SHEPHERD'S BUSH AREA

1938-1964

Wood Lane Jcn

1917

1917-1938

1920

1917-1964

WOOD LANE MILK DEPOT (?-1966)

1844

WOOD LANE STATION & DEPOT c.1920

1920

3 4

1920

2

1900

WOOD LANE
Plats. 1 & 2 (1908)
Plats. 3 & 4 (1920)

1

POWER STATION

WOOD LANE DEPOT (1900)

1908

1900

VIADUCT JUNCTION TO OLD OAK LANE BUILT 1917. ROUTE SHARED WITH CENTRAL LINE FROM 1920 VIA EXTENSION FROM WOOD LANE. ROUTE QUADRUPLED 1938, SEPARATING CENTRAL LINE FROM MAIN LINE. MAIN LINE ROUTE ABANDONED 1964

Viaduct Junction

LATIMER ROAD (1868)

Kensington Junction

1864

LATIMER RD TO UXBRIDGE RD SPUR:

OPENED 1864 BY THE METROPOLITAN AND GREAT WESTERN RAILWAYS. PASSENGER SERVICE WITHDRAWN 1940. NOT OFFICIALLY CLOSED UNTIL 1954

WHITE CITY (1947)

COUNCIL DEPOT

WOOD LANE (2008)

WHITE CITY Wood Lane (1908-1959)

1920

1947

* CONNECTION BETWEEN MAIN LINE AND WOOD LANE DEPOT (SEE INSET TO LEFT)

1947

WOOD LANE (1908-1947)

1864-1940

SHEPHERD'S BUSH (1864-1869)

1864

- Uxbridge Road Jcn

SHEPHERD'S BUSH MARKET
Shepherd's Bush **(1914)**

1908

1900

WHITE CITY DEPOT (1949-2007)
WOOD LANE DEPOT (1900-1949)
(On same site)

1844

SHEPHERD'S BUSH (1844-1844)

SHEPHERD'S BUSH (1864-1914)

WHITE CITY DEPOT (2007) (Under covered way)

UXBRIDGE ROAD GOODS (1869-1967)

SHEPHERD'S BUSH (2008)
UXBRIDGE ROAD (1869-1940) (On Same site)

GOLDHAWK ROAD (1914)

'Caxton Curve'

1900

SHEPHERD'S BUSH (1900)

SHEPHERD'S BUSH (1869-1916)

1869-1916

L&SWR FROM KENSINGTON OLYMPIA TO RAVENSCOURT PARK:

THE ROUTE BETWEEN KENSINGTON OLYMPIA (THEN ADDISON ROAD) AND RAVENSCOURT PARK (THEN SHAFTESBURY ROAD) WAS OPENED IN 1869 AND CLOSED TO ALL TRAFFIC IN 1916

1844

1869-1916

1864

Richmond Junction -

49

INSET FROM PAGE 31 - EARL'S COURT AREA

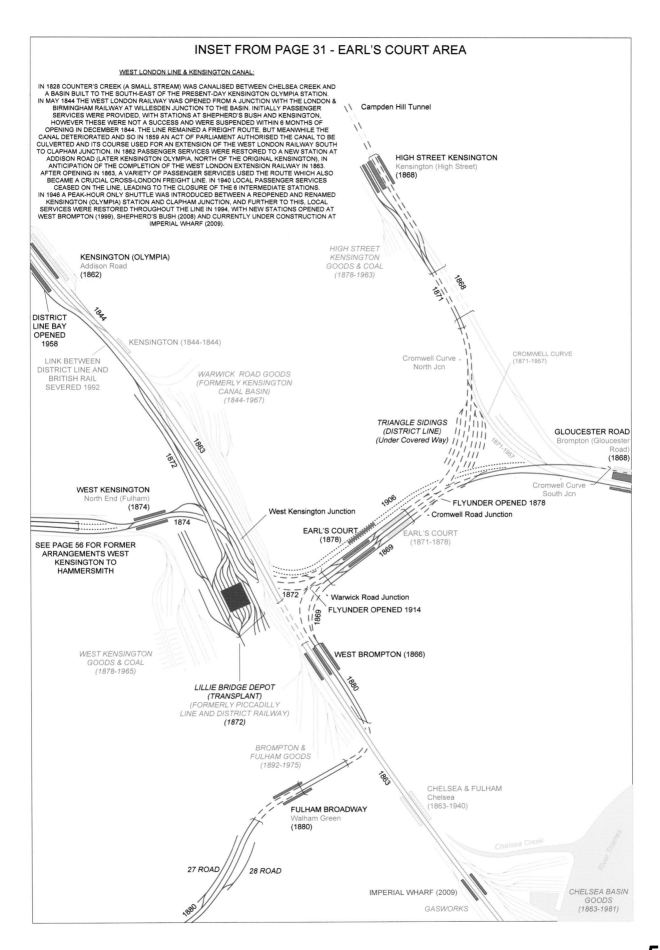

<u>WEST LONDON LINE & KENSINGTON CANAL:</u>

IN 1828 COUNTER'S CREEK (A SMALL STREAM) WAS CANALISED BETWEEN CHELSEA CREEK AND
A BASIN BUILT TO THE SOUTH-EAST OF THE PRESENT-DAY KENSINGTON OLYMPIA STATION.
IN MAY 1844 THE WEST LONDON RAILWAY WAS OPENED FROM A JUNCTION WITH THE LONDON &
BIRMINGHAM RAILWAY AT WILLESDEN JUNCTION TO THE BASIN. INITIALLY PASSENGER
SERVICES WERE PROVIDED, WITH STATIONS AT SHEPHERD'S BUSH AND KENSINGTON,
HOWEVER THESE WERE NOT A SUCCESS AND WERE SUSPENDED WITHIN 6 MONTHS OF
OPENING IN DECEMBER 1844. THE LINE REMAINED A FREIGHT ROUTE, BUT MEANWHILE THE
CANAL DETERIORATED AND SO IN 1859 AN ACT OF PARLIAMENT AUTHORISED THE CANAL TO BE
CULVERTED AND ITS COURSE USED FOR AN EXTENSION OF THE WEST LONDON RAILWAY SOUTH
TO CLAPHAM JUNCTION. IN 1862 PASSENGER SERVICES WERE RESTORED TO A NEW STATION AT
ADDISON ROAD (LATER KENSINGTON OLYMPIA, NORTH OF THE ORIGINAL KENSINGTON), IN
ANTICIPATION OF THE COMPLETION OF THE WEST LONDON EXTENSION RAILWAY IN 1863.
AFTER OPENING IN 1863, A VARIETY OF PASSENGER SERVICES USED THE ROUTE WHICH ALSO
BECAME A CRUCIAL CROSS-LONDON FREIGHT LINE. IN 1940 LOCAL PASSENGER SERVICES
CEASED ON THE LINE, LEADING TO THE CLOSURE OF THE 6 INTERMEDIATE STATIONS.
IN 1946 A PEAK-HOUR ONLY SHUTTLE WAS INTRODUCED BETWEEN A REOPENED AND RENAMED
KENSINGTON (OLYMPIA) STATION AND CLAPHAM JUNCTION, AND FURTHER TO THIS, LOCAL
SERVICES WERE RESTORED THROUGHOUT THE LINE IN 1994, WITH NEW STATIONS OPENED AT
WEST BROMPTON (1999), SHEPHERD'S BUSH (2008) AND CURRENTLY UNDER CONSTRUCTION AT
IMPERIAL WHARF (2009).

Campden Hill Tunnel

HIGH STREET KENSINGTON
Kensington (High Street)
(1868)

*HIGH STREET
KENSINGTON
GOODS & COAL
(1878-1963)*

1868

1871

KENSINGTON (OLYMPIA)
Addison Road
(1862)

1844

**DISTRICT
LINE BAY
OPENED
1958**

KENSINGTON (1844-1844)

LINK BETWEEN
DISTRICT LINE AND
BRITISH RAIL
SEVERED 1992

*WARWICK ROAD GOODS
(FORMERLY KENSINGTON
CANAL BASIN)
(1844-1967)*

Cromwell Curve -
North Jcn

CROMWELL CURVE
(1871-1957)

1863

1872

*TRIANGLE SIDINGS
(DISTRICT LINE)
(Under Covered Way)*

1871-1957

GLOUCESTER ROAD
Brompton (Gloucester
Road)
(1868)

WEST KENSINGTON
North End (Fulham)
(1874)

West Kensington Junction

1906

FLYUNDER OPENED 1878

Cromwell Curve
South Jcn

1874

Cromwell Road Junction

EARL'S COURT
(1878)

*EARL'S COURT
(1871-1878)*

1869

SEE PAGE 56 FOR FORMER
ARRANGEMENTS WEST
KENSINGTON TO
HAMMERSMITH

1872

Warwick Road Junction

1869

FLYUNDER OPENED 1914

*WEST KENSINGTON
GOODS & COAL
(1878-1965)*

WEST BROMPTON (1866)

*LILLIE BRIDGE DEPOT
(TRANSPLANT)
(FORMERLY PICCADILLY
LINE AND DISTRICT RAILWAY)
(1872)*

1880

*BROMPTON &
FULHAM GOODS
(1892-1975)*

1863

*CHELSEA & FULHAM
Chelsea
(1863-1940)*

FULHAM BROADWAY
Walham Green
(1880)

Chelsea Creek

27 ROAD   28 ROAD

1880

IMPERIAL WHARF (2009)

GASWORKS

*CHELSEA BASIN
GOODS
(1863-1981)*

River Thames

50

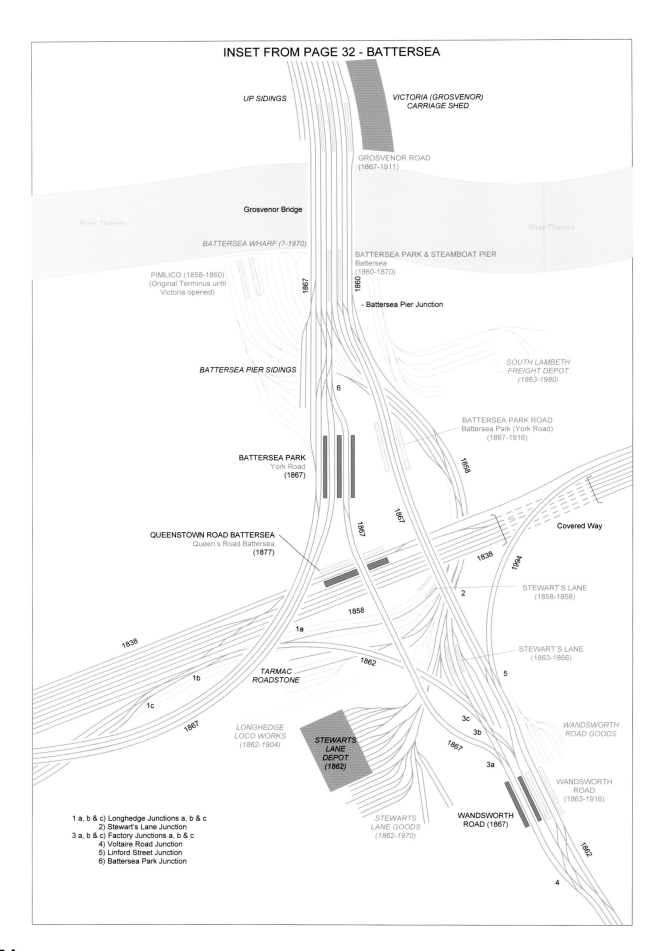

INSET FROM PAGE 32 - BATTERSEA

UP SIDINGS

**VICTORIA (GROSVENOR)
CARRIAGE SHED**

GROSVENOR ROAD
(1867-1911)

Grosvenor Bridge

River Thames

River Thames

BATTERSEA WHARF (?-1970)

BATTERSEA PARK & STEAMBOAT PIER
Battersea
(1860-1870)

PIMLICO (1858-1860)
(Original Terminus until
Victoria opened)

- Battersea Pier Junction

*SOUTH LAMBETH
FREIGHT DEPOT
(1863-1980)*

BATTERSEA PIER SIDINGS

1867

1860

6

BATTERSEA PARK ROAD
Battersea Park (York Road)
(1867-1916)

BATTERSEA PARK
York Road
(1867)

1858

QUEENSTOWN ROAD BATTERSEA
Queen's Road Battersea
(1877)

1867

1867

Covered Way

1838

1994

STEWART'S LANE
(1858-1858)

2

1858

1a

STEWART'S LANE
(1863-1866)

1838

1862

5

1b

*TARMAC
ROADSTONE*

1c

*WANDSWORTH
ROAD GOODS*

1867

3c

3b

*LONGHEDGE
LOCO WORKS
(1862-1904)*

**STEWARTS
LANE
DEPOT
(1862)**

1867

3a

WANDSWORTH
ROAD
(1863-1916)

WANDSWORTH
ROAD (1867)

1 a, b & c) Longhedge Junctions a, b & c
2) Stewart's Lane Junction
3 a, b & c) Factory Junctions a, b & c
4) Voltaire Road Junction
5) Linford Street Junction
6) Battersea Park Junction

*STEWARTS
LANE GOODS
(1862-1970)*

1862

4

INSET FROM PAGE 33 – NEW CROSS AREA

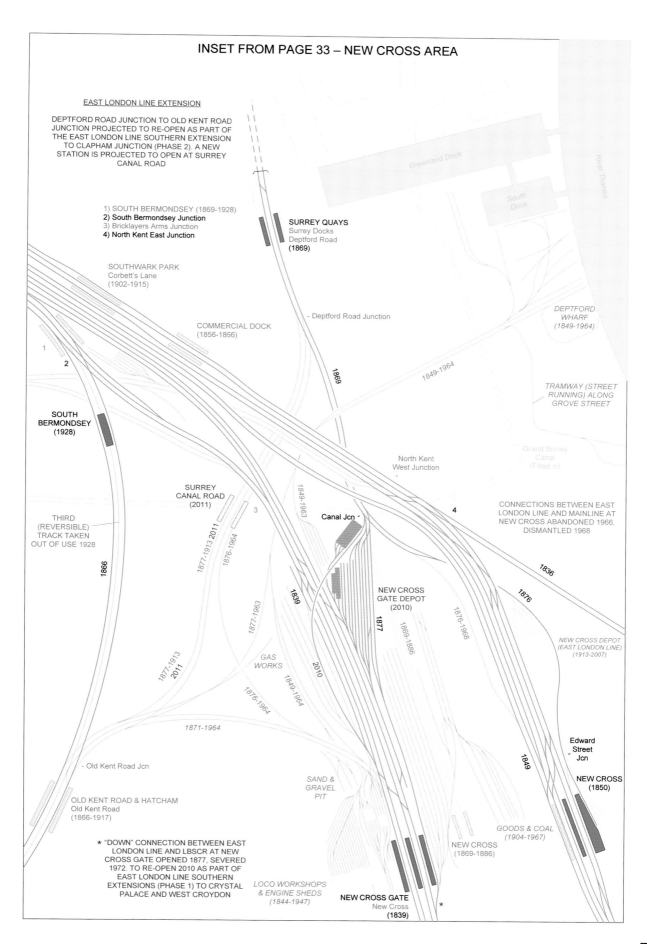

EAST LONDON LINE EXTENSION

DEPTFORD ROAD JUNCTION TO OLD KENT ROAD
JUNCTION PROJECTED TO RE-OPEN AS PART OF
THE EAST LONDON LINE SOUTHERN EXTENSION
TO CLAPHAM JUNCTION (PHASE 2). A NEW
STATION IS PROJECTED TO OPEN AT SURREY
CANAL ROAD

1) SOUTH BERMONDSEY (1869-1928)
2) South Bermondsey Junction
3) Bricklayers Arms Junction
4) North Kent East Junction

Greenland Dock

South
Dock

River Thames

SURREY QUAYS
Surrey Docks
Deptford Road
(1869)

SOUTHWARK PARK
Corbett's Lane
(1902-1915)

- Deptford Road Junction

DEPTFORD
WHARF
(1849-1964)

COMMERCIAL DOCK
(1856-1866)

1869

1849-1964

1

2

TRAMWAY (STREET
RUNNING) ALONG
GROVE STREET

SOUTH
BERMONDSEY
(1928)

North Kent
West Junction

Grand Surrey
Canal
(Filled in)

SURREY
CANAL ROAD
(2011)

3

1849-1963

4

Canal Jcn -

CONNECTIONS BETWEEN EAST
LONDON LINE AND MAINLINE AT
NEW CROSS ABANDONED 1966,
DISMANTLED 1968

THIRD
(REVERSIBLE)
TRACK TAKEN
OUT OF USE 1928

1877-1913 2011

1876-1964

1836

1866

1839

1877

1876

1877-1963

NEW CROSS
GATE DEPOT
(2010)

1869-1886

1876-1968

1877-1913
2011

GAS
WORKS

2010

1849-1964

NEW CROSS DEPOT
(EAST LONDON LINE)
(1913-2007)

1876-1964

1871-1964

Edward
Street
Jcn

- Old Kent Road Jcn

SAND &
GRAVEL
PIT

1849

NEW CROSS
(1850)

OLD KENT ROAD & HATCHAM
Old Kent Road
(1866-1917)

GOODS & COAL
(1904-1967)

★ "DOWN" CONNECTION BETWEEN EAST
LONDON LINE AND LBSCR AT NEW
CROSS GATE OPENED 1877, SEVERED
1972. TO RE-OPEN 2010 AS PART OF
EAST LONDON LINE SOUTHERN
EXTENSIONS (PHASE 1) TO CRYSTAL
PALACE AND WEST CROYDON

LOCO WORKSHOPS
& ENGINE SHEDS
(1844-1947)

NEW CROSS
(1869-1886)

NEW CROSS GATE
New Cross
(1839)

*

INSET FROM PAGES 23 & 24 – STRATFORD AREA

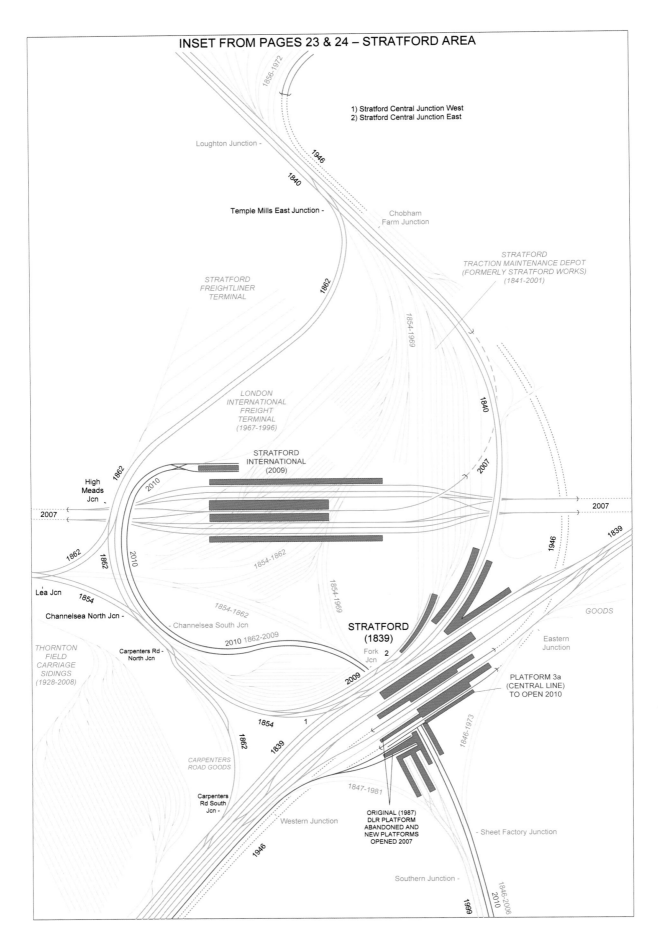

1) Stratford Central Junction West
2) Stratford Central Junction East

Loughton Junction -

1946

1840

Temple Mills East Junction -

Chobham
Farm Junction

STRATFORD
TRACTION MAINTENANCE DEPOT
(FORMERLY STRATFORD WORKS)
(1841-2001)

STRATFORD
FREIGHTLINER
TERMINAL

1862

1854-1969

LONDON
INTERNATIONAL
FREIGHT
TERMINAL
(1967-1996)

1840

STRATFORD
INTERNATIONAL
(2009)

2007

High
Meads
Jcn

1862

2010

2007

2007

1862

1946

1839

1854-1862

1854-1969

1862

1862

2010

GOODS

Lea Jcn

1854

Channelsea North Jcn -

STRATFORD
(1839)

Eastern
Junction

THORNTON
FIELD
CARRIAGE
SIDINGS
(1928-2008)

1854-1862

Channelsea South Jcn

Carpenters Rd -
North Jcn

2010 1862-2009

Fork
Jcn

2

PLATFORM 3a
(CENTRAL LINE)
TO OPEN 2010

2009

1846-1973

1854

1

CARPENTERS
ROAD GOODS

1862

1839

1847-1981

ORIGINAL (1987)
DLR PLATFORM
ABANDONED AND
NEW PLATFORMS
OPENED 2007

Carpenters
Rd South
Jcn -

Western Junction

- Sheet Factory Junction

Southern Junction -

1846-2006
2010

1999

53

INSET FROM PAGE 22 - KING'S CROSS & ST PANCRAS

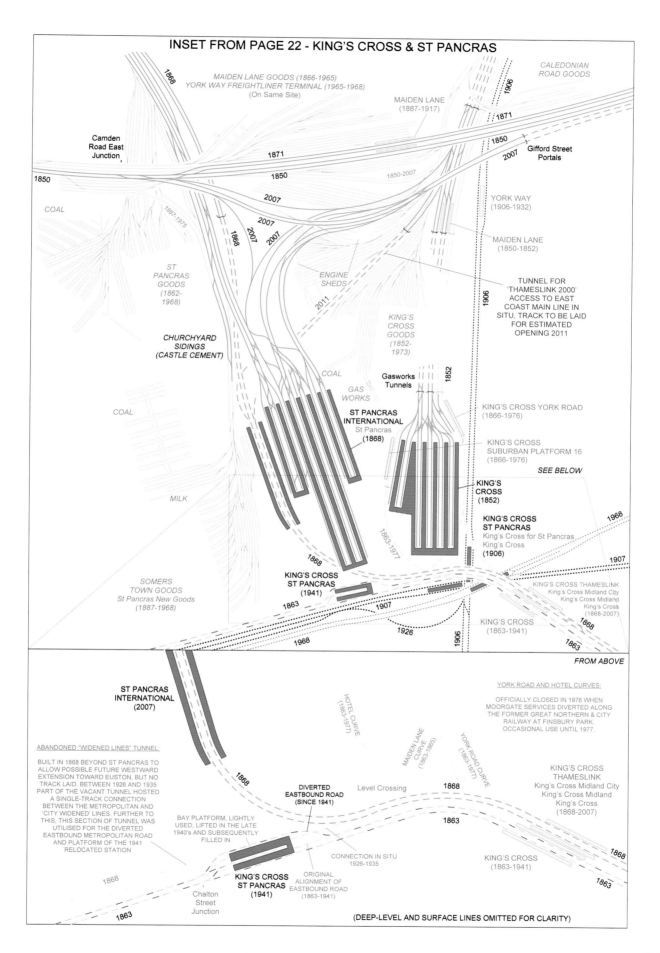

MAIDEN LANE GOODS (1866-1965)
YORK WAY FREIGHTLINER TERMINAL (1965-1968)
(On Same Site)

CALEDONIAN ROAD GOODS

MAIDEN LANE
(1887-1917)

1868

1906

1871

Camden
Road East
Junction

1871

1850

Gifford Street
Portals

1850

1850

2007

1850-2007

COAL

1887-1975

2007

*YORK WAY
(1906-1932)*

1868

2007

*ST
PANCRAS
GOODS
(1862-
1968)*

2007

2007

*ENGINE
SHEDS*

*MAIDEN LANE
(1850-1852)*

TUNNEL FOR
'THAMESLINK 2000'
ACCESS TO EAST
COAST MAIN LINE IN
SITU, TRACK TO BE LAID
FOR ESTIMATED
OPENING 2011

2011

*KING'S
CROSS
GOODS
(1852-
1973)*

1906

**CHURCHYARD
SIDINGS
(CASTLE CEMENT)**

COAL

1852

*GAS
WORKS*

Gasworks
Tunnels

COAL

**ST PANCRAS
INTERNATIONAL**
St Pancras
(1868)

KING'S CROSS YORK ROAD
(1866-1976)

KING'S CROSS
SUBURBAN PLATFORM 16
(1866-1976)

SEE BELOW

MILK

**KING'S
CROSS
(1852)**

**KING'S CROSS
ST PANCRAS**
King's Cross for St Pancras
King's Cross
(1906)

1968

*SOMERS
TOWN GOODS
St Pancras New Goods
(1887-1968)*

1868

**KING'S CROSS
ST PANCRAS**
(1941)

1863-1977

1907

KING'S CROSS THAMESLINK
King's Cross Midland City
King's Cross Midland
King's Cross
(1868-2007)

1863

1907

1868

KING'S CROSS
(1863-1941)

1926

1906

1968

1863

FROM ABOVE

**ST PANCRAS
INTERNATIONAL
(2007)**

*HOTEL
CURVE
(1863-1977)*

<u>YORK ROAD AND HOTEL CURVES:</u>

OFFICIALLY CLOSED IN 1976 WHEN
MOORGATE SERVICES DIVERTED ALONG
THE FORMER GREAT NORTHERN & CITY
RAILWAY AT FINSBURY PARK.
OCCASIONAL USE UNTIL 1977.

*MAIDEN LANE
CURVE
(1863-1885)*

*YORK ROAD CURVE
(1863-1977)*

<u>ABANDONED "WIDENED LINES" TUNNEL:</u>

BUILT IN 1868 BEYOND ST PANCRAS TO
ALLOW POSSIBLE FUTURE WESTWARD
EXTENSION TOWARD EUSTON, BUT NO
TRACK LAID. BETWEEN 1926 AND 1935
PART OF THE VACANT TUNNEL HOSTED
A SINGLE-TRACK CONNECTION
BETWEEN THE METROPOLITAN AND
'CITY WIDENED' LINES. FURTHER TO
THIS, THIS SECTION OF TUNNEL WAS
UTILISED FOR THE DIVERTED
EASTBOUND METROPOLITAN ROAD
AND PLATFORM OF THE 1941
RELOCATED STATION

1868

**DIVERTED
EASTBOUND ROAD
(SINCE 1941)**

Level Crossing

1868

**KING'S CROSS
THAMESLINK**
King's Cross Midland City
King's Cross Midland
King's Cross
(1868-2007)

BAY PLATFORM, LIGHTLY
USED, LIFTED IN THE LATE
1940's AND SUBSEQUENTLY
FILLED IN

1863

CONNECTION IN SITU
1926-1935

KING'S CROSS
(1863-1941)

1868

1868

**KING'S CROSS
ST PANCRAS**
(1941)

ORIGINAL
ALIGNMENT OF
EASTBOUND ROAD
(1863-1941)

1863

1863

Chalton
Street
Junction

1863

(DEEP-LEVEL AND SURFACE LINES OMITTED FOR CLARITY)

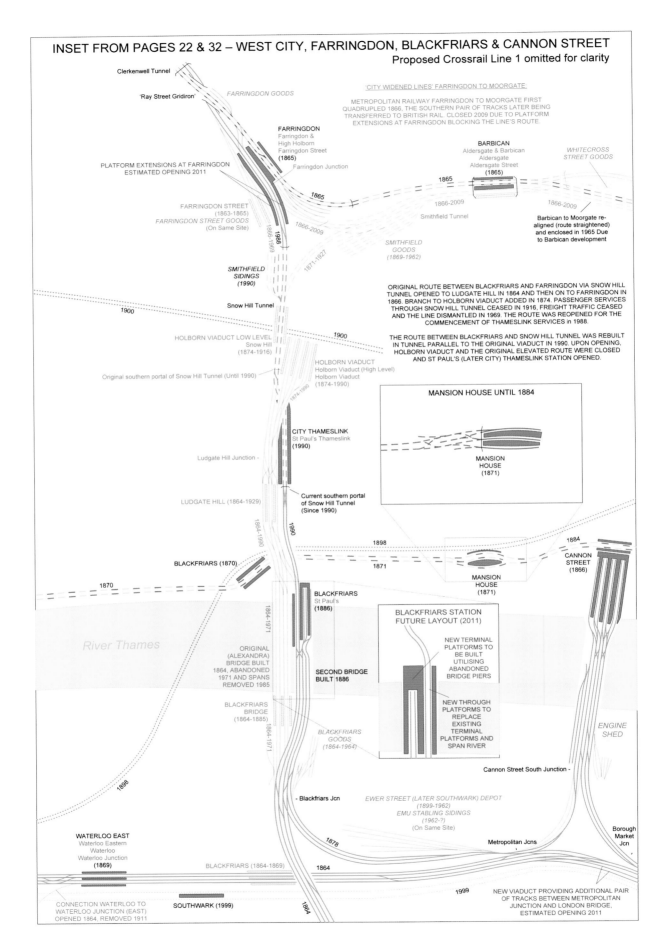

INSET FROM PAGES 22 & 32 – WEST CITY, FARRINGDON, BLACKFRIARS & CANNON STREET
Proposed Crossrail Line 1 omitted for clarity

Clerkenwell Tunnel

'Ray Street Gridiron'

FARRINGDON GOODS

'CITY WIDENED LINES' FARRINGDON TO MOORGATE:

METROPOLITAN RAILWAY FARRINGDON TO MOORGATE FIRST QUADRUPLED 1866, THE SOUTHERN PAIR OF TRACKS LATER BEING TRANSFERRED TO BRITISH RAIL. CLOSED 2009 DUE TO PLATFORM EXTENSIONS AT FARRINGDON BLOCKING THE LINE'S ROUTE.

FARRINGDON
Farringdon &
High Holborn
Farringdon Street
(1865)

BARBICAN
Aldersgate & Barbican
Aldersgate
Aldersgate Street
(1865)

*WHITECROSS
STREET GOODS*

PLATFORM EXTENSIONS AT FARRINGDON
ESTIMATED OPENING 2011

Farringdon Junction

1865

1865

1866-2009

1866-2009

Barbican to Moorgate re-
aligned (route straightened)
and enclosed in 1965 Due
to Barbican development

*FARRINGDON STREET
(1863-1865)*
FARRINGDON STREET GOODS
(On Same Site)

Smithfield Tunnel

1866-1969

1988

1871-1927

*SMITHFIELD
GOODS
(1869-1962)*

*SMITHFIELD
SIDINGS
(1990)*

Snow Hill Tunnel

ORIGINAL ROUTE BETWEEN BLACKFRIARS AND FARRINGDON VIA SNOW HILL
TUNNEL OPENED TO LUDGATE HILL IN 1864 AND THEN ON TO FARRINGDON IN
1866. BRANCH TO HOLBORN VIADUCT ADDED IN 1874. PASSENGER SERVICES
THROUGH SNOW HILL TUNNEL CEASED IN 1916, FREIGHT TRAFFIC CEASED
AND THE LINE DISMANTLED IN 1969. THE ROUTE WAS REOPENED FOR THE
COMMENCEMENT OF THAMESLINK SERVICES in 1988.

1900

1900

THE ROUTE BETWEEN BLACKFRIARS AND SNOW HILL TUNNEL WAS REBUILT
IN TUNNEL PARALLEL TO THE ORIGINAL VIADUCT IN 1990. UPON OPENING,
HOLBORN VIADUCT AND THE ORIGINAL ELEVATED ROUTE WERE CLOSED
AND ST PAUL'S (LATER CITY) THAMESLINK STATION OPENED.

HOLBORN VIADUCT LOW LEVEL
Snow Hill
(1874-1916)

HOLBORN VIADUCT
Holborn Viaduct (High Level)
Holborn Viaduct
(1874-1990)

Original southern portal of Snow Hill Tunnel (Until 1990)

1874-1990

MANSION HOUSE UNTIL 1884

CITY THAMESLINK
St Paul's Thameslink
(1990)

MANSION
HOUSE
(1871)

Ludgate Hill Junction -

Current southern portal
of Snow Hill Tunnel
(Since 1990)

LUDGATE HILL (1864-1929)

1864-1990

1990

1898

1884

**CANNON
STREET
(1866)**

1871

BLACKFRIARS (1870)

1870

MANSION
HOUSE
(1871)

BLACKFRIARS
St Paul's
(1886)

**BLACKFRIARS STATION
FUTURE LAYOUT (2011)**

NEW TERMINAL
PLATFORMS TO
BE BUILT
UTILISING
ABANDONED
BRIDGE PIERS

River Thames

ORIGINAL
(ALEXANDRA)
BRIDGE BUILT
1864, ABANDONED
1971 AND SPANS
REMOVED 1985

**SECOND BRIDGE
BUILT 1886**

1864-1971

NEW THROUGH
PLATFORMS TO
REPLACE
EXISTING
TERMINAL
PLATFORMS AND
SPAN RIVER

*BLACKFRIARS
BRIDGE
(1864-1885)*

*BLACKFRIARS
GOODS
(1864-1964)*

1864-1971

*ENGINE
SHED*

Cannon Street South Junction -

- Blackfriars Jcn

*EWER STREET (LATER SOUTHWARK) DEPOT
(1899-1962)*
*EMU STABLING SIDINGS
(1962-?)*
(On Same Site)

Borough
Market
Jcn

WATERLOO EAST
Waterloo Eastern
Waterloo
Waterloo Junction
(1869)

1878

Metropolitan Jcns

BLACKFRIARS (1864-1869)

1864

1999

CONNECTION WATERLOO TO
WATERLOO JUNCTION (EAST)
OPENED 1864, REMOVED 1911

SOUTHWARK (1999)

1864

NEW VIADUCT PROVIDING ADDITIONAL PAIR
OF TRACKS BETWEEN METROPOLITAN
JUNCTION AND LONDON BRIDGE,
ESTIMATED OPENING 2011

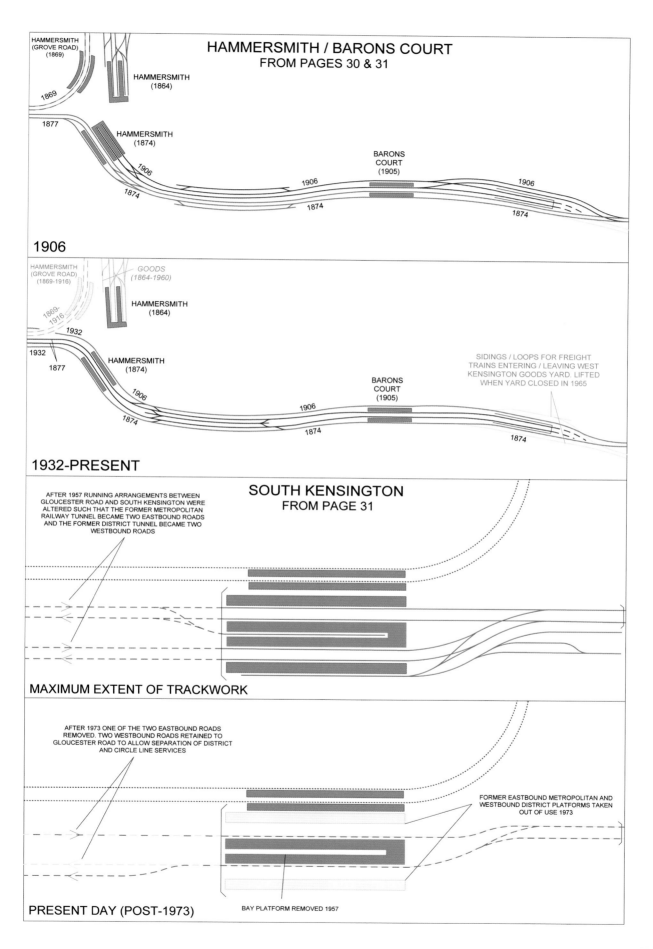

HAMMERSMITH / BARONS COURT
FROM PAGES 30 & 31

HAMMERSMITH
(GROVE ROAD)
(1869)

HAMMERSMITH
(1864)

1869

1877

HAMMERSMITH
(1874)

1906

1874

1906

BARONS
COURT
(1905)

1906

1874

1906

1874

1906

HAMMERSMITH
(GROVE ROAD)
(1869-1916)

GOODS
(1864-1960)

HAMMERSMITH
(1864)

1869-
1916

1932

1932

1877

HAMMERSMITH
(1874)

1906

1874

1906

BARONS
COURT
(1905)

1874

SIDINGS / LOOPS FOR FREIGHT
TRAINS ENTERING / LEAVING WEST
KENSINGTON GOODS YARD. LIFTED
WHEN YARD CLOSED IN 1965

1874

1932-PRESENT

SOUTH KENSINGTON
FROM PAGE 31

AFTER 1957 RUNNING ARRANGEMENTS BETWEEN
GLOUCESTER ROAD AND SOUTH KENSINGTON WERE
ALTERED SUCH THAT THE FORMER METROPOLITAN
RAILWAY TUNNEL BECAME TWO EASTBOUND ROADS
AND THE FORMER DISTRICT TUNNEL BECAME TWO
WESTBOUND ROADS

MAXIMUM EXTENT OF TRACKWORK

AFTER 1973 ONE OF THE TWO EASTBOUND ROADS
REMOVED. TWO WESTBOUND ROADS RETAINED TO
GLOUCESTER ROAD TO ALLOW SEPARATION OF DISTRICT
AND CIRCLE LINE SERVICES

FORMER EASTBOUND METROPOLITAN AND
WESTBOUND DISTRICT PLATFORMS TAKEN
OUT OF USE 1973

PRESENT DAY (POST-1973)

BAY PLATFORM REMOVED 1957

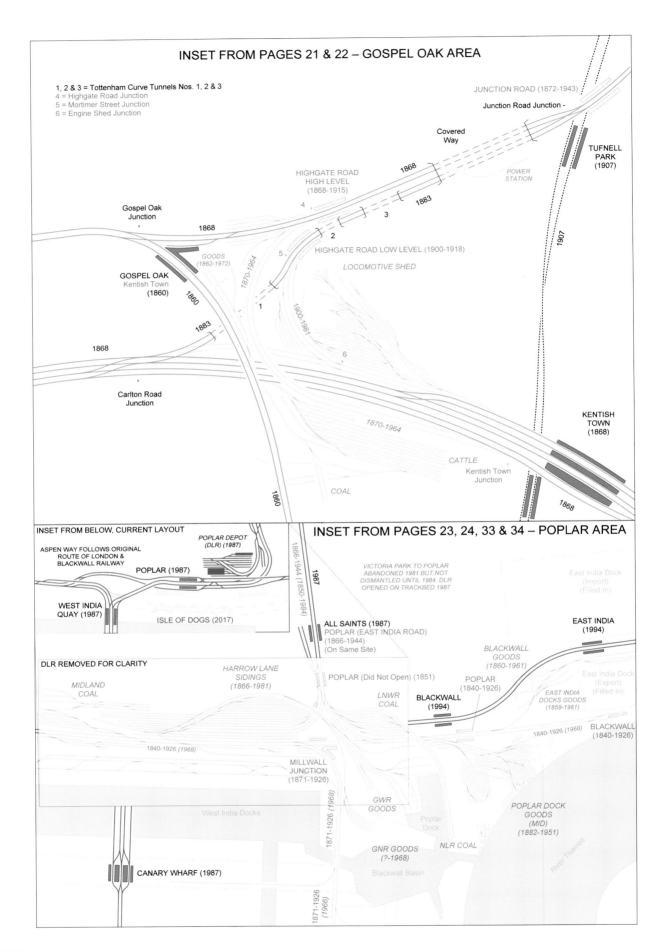

INSET FROM PAGES 21 & 22 – GOSPEL OAK AREA

1, 2 & 3 = Tottenham Curve Tunnels Nos. 1, 2 & 3
4 = Highgate Road Junction
5 = Mortimer Street Junction
6 = Engine Shed Junction

JUNCTION ROAD (1872-1943)

Junction Road Junction -

Covered
Way

TUFNELL
PARK
(1907)

HIGHGATE ROAD
HIGH LEVEL
(1868-1915)

1868

1883

POWER
STATION

Gospel Oak
Junction

1868

4

3

1907

1883

HIGHGATE ROAD LOW LEVEL (1900-1918)

GOSPEL OAK
Kentish Town
(1860)

GOODS
(1862-1972)

5

1870-1964

2

LOCOMOTIVE SHED

1860

1

1900-1981

6

1868

Carlton Road
Junction

1868

1870-1964

KENTISH
TOWN
(1868)

1860

CATTLE
Kentish Town
Junction

COAL

1868

INSET FROM BELOW, CURRENT LAYOUT

ASPEN WAY FOLLOWS ORIGINAL
ROUTE OF LONDON &
BLACKWALL RAILWAY

POPLAR DEPOT
(DLR) (1987)

POPLAR (1987)

WEST INDIA
QUAY (1987)

ISLE OF DOGS (2017)

INSET FROM PAGES 23, 24, 33 & 34 – POPLAR AREA

1866-1944 (1850-1984)

1987

VICTORIA PARK TO POPLAR
ABANDONED 1981 BUT NOT
DISMANTLED UNTIL 1984. DLR
OPENED ON TRACKBED 1987

East India Dock
(Import)
(Filled In)

ALL SAINTS (1987)
POPLAR (EAST INDIA ROAD)
(1866-1944)
(On Same Site)

BLACKWALL
GOODS
(1860-1961)

EAST INDIA
(1994)

DLR REMOVED FOR CLARITY

MIDLAND
COAL

HARROW LANE
SIDINGS
(1866-1981)

POPLAR (Did Not Open) (1851)

LNWR
COAL

POPLAR
(1840-1926)

BLACKWALL
(1994)

EAST INDIA
DOCKS GOODS
(1859-1961)

East India Dock
(Export)
(Filled In)

BLACKWALL
(1840-1926)

1840-1926 (1968)

1840-1926 (1968)

West India Docks

MILLWALL
JUNCTION
(1871-1926)

1871-1926 (1968)

GWR
GOODS

Poplar
Dock

POPLAR DOCK
GOODS
(MID)
(1882-1951)

River Thames

CANARY WHARF (1987)

GNR GOODS
(?-1968)

NLR COAL

Blackwall Basin

1871-1926
(1966)

57

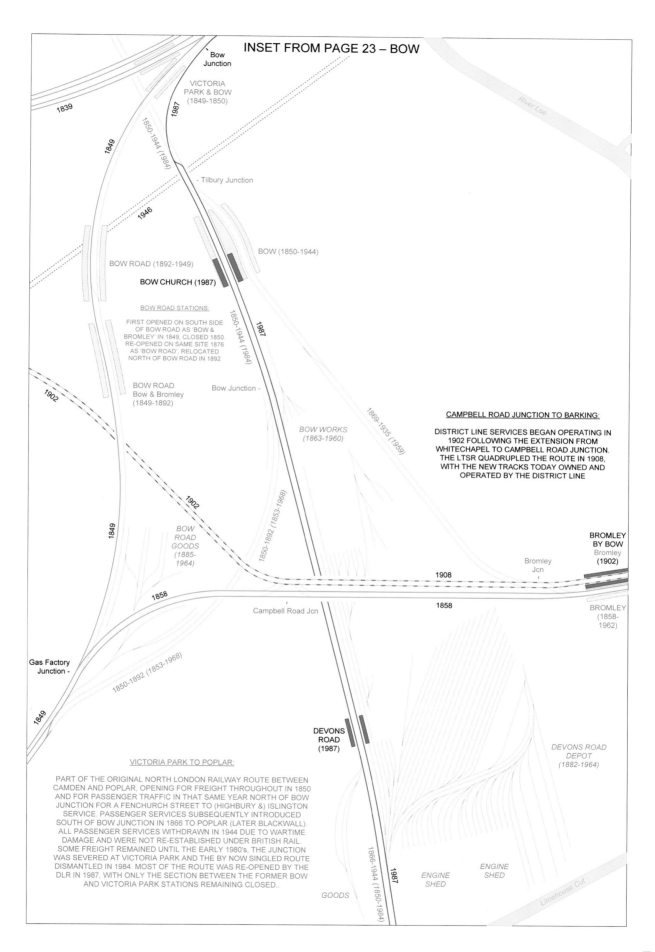

INSET FROM PAGE 23 – BOW

Bow
Junction

VICTORIA
PARK & BOW
(1849-1850)

1839

1849

1987

1850-1944 (1984)

1946

- Tilbury Junction

BOW (1850-1944)

BOW ROAD (1892-1949)

BOW CHURCH (1987)

1850-1944 (1984)

1987

BOW ROAD STATIONS:

FIRST OPENED ON SOUTH SIDE
OF BOW ROAD AS 'BOW &
BROMLEY' IN 1849, CLOSED 1850.
RE-OPENED ON SAME SITE 1876
AS 'BOW ROAD', RELOCATED
NORTH OF BOW ROAD IN 1892

BOW ROAD
Bow & Bromley
(1849-1892)

Bow Junction -

1902

1869-1935 (1959)

BOW WORKS
(1863-1960)

CAMPBELL ROAD JUNCTION TO BARKING:

DISTRICT LINE SERVICES BEGAN OPERATING IN
1902 FOLLOWING THE EXTENSION FROM
WHITECHAPEL TO CAMPBELL ROAD JUNCTION.
THE LTSR QUADRUPLED THE ROUTE IN 1908,
WITH THE NEW TRACKS TODAY OWNED AND
OPERATED BY THE DISTRICT LINE

1902

1849

BOW
ROAD
GOODS
(1885-
1964)

1850-1892 (1853-1968)

BROMLEY
BY BOW
Bromley
(1902)

Bromley
Jcn

1908

1858

1858

BROMLEY
(1858-
1962)

Gas Factory
Junction -

1850-1892 (1853-1968)

Campbell Road Jcn

1849

DEVONS
ROAD
(1987)

DEVONS ROAD
DEPOT
(1882-1964)

VICTORIA PARK TO POPLAR:

PART OF THE ORIGINAL NORTH LONDON RAILWAY ROUTE BETWEEN
CAMDEN AND POPLAR, OPENING FOR FREIGHT THROUGHOUT IN 1850
AND FOR PASSENGER TRAFFIC IN THAT SAME YEAR NORTH OF BOW
JUNCTION FOR A FENCHURCH STREET TO (HIGHBURY &) ISLINGTON
SERVICE. PASSENGER SERVICES SUBSEQUENTLY INTRODUCED
SOUTH OF BOW JUNCTION IN 1866 TO POPLAR (LATER BLACKWALL).
ALL PASSENGER SERVICES WITHDRAWN IN 1944 DUE TO WARTIME
DAMAGE AND WERE NOT RE-ESTABLISHED UNDER BRITISH RAIL.
SOME FREIGHT REMAINED UNTIL THE EARLY 1980's, THE JUNCTION
WAS SEVERED AT VICTORIA PARK AND THE BY NOW SINGLED ROUTE
DISMANTLED IN 1984. MOST OF THE ROUTE WAS RE-OPENED BY THE
DLR IN 1987, WITH ONLY THE SECTION BETWEEN THE FORMER BOW
AND VICTORIA PARK STATIONS REMAINING CLOSED..

ENGINE
SHED

ENGINE
SHED

1866-1944 (1850-1984)

1987

GOODS

River Lee

Limehouse Cut

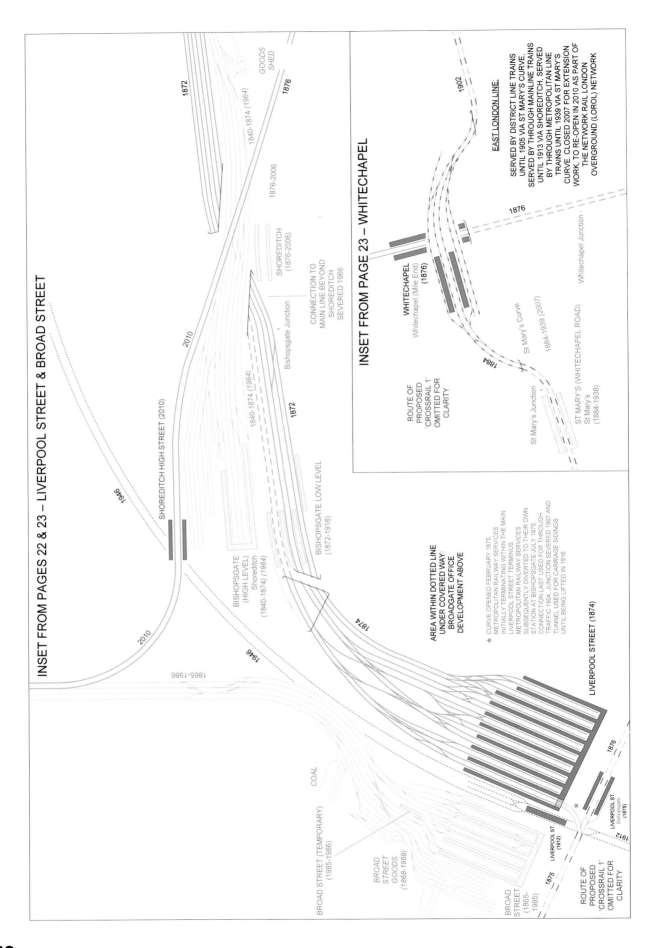

INSET FROM PAGES 22 & 23 – LIVERPOOL STREET & BROAD STREET

GOODS SHED

1872

1840-1874 (1964)

1876

1876-2006

SHOREDITCH
(1876-2006)

Bishopsgate Junction

CONNECTION TO
MAIN LINE BEYOND
SHOREDITCH
SEVERED 1966

2010

1840-1874 (1964)

1872

BISHOPSGATE LOW LEVEL
(1872-1916)

SHOREDITCH HIGH STREET (2010)

1946

2010

BISHOPSGATE
(HIGH LEVEL)
Shoreditch
(1840-1874) (1964)

1946

1865-1986

COAL

1874

AREA WITHIN DOTTED LINE
UNDER COVERED WAY:
BROADGATE OFFICE
DEVELOPMENT ABOVE

* CURVE OPENED FEBRUARY 1875,
METROPOLITAN RAILWAY SERVICES
INITIALLY TERMINATING WITHIN THE MAIN
LIVERPOOL STREET TERMINUS.
METROPOLITAN RAILWAY SERVICES
SUBSEQUENTLY DIVERTED TO THEIR OWN
STATION AT BISHOPSGATE JULY 1875.
CONNECTION LAST USED FOR THROUGH
TRAFFIC 1904, JUNCTION SEVERED 1907 AND
TUNNEL USED FOR CARRIAGE SIDINGS
UNTIL BEING LIFTED IN 1916

LIVERPOOL STREET (1874)

BROAD STREET (TEMPORARY)
(1985-1986)

BROAD
STREET
GOODS
(1868-1969)

BROAD
STREET
(1865-
1985)

ROUTE OF
PROPOSED
'CROSSRAIL 1'
OMITTED FOR
CLARITY

LIVERPOOL ST.
(1912)

LIVERPOOL ST.
Bishopsgate
(1875)

1876

1875

1912

*

INSET FROM PAGE 23 – WHITECHAPEL

1902

EAST LONDON LINE:

SERVED BY DISTRICT LINE TRAINS
UNTIL 1905 VIA ST MARY'S CURVE.
SERVED BY THROUGH MAINLINE TRAINS
UNTIL 1913 VIA SHOREDITCH, SERVED
BY THROUGH METROPOLITAN LINE
TRAINS UNTIL 1939 VIA ST MARY'S
CURVE. CLOSED 2007 FOR EXTENSION
WORK, TO RE-OPEN IN 2010 AS PART OF
THE NETWORK RAIL LONDON
OVERGROUND (LOROL) NETWORK

1876

WHITECHAPEL
Whitechapel (Mile End)
(1876)

St Mary's Curve
1884-1939 (2007)

1884

Whitechapel Junction -

ST MARY'S (WHITECHAPEL ROAD)
St Mary's
(1884-1938)

St Mary's Junction

ROUTE OF
PROPOSED
'CROSSRAIL 1'
OMITTED FOR
CLARITY

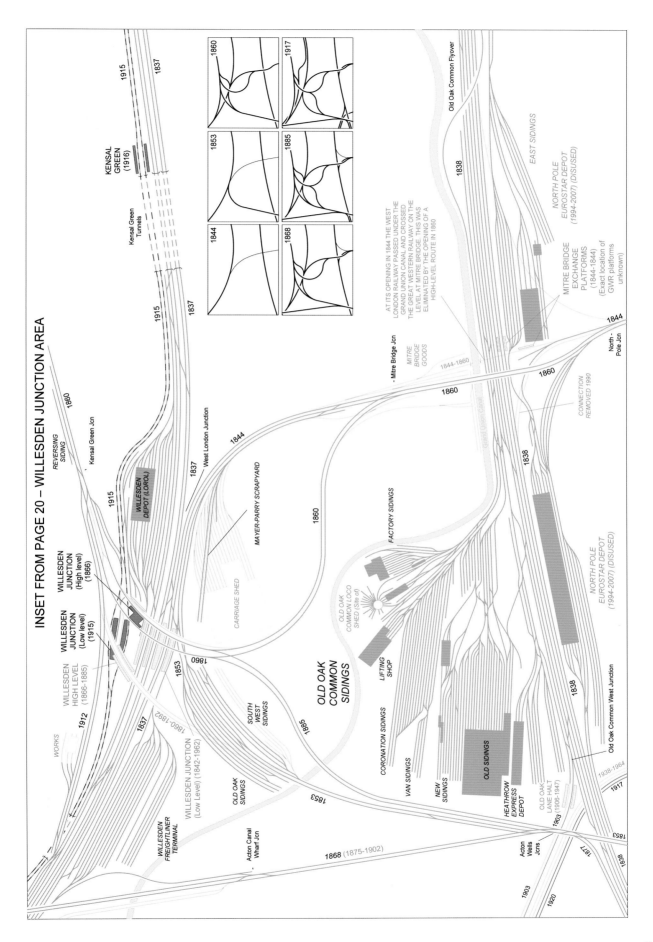

INSET FROM PAGE 20 – WILLESDEN JUNCTION AREA

1915
1837

KENSAL GREEN (1916)

Kensal Green Tunnels

1860 1853 1844

1917 1885 1868

AT ITS OPENING IN 1844 THE WEST LONDON RAILWAY PASSED UNDER THE GRAND UNION CANAL AND CROSSED THE GREAT WESTERN RAILWAY ON THE LEVEL AT MITRE BRIDGE. THIS WAS ELIMINATED BY THE OPENING OF A HIGH-LEVEL ROUTE IN 1860

1915

1837

Old Oak Common Flyover

1838

EAST SIDINGS

NORTH POLE EUROSTAR DEPOT (1994-2007) (DISUSED)

MITRE BRIDGE EXCHANGE PLATFORMS (1844-1844) (Exact location of GWR platforms unknown)

- Mitre Bridge Jcn

MITRE BRIDGE GOODS

1844-1860

1860

1860

1844

North-Pole Jcn

CONNECTION REMOVED 1990

REVERSING SIDING

1860

Kensal Green Jcn

WILLESDEN DEPOT (LOROL)

1837

West London Junction

1844

MAYER-PARRY SCRAPYARD

1915

WILLESDEN JUNCTION (High level) (1866)

WILLESDEN JUNCTION (Low level) (1915)

WILLESDEN HIGH LEVEL (1866-1885)

1912

WORKS

CARRIAGE SHED

1853

1860

1860

FACTORY SIDINGS

OLD OAK COMMON LOCO SHED (Site of)

LIFTING SHOP

Grand Union Canal

1838

1838

NORTH POLE EUROSTAR DEPOT (1994-2007) (DISUSED)

OLD OAK COMMON SIDINGS

WILLESDEN JUNCTION (Low Level) (1842-1962)

1860-1892

1837

OLD OAK SIDINGS

SOUTH WEST SIDINGS

1885

CORONATION SIDINGS

VAN SIDINGS

NEW SIDINGS

OLD SIDINGS

HEATHROW EXPRESS DEPOT

OLD OAK LANE HALT (1906-1947)

1903

Old Oak Common West Junction

1938-1964

WILLESDEN FREIGHTLINER TERMINAL

Acton Canal Wharf Jcn

1853

1868 (1875-1902)

Acton Wells Jcns

1877

1903

1920

1917

1853

1838

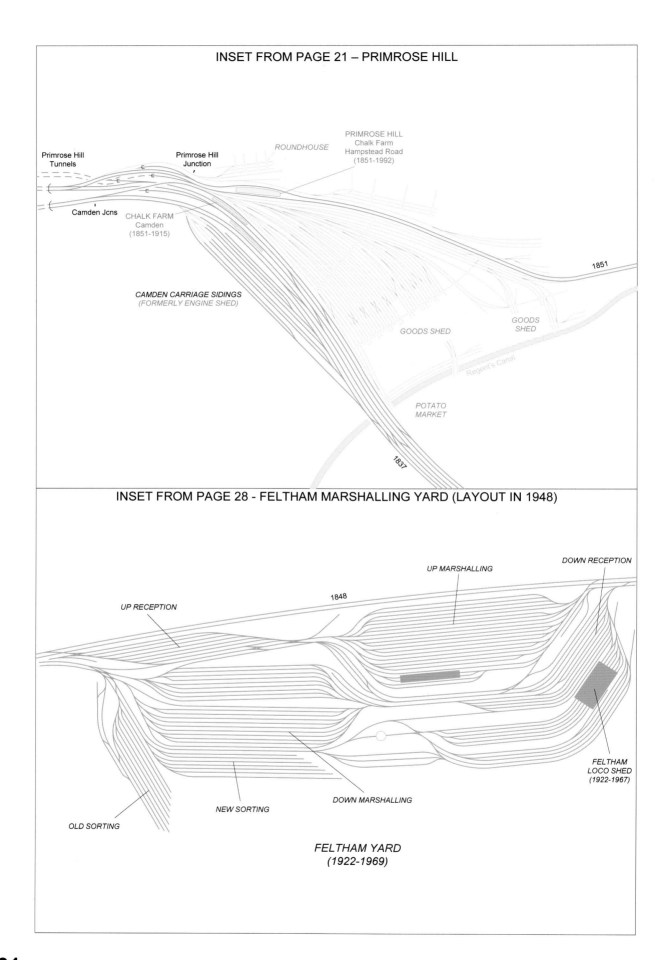

INSET FROM PAGE 21 – PRIMROSE HILL

Primrose Hill
Tunnels

Primrose Hill
Junction

ROUNDHOUSE

PRIMROSE HILL
Chalk Farm
Hampstead Road
(1851-1992)

Camden Jcns

CHALK FARM
Camden
(1851-1915)

1851

CAMDEN CARRIAGE SIDINGS
(FORMERLY ENGINE SHED)

GOODS SHED

GOODS
SHED

Regent's Canal

POTATO
MARKET

1837

INSET FROM PAGE 28 - FELTHAM MARSHALLING YARD (LAYOUT IN 1948)

UP MARSHALLING

DOWN RECEPTION

UP RECEPTION

1848

FELTHAM
LOCO SHED
(1922-1967)

OLD SORTING

NEW SORTING

DOWN MARSHALLING

FELTHAM YARD
(1922-1969)

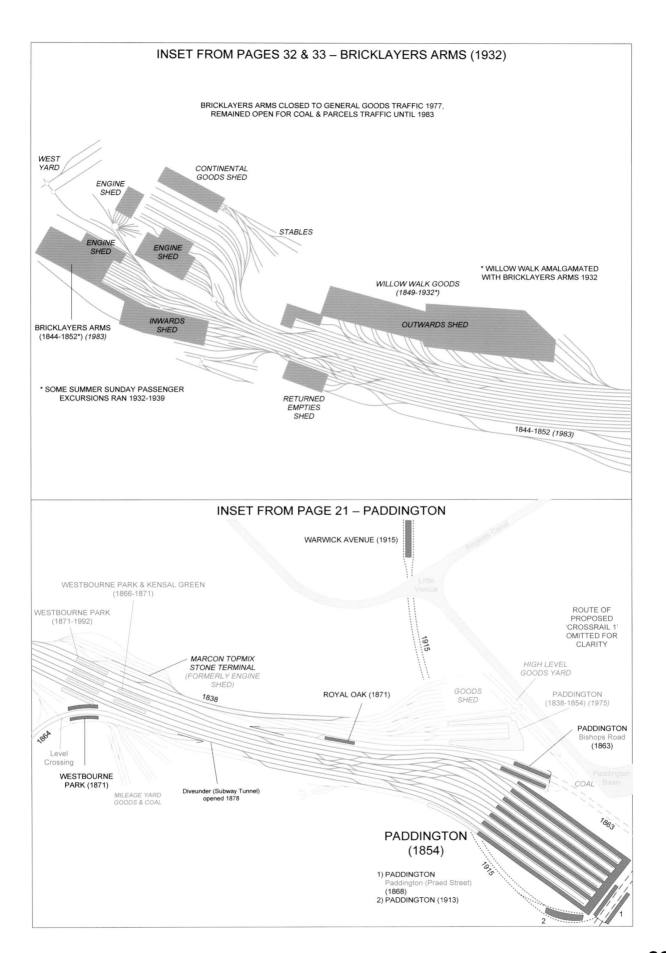

INSET FROM PAGES 32 & 33 – BRICKLAYERS ARMS (1932)

BRICKLAYERS ARMS CLOSED TO GENERAL GOODS TRAFFIC 1977,
REMAINED OPEN FOR COAL & PARCELS TRAFFIC UNTIL 1983

WEST
YARD

ENGINE
SHED

CONTINENTAL
GOODS SHED

STABLES

ENGINE
SHED

ENGINE
SHED

* WILLOW WALK AMALGAMATED
WITH BRICKLAYERS ARMS 1932

WILLOW WALK GOODS
(1849-1932*)

INWARDS
SHED

OUTWARDS SHED

BRICKLAYERS ARMS
(1844-1852*) (1983)

* SOME SUMMER SUNDAY PASSENGER
EXCURSIONS RAN 1932-1939

RETURNED
EMPTIES
SHED

1844-1852 (1983)

INSET FROM PAGE 21 – PADDINGTON

WARWICK AVENUE (1915)

Regents Canal

WESTBOURNE PARK & KENSAL GREEN
(1866-1871)

WESTBOURNE PARK
(1871-1992)

Little
Venice

ROUTE OF
PROPOSED
'CROSSRAIL 1'
OMITTED FOR
CLARITY

1915

MARCON TOPMIX
STONE TERMINAL
(FORMERLY ENGINE
SHED)

1838

ROYAL OAK (1871)

GOODS
SHED

HIGH LEVEL
GOODS YARD

PADDINGTON
(1838-1854) (1975)

1864

Level
Crossing

WESTBOURNE
PARK (1871)

MILEAGE YARD
GOODS & COAL

Diveunder (Subway Tunnel)
opened 1878

PADDINGTON
Bishops Road
(1863)

Paddington
COAL   Basin

PADDINGTON
(1854)

1) PADDINGTON
Paddington (Praed Street)
(1868)
2) PADDINGTON (1913)

1915

1863

2   1

Index

Entries in black plain capital text denote open passenger stations, red closed, blue under construction or proposed (2009). Previous names are listed in reverse chronological order in red lower-case indented text below .

Entries in black italic capital text denote open non-passenger facilities, red closed, blue under construction or proposed (2009). Entries in black lower-case text denote in-use railway features, e.g. junctions or tunnels, red disused

Although UERL was formed in 1902, the constituent four railways are referred to by their original names prior to 1910 to acknowledge the huge growth of Underground Electric Railways in the 1900's

and the independent identities then retained in line nomenclature. Developments between 1910 and 1933 are referred to under the banner 'UERL' whilst the Metropolitan and Central London Railways

are referred to independently. After 1933 all developments to the Underground network are referred to under the banner 'LT', then 'LUL' post-1985.

A

NAME: (Previous names indented below)	PAGE / GRID:	YEAR OPENED:	YEAR CLOSED:	OPENED BY:	NOTES:
AA OIL SIDINGS (ANGERSTEIN WHARF)	34 / 1A	?	?	PRIV	
Abbey Mills Lower Junction	24 / 4A	1858	1958	LTSR	Abbey Mills Curve closed to passengers 1940, freight 1958
Abbey Mills Upper Junction	24 / 3A	1858	1958	LTSR	Abbey Mills Curve closed to passengers 1940, freight 1958
ABBEY ROAD	24/3A	2010	N/A	DLR	Canning Town to Stratford International DLR extension to open 2010
ABBEY WOOD	35 / 1B	1850	N/A	SER	Goods yard closed 1960
Acton Canal Wharf Junction	20 / 3B & 60	1868	N/A	MID	
ACTON CENTRAL	30 / 1A	1853	N/A	N&SWJ	'Central' suffix added 1925
Acton					
ACTON COAL	30 / 1A	?	1965	N&SWJ	
Acton Curve	40 / 2A	1878	1965	LSWR	
Acton Gatehouse Junction	30 / 1A	1857	1965	N&SWJ	Hammersmith & Chiswick Branch closed 1965
ACTON LANE (WILLESDEN)	20 / 3A	1861	1866	LNWR	Adjacent to current Harlesden Station
Acton Lane East Junction	30 / 2A & 40 / 2A	1879	1965	LSWR	
Acton Lane West Junction	30 / 2A & 40 / 2A	1878	1965	LSWR	
ACTON MAIN LINE	20 / 4A	1868	N/A	GWR	
Acton					
ACTON TOWN	30 / 1A	1879	N/A	MDR	Rebuilt and renamed 1910, further rebuilt 1933. First served by Piccadilly Line 1932.
Mill Hill Park					South Acton Shuttle served bay platform 5 until 1959.
Acton Town North Junction	30 / 1A	1883	N/A	MDR	Extensively remodelled 1932 during Turnham Green to Northfields quadrupling
Acton Town South Junction	30 / 1A & 40 / 1A	1899 (1905)	(1914) 1959	MDR	First passenger use 1905, last freight use 1914
Acton Wells Junction	20 / 4B & 60	1877	N/A	N&SWJ	
ACTON WORKS (RAILWAY ENGINEERING WORKS)	30 / 1A	1923	N/A	UERL	
ACTON YARD (YEOMAN AGGREGATES)	20 / 4A	?	N/A	PRIV	
ADDINGTON VILLAGE	48 / 2B	2000	N/A	CTL	
ADDISCOMBE (SER)	48 / 1A	1864	1997	SER	Renamed 'Addiscombe (Croydon)' 1925, 'Croydon' suffix dropped 1955
Addiscombe (Croydon)					Goods Yard closed 1968. Elmers End to Addiscombe closed 1997
Croydon (Addiscombe)					
Croydon (Addiscombe Road)					
ADDISCOMBE (CTL)	48 / 1A	2000	N/A	CTL	
ADDISCOMBE EMU SHED	48 / 1A	1926	1992	SR	On site of former Loco Shed
AEC MOTOR WORKS	29 / 1A	?	?	PRIV	
AGGREGATE INDUSTRIES LTD (ANGERSTEIN WHARF)	34 / 1A	?	N/A	PRIV	
AGGREGATE INDUSTRIES LTD (NEASDEN)	20 / 2B	?	N/A	PRIV	On site of former Loco Shed
AIRCRAFT SIDINGS Nos 1 & 2 (KIDBROOKE)	34 / 3A	?	?	PRIV	War Depot established at Kidbrooke during WWI
ALBANY PARK	35 / 4B	1935	N/A	SER	
ALDERSBROOK (UP) CAR HOLDING SIDINGS	24 / 1B	?	N/A	BR	
ALDGATE	23 / 4A & 7 / 2A	1876	N/A	MET	
Aldgate Junction	23 / 4A & 7 / 2A	1884	N/A	MET	
ALDGATE EAST (1st)	23 / 4A & 7 / 2A	1884	1938	MDR & MET	Relocated East 1938 (Junction Remodelling)
ALDGATE EAST (2nd)	23 / 4A & 7 / 2A	1938	N/A	LT (DIS & MET)	
Aldgate East Junction	23 / 4A & 7 / 2A	1884	N/A	MDR & MET	Junction relocated East 1938
ALDWYCH	22 / 4A	1907	1994	GNP&BR	Aldwych Branch closed to passengers 1994, but track and a train retained for filming work
Strand (Aldwych)					
Strand					
Alexandra Bridge	55	1864	1971	LCDR	Spans removed 1985, piers remain. Some piers to be used for Blackfriars station redevelopment
ALEXANDRA PALACE	12 / 3A	1873	1954	GNR	Nominally opened by Muswell Hill & Palace Railway, but operated by GNR from opening.
Alexandra Park (1891-1892 only)					Closed and re-opened several times during its existence, known as Alexandra Park 1891-1892
Alexandra Palace					Closed when Alexandra Palace to Finsbury park service withdrawn 1954. Had been intended
					for electrification and transfer to LT Northern Line, but works abandoned post-WW2.
ALEXANDRA PALACE	12 / 3A	1859	N/A	GNR	Renamed 'Wood Green (Alexandra Palace)' 1971, renamed 'Alexandra Palace' 1982
Wood Green (Alexandra Palace)					
Wood Green					
ALL SAINTS	23 / 4B & 57	1987	N/A	DLR	On Site of former NLR Poplar Station
ALPERTON	19 / 3B	1903	N/A	MDR	Renamed 'Alperton' 1910. First served Piccadilly Line 1932, last served District Line 1933
Perivale & Alperton					
Perivale Alperton					
AMERSHAM	1 / 2A	1892	N/A	MET	'& Chesham Bois' 1922-1934. Metropolitan Line services beyond Amersham ceased 1961
Amersham & Chesham Bois					
Amersham					
AMPERE WAY	47 / 1A	2000	N/A	CTL	

NAME: (Previous names indented below)	PAGE / GRID:	YEAR OPENED:	YEAR CLOSED:	OPENED BY:	NOTES:
ANERLEY	43 / 2A	1839	N/A	LCR	East London Line projected to serve from 2010
Anerley Bridge					
Annerley					
ANGEL	22 / 3B	1901	N/A	C&SLR	Closed 1922-1924 (tunnel widening). Rebuilt with Northbound road routed via new tunnel 1992
ANGEL ROAD	13 / 2A	1840	N/A	ECR	
Water Lane					
Edmonton					
Angerstein Junction	34 / 2A	1852	N/A	SER	
ANGERSTEIN WHARF	34 / 1A	1852	N/A	SER	
ARCHWAY	22 / 1A	1907	N/A	CCE&HR	Terminus 1907-1939, opened as 'Highgate'. 'Archway' prefix added 1939, reversed 1941,
Highgate (Archway)					'Highgate' prefix dropped 1947
Archway (Highgate)					
Highgate					
ARENA	43 / 4A	2000	N/A	CTL	
ARNOS GROVE	12 / 2A	1932	N/A	UERL (PIC)	Terminus of extension from Finsbury Park 1932-1933
ARNOS GROVE SIDINGS	12 / 2A	1932	N/A	UERL (PIC)	Stabling Sidings for Piccadilly Line
ARSENAL	22 / 1B	1906	N/A	GNP&BR	Opened as 'Gillespie Road', renamed 'Arsenal (for Highbury Hill)' 1932, suffix gradually dropped
Arsenal (for Highbury Hill)					
Gillespie Road					
ASCOT ROAD	2 / 4A	N/A	N/A	LUL (MET)	Proposed station on Metropolitan Line Watford Junction Extension
ASHBURTON GROVE GOODS	22 / 2B & 15 / 4B	1876	1960	GNR	
ASHFORD (MIDDX.)	37 / 1B	1848	N/A	LSWR	Goods yard closed 1965
ASHTEAD	45 / 4A	1859	N/A	LSWR & LBSCR	
AVENUE ROAD	43 / 3A	2000	N/A	CTL	

B

NAME: (Previous names indented below)	PAGE / GRID:	YEAR OPENED:	YEAR CLOSED:	OPENED BY:	NOTES:
BAKER STREET	21 / 4B	1863	N/A	MET	Platforms to Swiss Cottage opened 1868 (Now Metropolitan Line Platforms)
					Baker Street & Waterloo Railway opened 1906, Jubilee Line opened 1979
BALHAM	42 / 1A	1856	N/A	LBSCR	Opened by West End of London & Crystal Palace Railway, but operated by LBSCR from outset
Balham & Upper Tooting					Northern Line Station and interchange opened 1926. '& Upper Tooting' suffix dropped 1969
Balham					
BANDON HALT	47 / 2A	1906	1914	LBSCR	
BANK	22 / 4B	1898	N/A	LSWR (W&C)	Opened by LSWR (Waterloo & City Line). C&SLR and CLR platforms opened 1900, DLR
City (W&C only)					platforms opened 1991. Waterloo & City platforms renamed from 'City' to 'Bank' 1940
BANSTEAD	46 / 4A	1865	N/A	LBSCR	'& Burgh Heath' suffix 1898-1928. Goods yard in use 1880-1964
Banstead & Burgh Heath					
BARBICAN	22 / 4B & 55	1865	N/A	MET	Opened as 'Aldersgate Street', City Widened Lines platforms added 1866 (later Network Rail)
Aldersgate & Barbican					'Street' suffix dropped 1910, '& Barbican' suffix added 1923, 'Aldersgate' prefix dropped 1968.
Aldersgate					Network Rail platforms closed 2009, although westbound NR services had ceased stopping
Aldersgate Street					prior to this
BARKING	25 / 2A	1854	N/A	LTSR	Served by District Railway since 1902 (no service 1905-1908), Served by Metropolitan Railway
					since 1936 ('Hammersmith & City Line' since 1990). Extensively rebuilt 1959-1961
Barking East Junction	25 / 2B	1961	N/A	BR	All junctions in Barking area extensively remodelled 1959-1961
BARKING GOODS	25 / 1B	1854	1957	LTSR	
BARKING POWER STATION	25 / 4B	1925	1981	PRIV	
BARKING RIVERSIDE	25 / 4B	2017	N/A	DLR	Gallions Reach to Dagenham Dock proposed to open c.2017
BARKINGSIDE (GER)	15 / 3A	1903	1947	GER	Closed 1916-1919. Fairlop Loop closed 1947 to allow electrification & transfer to LT Central Line
					Freight traffic remained until 1965
BARKINGSIDE (LT)	15 / 3A	1948	N/A	LT (CEN)	First served by LT Central Line Trains 1948. Goods yard closed 1965
BARKING SIDINGS	25 / 2A	1958	N/A	LT (DIS)	Stabling sidings for District and Hammersmith & City Line Trains
Barking Station Junction	25 / 1A	1961	N/A	BR	Junction for Bay Platform used by Gospel Oak (formerly Kentish Town) trains
Barking Tilbury Line Junction East	25 / 2A	1961	N/A	BR	All junctions in Barking area extensively remodelled 1959-1961
Barking Tilbury Line Junction West	25 / 1A	1961	N/A	BR	All junctions in Barking area extensively remodelled 1959-1961
Barking West Junction	25 / 1A	1961	N/A	BR	All junctions in Barking area extensively remodelled 1959-1961
BARNEHURST	36 / 3A	1895	N/A	SER	Goods Yard closed 1968
BARNES	30 / 3B	1846	N/A	LSWR	Goods yard closed 1969
BARNES BRIDGE	30 / 3B	1916	N/A	LSWR	
Barnes Bridge	30 / 3B	1849	N/A	LSWR	
Barnes Junction	30 / 3B	1849	N/A	LSWR	
Barnet Tunnels	11 / 1B	1850	N/A	GNR	
BARONS COURT	31 / 2A & 56	1905	N/A	MDR	GNP&BR platforms opened 1906
BATH ROAD	30 / 1B	1909	1917	N&SWJR	Passenger services withdrawn from Hammersmith & Chiswick Branch 1917
BATTERSEA	31 / 3B	1863	1940	WLER	Passenger service withdrawn Willesden Jcn to Clapham Jcn 1940
BATTERSEA PARK & STEAMBOAT PIER	32 / 2A & 51	1860	1870	LBSCR	
Battersea					
BATTERSEA PARK (2nd)	32 / 3A & 51	1867	N/A	LBSCR	Renamed 'Battersea Park' 1870
Battersea Park & York Road					
York Road & Battersea Park					
York Road					
Battersea Park Junction	51	1867	N/A	LBSCR	
BATTERSEA PARK ROAD	32 / 2A & 51	1867	1916	LCDR	Renamed 1877
Battersea Park (York Road)					

NAME: (Previous names indented below)	PAGE / GRID:	YEAR OPENED:	YEAR CLOSED:	OPENED BY:	NOTES:
Battersea Pier Junction	32 / 2A & 51	1867	N/A	LCDR	
BATTERSEA PIER SIDINGS	51	?	N/A	LBSCR	
BATTERSEA WHARF	51	?	1970	LBSCR	
BAYSWATER	21 / 4A	1868	N/A	MET	Opened as 'Bayswater', renamed 'Bayswater (Queens Road) & Westbourne Grove' 1923,
Bayswater (Queensway)					'& Westbourne Grove' suffix dropped 1933, renamed 'Bayswater (Queensway)' 1946,
Bayswater (Queens Road)					suffix gradually dropped
Bayswater (Queens Road) & Westbourne Grove					
Bayswater					
BECKENHAM HILL	43 / 2B	1892	N/A	LCDR	
BECKENHAM HILL CARRIAGE SIDINGS	43 / 2B	?	N/A	SR	
BECKENHAM JUNCTION	43 / 3B	1857	N/A	SER	Built by the Mid Kent Railway, but operated by SER from opening. Goods yard closed 1964
Beckenham					Croydon Tramlink served since 2000
BECKENHAM ROAD	43 / 3A	2000	N/A	CTL	
BECKTON (GER)	25 / 4A	1873	1940	GER	Passenger services withdrawn from Beckton and Gallions 1940
BECKTON (DLR)	24 / 4B	1994	N/A	DLR	
BECKTON DEPOT	25 / 4A	1994	N/A	DLR	DLR Depot
BECKTON GAS WORKS	25 / 4A	1872	1971	PRIV	
Beckton Junction	24 / 4B	1880	1940	GER	Divergence of Beckton and Gallions Branches
BECKTON PARK	24 / 4B	1994	N/A	DLR	
BECKTON RIVERSIDE	25 / 4A	2017	N/A	DLR	Gallions Reach to Dagenham Dock proposed to open c.2017
BECONTREE (LMS)	25 / 2B	1926	1962	LMS	Opened on existing LTSR Main Line. First served by District Line after quadrupling in 1932.
Gale Street Halt					Last served by British Rail 1962 and 'Fast' Platforms abandoned. Owned by LT since 1970.
BECONTREE (LT)	25 / 2B	1932	N/A	LMS	Barking to Upminster quadrupled by LMS 1932, new platforms at Becontree served by
					District Line from opening. Ownership transferred to LT 1970.
BECONTREE ESTATE RAILWAY	25 / 1B	1921	1934	LCC	Transported building materials during construction of Becontree Estate. Extended to Thames
BEDDINGTON LANE (WCR)	42 / 4A	1855	1997	WCR	Opened as 'Beddington', 'Lane' suffix added 1887
Beddington Lane Halt					Wimbledon to West Croydon closed 1997 prior to conversion to Tramlink
Beddington					
BEDDINGTON LANE (CTL)	42 / 4A	2000	N/A	CTL	On site of former Beddington Lane Station
BELGRAVE WALK	41 / 3B	2000	N/A	CTL	
BELLINGHAM	43 / 1B	1892	N/A	LCDR	
BELMONT (MIDDX.)	9 / 3B	1932	1964	LNWR	Belmont to Harrow & Wealdstone withdrawn 1964 and entire branch closed to freight
BELMONT (SURREY)	46 / 3A	1865	N/A	LBSCR	Renamed 1875. Goods Yard in use 1880-1969
California					
BELSIZE PARK	21 / 2B	1907	N/A	CCE&HR	
Belsize Tunnels	21 / 2B	1868	N/A	MID	
BELVEDERE	36 / 1A	1859	N/A	SER	
BERMONDSEY	33 / 1A	1999	N/A	LUL (JUB)	
BERRYLANDS	40 / 4A	1933	N/A	SR	
BETHNAL GREEN (GER)	23 / 3A	1872	N/A	GER	
Bethnal Green Junction					
BETHNAL GREEN (LT)	23 / 3A	1946	N/A	LT (CEN)	
BEXLEY	36 / 4A	1866	N/A	SER	Goods Yard closed 1963
BEXLEYHEATH	35 / 3B	1895	N/A	SER	Goods Yard situated 1/4 Mile West of passenger station, closed 1968
Bexley Heath					
BICKLEY	44 / 3B	1858	N/A	LCDR	
Southborough Road					
Bickley Junctions	44 / 3B	1902	N/A	SECR	
BINGHAM ROAD	48 / 1A	1906	1983	SER	Closed 1915-1935, finally closed 1983
BIRKBECK	43 / 3A	1930	N/A	SR	Croydon Tramlink opened 2000
BISHOPSGATE (HIGH LEVEL)	23 / 4A & 59	1840 *(1882)*	1874 *(1964)*	ECR	Terminus for Eastern Counties (later Great Eastern) Railway 1840-1874
Bishopsgate					Goods traffic commenced 1882 and remained until 1964
Shoreditch					
Bishopsgate Junction	59	1876	1916 *(1966)*	ELR	Link between East London Line and GER main line. Last passenger service 1916, severed 1966
BISHOPSGATE (LOW LEVEL)	23 / 4A & 59	1872	1916	GER	
BLACKFRIARS (SER)	32 / 1B & 55	1864	1869	SER	Replaced by Waterloo Junction (=East) to West
Great Surrey Street					
BLACKFRIARS (MDR)	22 / 4B	1870	N/A	MDR	Main Line station opened by LCDR 1886 as 'St Paul's', renamed 'Blackfriars' 1937
St Paul's					LU platforms closed 2009-2011 due to redevelopment works
BLACKFRIARS BRIDGE	32 / 1B & 55	1864	1885	LCDR	Replaced by St Paul's (=Blackfriars) on North bank of Thames
BLACKFRIARS GOODS	55	1864	1964	LCDR	
Blackfriars Junction	32 / 1B & 55	1878	N/A	LCDR	
BLACKHEATH	34 / 3A	1849	N/A	SER	
BLACKHEATH HILL	33 / 3B	1871	1917	LCDR	Terminus 1871-1888. Passenger service withdrawn Nunhead to Greenwich Park 1917
Blackheath Junction	34 / 3A	1895	N/A	SER	
Blackheath Tunnel	34 / 2A	1849	N/A	SER	
BLACKHORSE LANE	43 / 4A	2000	N/A	CTL	
BLACKHORSE ROAD	13 / 4A	1894	N/A	T&FG	Victoria Line station opened & BR platforms resited west 1968
Black Horse Road					
BLACKWALL (LBR)	24 / 4A & 57	1840	1926	LBR	Passenger service to Blackwall withdrawn 1926
BLACKWALL (DLR)	23 / 4B & 57	1994	N/A	DLR	
BLACKWALL GOODS	57	1860	1961	GNR	
BLAKE HALL	6 / 2B	1865	1981	GER	Epping to Ongar transferred to LT 1949, Electrified 1956, Blake Hall closed 1981
Bollo Lane Junction	30 / 2A & 40 / 2A	1878	1965	LSWR	Acton Curve dismantled 1965

NAME: (Previous names indented below)	PAGE / GRID:	YEAR OPENED:	YEAR CLOSED:	OPENED BY:	NOTES:
BOND STREET	22 / 4A	1900	N/A	CLR	Jubilee Line platforms opened 1979. Platforms for 'Crossrail 1' proposed to open 2017
BOROUGH	32 / 1B	1890	N/A	C&SLR	Closed 1922-1925
Great Dover Street					
Borough Market Junction	32 / 1B & 55	1866	N/A	SER	
BOROUGH ROAD	32 / 1B	1864	1907	LCDR	
BOSTON MANOR	29 / 1B	1883	N/A	MDR	Renamed 1911. First served by Piccadilly Line 1933. Last served by District Line 1964
Boston Road					
BOUNDS GREEN	12 / 2A	1932	N/A	UERL (PIC)	
BOUNDS GREEN DEPOT	12 / 3A	1929	N/A	LNER	
BOW	23 / 3B & 57	1850	1944	NLR	Passenger service Dalston Junction to Poplar withdrawn 1944
BOW CHURCH	23 / 3B & 57	1987	N/A	DLR	On site of former NLR Bow Station
BOW GOODS	23 / 3B	?	N/A	GER	Plasmor, Aggregate Industries & Midland Waste
BOW GOODS	23 / 3B	?	?	NLR	
BOWES PARK	12 / 2A	1880	N/A	GNR	
Bow Junction	23 / 3B & 57	1849	N/A	LBR & ECR	Junction between Eastern Counties Railway and Blackwall Extension Railway (LBR)
Bow Junction	23 / 3B & 57	1850	1968	NLR	Junction of NLR routes to Poplar and Fenchurch Street
BOW ROAD (GER) (1st)	23 / 3B & 57	1849	1892	LBR	Blackwall Extension Railway (London & Blackwall Rly) opened to passengers 1849, closed 1850
Bow & Bromley					Re-opened 1876 as 'Bow Road', closed and re-sited north 1892
BOW ROAD (GER) (2nd)	23 / 3B & 57	1892	1949	GER	Closed 1941-1946. Passenger services Fenchurch Street to Stratford withdrawn 1949
BOW ROAD (MDR)	23 / 3B	1902	N/A	MDR & LTSR	Served by Metropolitan Line since 1936 ('Hammersmith & City Line' since 1990)
BOW ROAD GOODS	23 / 3B & 57	1885	1964	GER	
BOW WORKS	23 / 4B & 57	1863	1960	NLR	North London Railway Loco Works
BOYERS SIDING (FELTHAM)	38 / 1A	?	?	PRIV	Market garden
BRENT CROSS	11 / 4A	1923	N/A	UERL (CCE&HR)	Renamed 1976
Brent					
BRENT CROSS THAMESLINK	20 / 1B	?	N/A	NR	Proposed new station in connection with regeneration project
Brent Curve Junction	20 / 1B	1868	N/A	MID	
BRENTFORD (GWR)	29 / 2B	1860	1942	GWR	Closed 1915-1920. Passenger service on GWR Brentford Branch withdrawn 1942
BRENTFORD (LSWR)	29 / 2B	1849	N/A	LSWR	'Brentford Central' 1950-1980. Goods yard closed 1965
Brentford Central					
Brentford					
BRENTFORD DOCK	29 / 2B	1859	1964	GWR	
BRENTFORD GOODS	29 / 2B	1930	N/A	GWR	
BRENTFORD STONE TERMINAL	29 / 2B	?	N/A	PRIV	Aggregate Industries
BRENTFORD WASTE TERMINAL	29 / 2B	1977	N/A	PRIV	West London Waste
BRENTHAM (FOR NORTH EALING)	19 / 3B	1911	1947	GWR	Replaced Twyford Abbey Halt. Closed 1915-1920
Brentham					
BRENT WASTE TERMINAL	21 / 1A	?	N/A	PRIV	Shanks & McEwan Ltd
BREWERY SIDINGS (ROMFORD)	16 / 4B	1853	1963	PRIV	
BRICKLAYERS ARMS	32 / 1B & 62	1844	1852 (1983)	LGR & LCR	Closed to passengers 1852, remained in use for Goods until 1983
Bricklayers Arms Junction	52	1844	1983	LGR & LCR	
BRIMSDOWN	5 / 3B	1884	N/A	GER	
BRITISH MUSEUM	22 / 4A	1900	1933	CLR	Closed when Central Line platforms opened at Holborn (Kingsway) 1933
BRIXTON (LCDR)	32 / 3B	1862	N/A	LCDR	Platforms on route to Denmark Hill closed 1929
Brixton & South Stockwell					
Brixton					
BRIXTON (LT)	32 / 3B	1971	N/A	LT (VIC)	Southern terminus of Victoria Line
Brixton Junction	32 / 3B	1864	N/A	LCDR	
BROAD STREET	22 / 4B & 59	1865	1985	NLR	
BROAD STREET GOODS	22 / 4B & 59	1868	1969	LNWR	
BROAD STREET (TEMPORARY)	22 / 4B & 59	1985	1986	BR	Opened due to demolition of Broad Street, prior to diversion of trains to Liverpool Street
BROCKLEY	33 / 3B	1871	N/A	LBSCR	East London Line projected to serve from 2010
BROCKLEY HILL	10 / 1A	N/A	N/A	LT (NOR)	On Northern Line extension to Bushey Heath from Edgware. Construction abandoned 1940
BROCKLEY LANE	33 / 3B	1872	1917	LCDR	Passenger service withdrawn Nunhead to Greenwich Park 1917
BROCKLEY LANE DEPOT	33 / 3A	1883	1970	GNR & LNWR	'Martins Siding' on Down Side LNWR Coal Yard 1885-1970
BROMLEY	23 / 4B & 57	1858	1962	LTSR	Damaged by fire 1892, rebuilt to West 1894. Main Line services non-stopped since 1962
					and Fast Platforms abandoned
BROMLEY-BY-BOW	23 / 4B & 57	1902	N/A	MDR	First served by District Railway 1902, line quadrupled 1908, District Trains using Slow Lines
Bromley					Served by Metropolitan Line since 1936 ('Hammersmith & City Line' since 1990), renamed 1967
Bromley Down Junction	43 / 3A	1857	N/A	LBSCR	
Bromley Junction	23 / 4B & 57	1869	1959	LTSR	Resited to the West with Bromley Station 1894
BROMLEY GOODS	24 / 4A	1898	?	LTSR	
BROMLEY NORTH	44 / 3A	1878	N/A	SER	Renamed 1899. Goods yard closed 1968
Bromley					
BROMLEY SOUTH	44 / 3A	1858	N/A	LCDR	Renamed 'Bromley South' 1899
Bromley					
Bromley Common					
Bromley Up Junction	43 / 3A	1857	N/A	LBSCR	
BROMPTON & FULHAM GOODS	31 / 2A & 50	1892	1975	LNWR	
BROMPTON ROAD	31 / 1B	1906	1934	GNP&BR	
BRONDESBURY	21 / 2A	1860	N/A	HJR	Opened as 'Edgeware Road (Kilburn)', '& Brondesbury' suffix added 1872, renamed
Brondesbury (Edgware Road)					'Brondesbury (Edgware Road)' 1873, renamed 'Brondesbury' 1883. Closed 1995-1996
Edgware Road & Brondesbury					
Edgware Road					
Edgeware Road (Kilburn)					

NAME: (Previous names indented below)	PAGE / GRID:	YEAR OPENED:	YEAR CLOSED:	OPENED BY:	NOTES:
BRONDESBURY PARK	21 / 3A	1908	N/A	LNWR	Closed 1995-1996
BRUCE GROVE	13 / 3A	1872	N/A	GER	
BUCKHURST HILL (ECR)	14 / 1B	1856	1970	ECR	Majority of Passenger services transferred to LT in 1948. First Trains in the morning remained British Rail services until 1970
BUCKHURST HILL (LT)	14 / 1B	1948	N/A	LT (CEN)	First served by Central Line Trains 1948. Goods Yard closed 1964
BURDETT ROAD	23 / 4B	1871	1941	GER	
BURNT OAK	10 / 3A	1924	N/A	UERL (CCE&HR)	'Watling' suffix introduced 1928, gradually dropped
Burnt Oak (Watling)					
Burnt Oak					
Burroughs Tunnels	10 / 4B	1924	N/A	UERL (CCE&HR)	
Bury Street Junction	5 / 4A	1891	N/A	GER	
BUSHEY	2 / 4B	1841	N/A	L&B	Served by London Underground Bakerloo Line Trains 1917-1982. '& Oxhey' dropped 1974
Bushey & Oxhey					Goods yard closed 1969
Bushey					
BUSHEY HEATH	9 / 1B	N/A	N/A	LT (NOR)	Intended terminus of Northern Line extension from Edgware. Construction abandoned 1940
BUSHEY HEATH DEPOT	9 / 1B	N/A	N/A	LT (NOR)	Was to replace Golders Green Depot. Sheds constructed but track never laid, abandoned 1940
BUSH HILL PARK	5 / 4A	1880	N/A	GER	

C

CALEDONIAN ROAD (NLR)	22 / 2A	1852	1870	NLR	Original station, resited West and renamed 'Barnsbury' 1870
CALEDONIAN ROAD (GNP&BR)	22 / 2A	1906	N/A	GNP&BR	
CALEDONIAN ROAD & BARNSBURY	22 / 2A	1870	N/A	NLR	Replaced original Caledonian Road Station to East. Renamed 'Caledonian Road & Barnsbury' in 1893
Barnsbury					
CALEDONIAN ROAD GOODS	22 / 2A & 54	?	?	GNR	
CAMBERWELL	32 / 3B	1862	1916	LCDR	Opened as 'Camberwell', 'New Road' suffix added 1863, dropped 1908
Camberwell New Road					
Camberwell					
CAMBERWELL GOODS & COAL	32 / 2B	?	1964	LCDR	
Cambria Junction	32 / 3B	1872	N/A	LCDR	
CAMBRIDGE HEATH	23 / 3A	1884	N/A	GER	Closed during World War I, re-opening 1919
CAMDEN CARRIAGE SIDINGS	21 / 3B & 61	?	N/A	LNWR	Formerly engine shed
Camden Junctions	21 / 2B & 61	1851	N/A	LNWR	
CAMDEN ROAD (NLR) (1st)	22 / 2A	1850	1870	NLR	Original station on St Pancras Way. Replaced by Camden Town Station to West
CAMDEN ROAD (MID)	22 / 2A	1868	1916	MID	
CAMDEN ROAD (NLR) (2nd)	22 / 2A	1870	N/A	NLR	Replaced first station to East. Renamed Camden Road 1950
Camden Town					
Camden Road East Junctions	54	1850	N/A	NLR	
CAMDEN TOWN	22 / 2A	1907	N/A	CCE&HR	
Camden Town Junctions	22 / 3A	1907	N/A	CCE&HR	Extensively remodelled 1924 due to extension of Bank Branch from Euston
Campbell Road Junction	23 / 4B & 57	1902	1959	LTSR & MDR	Junction between LTSR and District Railway, connection removed 1959
Campden Hill Tunnel	31 / 1A	1868	N/A	MET	
CANADA WATER	33 / 1A	1999	N/A	LUL (ELL)	Jubilee Line platforms opened 1 month after East London Line in 1999
Canal Junction	52	1876	N/A	ELR	
CANARY WHARF (DLR)	33 / 1B & 57	1987	N/A	DLR	
CANARY WHARF (LUL)	33 / 1B	1999	N/A	LUL (JUB)	
CANNING TOWN (1st)	24 / 4A	1847	1999	ECR	Renamed 1873. Relocated to the South in connection with Jubilee Line Extension
Barking Road					
CANNING TOWN (2nd)	24 / 4A	1999	N/A	RT / DLR / LUL	Replaced NLL station to North, NR platforms closed 2006 (to become DLR 2010)
CANNING TOWN GOODS	24 / 4A	1880	1967	LNWR	
CANNON STREET	22 / 4B & 55	1866	N/A	SER	District Railway station opened 1884
CANNON STREET ROAD	23 / 4A & 7 / 3B	1842	1848	LBR	
Cannon Street South Junction	32 / 1B & 55	1866	N/A	SER	
CANONBURY	22 / 2B	1870	N/A	NLR	
Canonbury West Junction	22 / 2B	1874	N/A	NLR & GNR	
CANONS PARK	9 / 2B	1932	N/A	MET	Opened by Metropolitan Railway. 'Edgware' Suffix dropped 1933
Canons Park (Edgware)					Transferred to Bakerloo Line 1939, Jubilee Line 1979
Canterbury Road Junction	32 / 3B	1865	N/A	LCDR	
Carlton Road Junction	21 / 2B & 57	1883	N/A	MID	
CARPENDERS PARK (1st)	8 / 1B	1914	1952	LNWR	Served by London Underground Bakerloo Line Trains 1917-1952
CARPENDERS PARK (2nd)	8 / 1B	1952	N/A	BR	Served by London Underground Bakerloo Line Trains 1952-1982
CARPENTERS ROAD GOODS	53	?	?	GER	
Carpenters Road North Junction	53	1862	N/A	ECR	
Carpenters Road South Junction	53	1862	N/A	ECR	
CARSHALTON	46 / 2B	1868	N/A	LBSCR	
CARSHALTON BEECHES	46 / 2B	1906	N/A	LBSCR	Renamed 1925
Beeches Halt					
CARTERHATCH LANE	5 / 3A	1916	1919	GER	
CASTLE BAR PARK	19 / 4A	1904	N/A	GWR	'Halt' suffix dropped 1969
Castle Bar Park Halt					
CATERHAM	48 / 4B	1856	N/A	CR	
CATFORD	33 / 4B	1892	N/A	LCDR	
CATFORD BRIDGE	33 / 4B	1857	N/A	SER	Built by the Mid Kent Railway, but operated by SER from opening. Goods yard closed 1968

NAME: (Previous names indented below)	PAGE / GRID:	YEAR OPENED:	YEAR CLOSED:	OPENED BY:	NOTES:
CENTRAL	24 / 4B	1880	1940	PLA	Passenger services withdrawn from Gallions Branch 1940
CENTRAL CROYDON	47 / 1B	1868	1890	LBSCR	Closed 1871-1886
CENTRALE	47 / 1B	2005	N/A	CTL	
CHADWELL HEATH	25 / 1B	1864	N/A	GER	
Chadwell Heath for Becontree					
Chadwell Heath					
CHAFFORD HUNDRED	16 / 3B	1993	N/A	BR	
CHALFONT & LATIMER	1 / 2A	1889	N/A	MET	Renamed 1915. Goods yard closed 1966
Chalfont Road					
CHALK FARM (CCE&HR)	21 / 2B	1907	N/A	CCE&HR	
CHALK FARM (LNWR)	21 / 2B & 61	1851	1915	LNWR	
Camden					
Chalton Street Junction	54	1926	1935	MET	Link between Metropolitan Line and City Widened Lines
CHANCERY LANE	22 / 4B	1900	N/A	CLR	'Gray's Inn' suffix introduced 1934, gradually dropped
Chancery Lane (Gray's Inn)					
Chancery Lane					
Channelsea North Junction	23 / 2B & 53	1862	N/A	GER	
Channelsea South Junction	53	1854	2009	ECR	Disconnected 2009 when LOROL services diverted into Stratford High Level
CHARING CROSS (SER)	22 / 4A	1864	N/A	SER	
CHARING CROSS (LT-JUB)	22 / 4A & 28 / 2A	1979	1999	LT (JUB)	Station closed when Jubilee Line extension opened 1999. Retained for emergencies.
CHARING CROSS (CCE&HR)	22 / 4A & 28 / 2A	1907	N/A	CCE&HR	Opened as 'Charing Cross'. Renamed 'Charing Cross (Strand)' 1914. Renamed 'Strand' 1915.
Strand					Closed 1973-1979 in connection with Jubilee Line construction, re-opened as 'Charing Cross'
Charing Cross (Strand)					1979 with interchange with Bakerloo and Jubilee Lines.
Charing Cross					
CHARING CROSS (BS&WR)	22 / 4A & 28 / 2A	1906	N/A	BS&WR	Station renamed and interchange with Jubilee and Northern Lines provided 1979
Trafalgar Square					
CHARLTON	34 / 2B	1849	N/A	SER	Suffix 'Junction' sometimes added. Goods yard closed 1963
Charlton Junction	34 / 2A	1873	N/A	SER	
Charlton Tunnel	34 / 1B	1849	N/A	SER	
CHEAM	46 / 2A	1847	N/A	LBSCR	Goods yard closed 1964
CHELSEA BASIN GOODS	31 / 3B & 50	1863	1981	LNWR & GWR	
CHELSEA & FULHAM	31 / 2A & 50	1863	1940	WLER	'& Fulham' after 1902. Passenger service withdrawn Willesden Jcn to Clapham Jcn 1940
Chelsea					
CHERTSEY	37 / 4A	1848	N/A	LSWR	
CHESHAM	1 / 1A	1889	N/A	MET & GCR	Goods yard closed 1966
CHESHUNT	5 / 1B	1846	N/A	GER	
Cheshunt Junction	5 / 1B	1891	N/A	GER	
CHESSINGTON NORTH	45 / 2A	1939	N/A	SR	
CHESSINGTON SOUTH	45 / 2A	1939	N/A	SR	
CHESSINGTON SOUTH SIDINGS	45 / 2A	1939	N/A	SR	Formerly Goods yard (closed 1963), then Coal depot (closed 1988)
CHIGWELL (GER)	14 / 1B	1903	1947	GER	Fairlop Loop closed 1947 to allow electrification and transfer to LT Central Line. Freight traffic remained until 1965
CHIGWELL (LT)	14 / 1B	1948	N/A	LT (CEN)	First served by LT Central Line Trains 1948
CHINGFORD	14 / 1A	1878	N/A	GER	
CHINGFORD (BULL LANE)	14 / 1A	1873	1878 (1965)	GER	Original terminus of extension from Walthamstow. Remained open to goods traffic until 1965
CHIPSTEAD					
Chipstead & Banstead Downs	47 / 3A	1897	N/A	SECR	Goods yard closed 1962
CHISLEHURST	44 / 3B	1865	N/A	SER	
Chislehurst & Bickley Park					
Chislehurst Junction	44 / 3B	1904	N/A	SECR	
Chislehurst Tunnels	44 / 2B	1865	N/A	SER	
CHISWICK	30 / 2A	1849	N/A	LSWR	Renamed 1948. Goods yard closed 1958
Chiswick & Grove Park					
Chiswick					
Chiswick Junction (1)	30 / 2A	1869	1932	LSWR	Chiswick Curve dismantled 1932
Chiswick Junction (2)	30 / 3B	1862	1881	LSWR	Barnes Curve disused since 1869 but not dismantled until 1881
CHISWICK PARK	30 / 2A & 40 / 1A	1879	N/A	MDR	Opened as Acton Green, renamed 'Chiswick Park & Acton Green' 1887, renamed 'Chiswick Park' 1910. Completely rebuilt 1933 due to quadrupling works
Chiswick Park & Acton Green					
Acton Green					
Chobham Farm Junction	53	1854	1969	GER	
CHORLEYWOOD	1 / 3B	1889	N/A	MET	Opened as 'Chorley Wood', '& Chenies' suffix in use 1915-1934, became 'Chorleywood' 1964
Chorley Wood					Goods yard closed 1966
Chorley Wood & Chenies					
Chorley Wood					
Christian Street Junction	23 / 4A & 7 / 3B	1886	N/A	LTSR	Originally Junction for Commercial Road Goods, Now point where 4 tracks become 2
CHRISTIE'S SIDING	34 / 2A	?	?	PRIV	
CHURCHBURY	5 / 4A	1891	1919	GER	Closed 1909-1915. Site now occupied by Southbury Station
CHURCH MANOR WAY HALT	35 / 1B	1917	1919	SECR	Provided for munitions workers
CHURCH STREET	47 / 1B	2000	N/A	CTL	
CHURCHYARD SIDINGS	54	1868	N/A	MID	Castle cement terminal
CITY GOODS	23 / 4A & 7 / 3A	1862	1949	MID	
CITY ROAD	22 / 3B	1901	1922	C&SLR	
CITY THAMESLINK	22 / 4B & 55	1990	N/A	BR	Renamed 1991
St Paul's Thameslink					

NAME: (Previous names indented below)	PAGE / GRID:	YEAR OPENED:	YEAR CLOSED:	OPENED BY:	NOTES:
CLAPHAM COMMON (LSWR)	31 / 4B	1838	1863	LSWR	Replaced by Clapham Junction Station to North
Wandsworth					
CLAPHAM COMMON (C&SLR)	32 / 3A	1900	N/A	C&SLR	Terminus of City & South London Railway 1900-1926. Closed 1923-1924
CLAPHAM GOODS	32 / 3A	?	1963	LCDR	
CLAPHAM HIGH STREET	32 / 3A	1862	N/A	LCDR	LBSCR platforms opened 1867, LCDR platforms closed 1916. Renamed 'Clapham High Street'
Clapham					1989. East London Line extension Phase 2 (LOROL) projected to serve from 2011.
Clapham & North Stockwell					LSWR timetables for trains serving the station to / from Ludgate Hill referred to
Clapham Road & North Stockwell					'Clapham Town'
Clapham & North Stockwell					
Clapham					
CLAPHAM JUNCTION	31 / 3B	1863	N/A	LSWR	East London Line extension Phase 2 (LOROL) projected to serve from 2011
CLAPHAM NORTH	32 / 3A	1900	N/A	C&SLR	Closed 1923-1924, Renamed 1926
Clapham Road					
CLAPHAM SOUTH	32 / 4A	1926	N/A	UERL (NOR)	
CLAPHAM YARD	31 / 4B	?	N/A	LSWR	
CLAPTON	23 / 1A	1872	N/A	GER	
CLAPTON GOODS	23 / 1A	1900	1964	GER	
Clapton Junction	23 / 1A	1872	N/A	GER	
Clapton Tunnel	23 / 1A	1872	N/A	GER	
CLARENCE YARD GOODS	22 / 1B & 15 / 3B	1875	1960	GNR	
Clerkenwell Tunnels	22 / 3B & 55	1863	N/A	MET	Quadrupled 1868
CLOCK HOUSE	43 / 3B	1890	N/A	SER	Goods yard closed 1964
COBORN ROAD	23 / 3B	1865	1882	GER	Renamed 1879. Closed and moved west 1882
Old Ford					
COBORN ROAD FOR OLD FORD	23 / 3B	1882	1946	GER	Closed 1916-1919
Coborn Road					
COCKFOSTERS	3 / 3B	1933	N/A	LT (PIC)	
COCKFOSTERS DEPOT	4 / 4A	1933	N/A	LT (PIC)	
COLINDALE	10 / 3B	1924	N/A	UERL (CCE&HR)	
COLLIERS WOOD	41 / 2B	1926	N/A	UERL (NOR)	
COLNBROOK	27 / 2A	1884	1965	GWR	Terminus of branch from West Drayton 1884-1885. Passenger service withdrawn between
					West Drayton and Staines West 1965
COLNBROOK ESTATE HALT	27 / 2A	1961	1965	BR	Passenger service West Drayton to Staines West withdrawn 1965
COLNBROOK GOODS	27 / 2A	1884	1966	GWR	
COLNBROOK LOGISTICS CENTRE	27 / 2A	2002	N/A	PRIV	Transfer point for Heathrow Airport construction materials
COLNBROOK OIL TERMINAL (ELF)	27 / 2A	1990	N/A	PRIV	Aviation Fuel terminal for Heathrow Airport
COMMERCIAL DOCK	33 / 1A & 52	1856	1866	SER	
COMMERCIAL ROAD GOODS	23 / 4A & 7 / 2B	1886	1967	LTSR	
Connaught Bridge	34 / 1B	1855	1967	GER	
CONNAUGHT ROAD	24 / 4B	1880	1940	PLA	Passenger services withdrawn from Gallions Branch 1940
Connaught Tunnel	24 / 4B	1876	2006	GER	North Woolwich Branch diverted underground due to construction of Royal Albert Dock
					Stratford to North Woolwich closed 2006, tunnel proposed to be re-used by Crossrail 1
COOMBE LANE	48 / 2A	2000	N/A	CTL	
COOMBE ROAD	48 / 2A	1885	1983	SER	Closed 1916-1935, Renamed upon re-opening, finally closed 1983
Coombe Lane					
Copenhagen Tunnels	22 / 2A	1850	N/A	GNR	
Coppermill North Junction	13 / 4A	1872	N/A	GER	Junction between Lea Valley Line and 1872 route from Hackney Downs
Coppermill South Junction	13 / 4A	1885	1960	GER	Junction between Lea Valley Line and 1885 curve to Chingford
CORY OIL (SELSDON)	47 / 2B	1968	1993	PRIV	Originally Selsdon Goods yard
Cottage Junction	42 / 4B	1983	N/A	BR	
COULSDON NORTH	47 / 4A	1899	1983	LBSCR	Renamed 'Coulsdon & Smitham Downs' 1911, renamed 'Coulsdon West' 1923 for 3 weeks,
Coulsdon West					then finally renamed 'Coulsdon North'. Goods yard closed 1968
Coulsdon & Smitham Downs					
Stoat's Nest & Cane Hill					
COULSDON SOUTH	48 / 3A	1889	N/A	SER	Renamed 'Coulsdon East' in 1923 for 3 weeks, then 'Coulsdon South'
Coulsdon East					
Coulsdon & Cane Hill					
Coulsdon					
Courthill Loop North Junction	33 / 3B	1929	N/A	SR	
Courthill Loop South Junction	33 / 3B	1929	N/A	SR	
COVENT GARDEN	22 / 4A	1907	N/A	GNP&BR	
COWLEY	17 / 4B	1904	1962	GWR	Passenger services withdrawn from Uxbridge Vine Street Branch 1962, freight in 1964
CRANLEY GARDENS	12 / 3A	1902 (1897)	1954 (1957)	GNR	Closed when Alexandra Palace to Finsbury park service withdrawn 1954. Had been intended
					for electrification and transfer to LT Northern Line, but works abandoned post-WW2. Also
					closed to passengers 1951-1952. Goods yard in operation 1897-1957.
CRAYFORD	36 / 4B	1866	N/A	SER	Goods yard closed 1965
Crayford Creek Junction	36 / 3B	1895	N/A	SER	
Crayford Spur "A" Junction	36 / 3B	1942	N/A	SER	
Crayford Spur "B" Junction	36 / 4B	1942	N/A	SER	
CREEKMOUTH	25 / 4B	2017	N/A	DLR	Gallions Reach to Dagenham Dock proposed to open c.2017
Cremorne Bridge	31 / 3B	1863	N/A	WLER	
Crescent Wood Tunnel	43 / 1A	1865	1954	LCDR	Closed 1917-1919. Nunhead to Crystal Palace (High Level) closed 1954 (Passengers and Goods)
CREWS HILL	4 / 1A	1910	N/A	GNR	

NAME: (Previous names indented below)	PAGE / GRID:	YEAR OPENED:	YEAR CLOSED:	OPENED BY:	NOTES:
CRICKLEWOOD	21 / 1A	1870	N/A	MID	
Childs Hill & Cricklewood					
Cricklewood Curve Junction	21 / 1A	1870	N/A	MID	
CRICKLEWOOD ENGINE SHEDS	20 / 1B	1882	1964	MID	1st shed 1882, 2nd added 1893
CRICKLEWOOD RECESS SIDINGS	20 / 1B	?	N/A	?	Disused
Cricklewood South Junction	21 / 2A	?	N/A	MID	
Watling Street Junction					
CROFTON PARK	33 / 4B	1892	N/A	LCDR	
Crofton Road Junction	32 / 3B	?	N/A	LCDR & LBSCR	
Cromwell Curve North Junction	31 / 2A & 50	1871	1957	MDR	Cromwell Curve lifted 1957. Area rafted over and Traingle Sidings built on site.
Cromwell Curve South Junction	31 / 2B & 50	1871	1957	MDR	Cromwell Curve lifted 1957. Area rafted over and Traingle Sidings built on site.
Cromwell Road Junction	50	1871	N/A	MDR	
CROSSHARBOUR	33 / 1B	1987	N/A	DLR	On site of former Millwall Docks Station. '& London Arena' suffix 1994-2007
Crossharbour & London Arena					
Crossharbour					
Cross Street Tunnel	35 / 1A	1849	N/A	SER	
CROUCH END	12 / 4A	1867	1954	GNR	Nominally opened by Edgware, Highgate & London Railway, but operated by GNR from opening
					Closed when Alexandra Palace to Finsbury park service withdrawn 1954. Had been intended
					for electrification and transfer to LT Northern Line, but works abandoned post-WW2
CROUCH HILL	12 / 4A	1868	N/A	T&HJ	
CROWLANDS	16 / 4A	N/A	N/A	GER	Platform foundations built west of Jutsums Lane 1900, but station never completed
CROXLEY	1 / 4B	1925	N/A	MET & LNER	'Green' suffix dropped 1949. Goods yard closed 1966
Croxley Green					
CROXLEY GREEN	2 / 4A	1912	1996	LNWR	Croxley Green Branch service suspended 1996
CROXLEY TIP	1 / 4B	1902	1970	MET	London Transport refuse tip. Formerly Gravel Pit
CROYDON 'A' POWER STATION	47 / 1B	1896	1973	PRIV	
CROYDON 'B' POWER STATION	47 / 1A	1950	1981	PRIV	
CRYSTAL PALACE	43 / 2A	1854	N/A	LBCSR	'Low Level' 1923-1955. East London Line projected to serve from 2010
Crystal Palace Low Level					Goods yard closed 1965
Crystal Palace					
CRYSTAL PALACE HIGH LEVEL	43 / 2A	1865	1954	LCDR	'& Upper Norwood' added 1898. Closed 1917-1919 and 1944-1946.
Crystal Palace & Upper Norwood					Nunhead to Crystal Palace (High Level) closed 1954 (Passengers and Goods)
Crystal Palace High Level & Upper Norwood					
Crystal Palace High Level					
Crytsal Palace Tunnel	43 / 2A	1856	N/A	LBSCR	
Crystal Palace Tunnel Junction	43 / 2A	1856	N/A	LBSCR	
CUSTOM HOUSE	24 / 4A	1855	N/A	ECR	DLR Platforms opened 1994. NR platforms closed 2006, Proposed to re-open 2017
Custom House Victoria Dock					(Crossrail 1)
Custom House					
CUTTY SARK	33 / 2B	1999	N/A	DLR	
CYPRUS	24 / 4B	1994	N/A	DLR	

D

NAME: (Previous names indented below)	PAGE / GRID:	YEAR OPENED:	YEAR CLOSED:	OPENED BY:	NOTES:
DAGENHAM DOCK	26 / 3A	1908	N/A	LTSR	Gallions Reach to Dagenham Dock DLR extension proposed to open c.2017
DAGENHAM DOCK	26 / 4A	1887	?	PRIV	
DAGENHAM EAST (LTSR)	26 / 2A	1885	1962	LTSR	Served by District Railway trains 1902-1905. British Rail services withdrawn 1962 and 'Fast'
Dagenham					platforms abandoned
DAGENHAM EAST (MDR)	26 / 2A	1902	N/A	MDR	1902 date denotes first time District railway served original LTSR platforms at Dagenham.
Dagenham					District trains withdrawn East Ham to Upminster 1905, reinstated Barking to Upminster 1932.
					Current District platforms constructed 1932 during LMS quadrupling of route.
					Renamed 1949, ownership of 'Slow' platforms transferred to LT 1970.
					Goods yard closed 1968
DAGENHAM HEATHWAY	26 / 2A	1932	N/A	LMS	Barking to Upminster quadrupled by the LMS in 1932 and 4 new stations opened.
Heathway					Served by District Line from opening. Renamed 1949, ownership transferred to LT in 1970
DAGENHAM VALE	25 / 3B	2017	N/A	DLR	Gallions Reach to Dagenham Dock proposed to open c.2017
DALSTON	23 / 2A & 18 / 4B	2010	N/A	NR (LOROL)	Projected northern terminus of East London Line Extension Phase 1. On site of former
					Dalston Junction Station
Dalston Eastern Junction	23 / 2A & 18 / 3B	1865	1965	NLR	Dalston Eastern Curve closed to passengers 1944, freight 1965
DALSTON JUNCTION	23 / 2A & 18 / 4B	1865	1986	NLR	Platforms 5 & 6 closed 1944, 3 & 4 closed 1976. To re-open 2010 as 'Dalston'
Dalston Junction	23 / 2A & 18 / 4B	1865	1965	NLR	Dalston Eastern Curve closed to passengers 1944, freight 1965
DALSTON KINGSLAND	23 / 2A & 18 / 3A	1983	N/A	BR	On site of former Kingsland Station
Dalston Western Junction	23 / 2A & 18 / 3A	1865	1986	NLR	Expected to be reinstated 2011 when East London Line extended beyond Dalston
Dartford Junction	36 / 4B	1886	N/A	SER	
DAY & SONS GRAVEL (PURLEY)	47 / 4B	?	N/A	PRIV	
DBS STONE TERMINAL (TOLWORTH)	45 / 1A	1981	N/A	BR	Former Goods yard (open 1939-1965), then Coal Terminal (open 1965-1989)
DEBDEN (GER)	6 / 3A	1865	1970	GER	Majority of Passenger services transferred to LT and station became 'Debden' in 1949
Chigwell Lane					First Trains in the morning remained British Rail services until 1970
Chigwell Road					
DEBDEN (LT)	6 / 3A	1949	N/A	LT (CEN)	First served by Central Line Trains 1949. Goods yard closed 1966
DENHAM	7 / 4A	1906	N/A	GCR & GWR	Projected terminus of Central Line extension from West Ruislip, but works cancelled post-WW2
Denham For Harefield					
Denham East Junction	17 / 1B	1907	1916	GCR & GWR	
Denham South Junction	17 / 1A	1907	1916	GCR & GWR	

NAME: (Previous names indented below)	PAGE / GRID:	YEAR OPENED:	YEAR CLOSED:	OPENED BY:	NOTES:
Denham West Junction	17 / 1A	1907	1962	GCR & GWR	
DENMARK HILL	32 / 3B	1865	N/A	LCDR	East London Line extension phase 2 (LOROL) projected to serve from 2011
DEPTFORD	33 / 2B	1836	N/A	LGR	Terminus 1836-1838, closed 1915-1926
DEPTFORD BRIDGE	33 / 3B	1999	N/A	DLR	
Deptford Road Junction	33 / 2A & 52	1871	1964	ELR	Projected to re-open as part of East London Line Extension Phase 2 in 2011
DEPTFORD WHARF	33 / 1B & 52	1849	1964	LBSCR	
DEVONSHIRE STREET (MILE END)	23 / 3A	1839	1843	ECR	London Terminus of ECR 1839-1840. Replaced by Mile End to West
DEVONS ROAD	23 / 4B & 57	1987	N/A	DLR	
DEVONS ROAD DEPOT	23 / 4B & 57	1882	1964	NLR	Locomotive Depot
District Junction (South Acton)	40 / 1A	1899	1932	MDR	'Clipped' out of use since 1914, not physically removed until 1932
Dockyard Tunnel	34 / 1B	1849	N/A	SER	
DOLLIS HILL	20 / 2B	1909	N/A	MET	Last served Metropolitan Line 1940. Served by Bakerloo Line 1939-1979, Jubilee thereafter
Dollis Hill & Gladstone Park					
Dollis Hill					
DOWN SIDINGS (PLUMSTEAD)	35 / 1A	?	N/A	SER	
DOWN SIDINGS (WIMBLEDON)	41 / 2A	?	N/A	LSWR	
DOWN STREET	32 / 1A	1907	1932	GNP&BR	
Down Street, Mayfair					
DOWN YARD (SOUTHALL)	28 / 1B	1859	N/A	GWR	
DRAYTON GREEN	19 / 4A	1905	N/A	GWR	
Drayton Green Ealing Halt					
Drayton Green Junction	19 / 4A	1903	N/A	GWR	
Drayton Green Tunnel	19 / 4A	1974	N/A	BR	Covered Way over line in connection with housing development
DRAYTON PARK	22 / 2B	1904	N/A	GN&CR	Opened by GN&CR, bought by Metropolitan Railway 1913, transferred to Northern Line 1939, closed by London Underground 1975, re-opened by British Rail 1976
DRAYTON PARK DEPOT	22 / 2B	1904	1975	GN&CR	
DUDDING HILL FOR WILLESDEN & NEASDEN	20 / 2B	1875	1902	MID	Closed 1888-1893
Dudding Hill					
Dudding Hill for Church End Willesden					
Willesden & Dudden Hill					
Dudding Hill Junction	20 / 1B	1870	N/A	MID	
DUNDONALD ROAD	41 / 2A	2000	N/A	CTL	
DURNSFORD ROAD POWER STATION	41 / 1A	1915	1965	LSWR	LSWR power station
DURNSFORD ROAD SIDINGS	41 / 1A	1914	N/A	LSWR	Part of Wimbledon Traincare Depot (SWT). Current layout from 1976

E

NAME:	PAGE / GRID:	YEAR OPENED:	YEAR CLOSED:	OPENED BY:	NOTES:
EAGLE LANE GOODS	14 / 3A	1899	1966	GER	
EALING BROADWAY	19 / 4B	1838	N/A	GWR	Served by District Railway since 1879. Served by Central London Railway since 1920.
Ealing					
EALING COMMON	30 / 1A	1879	N/A	MDR	'& West Acton' 1886-1910. Served by Piccadilly Line since 1932
Ealing Common & West Acton					
Ealing Common					
EALING COMMON DEPOT	30 / 1A	1905	N/A	MDR	District Line Depot. Used also for Piccadilly Line 1932-1964.
EARDLEY CARRIAGE SIDINGS	42 / 2A	?	1960	LBSCR	
EARL'S COURT (1st)	31 / 2A & 50	1871	1878	MDR	Resited West 1878
EARL'S COURT (2nd)	31 / 2A & 50	1878	N/A	MDR	GNP&BR platforms opened 1906. Closed 1997-1998 (Piccadilly Line only)
EARLSFIELD	41 / 1B	1884	N/A	LSWR	Renamed 1902
Earlsfield & Summerstown					
Earlsfield					
EAST ACTON	20 / 4B	1920	N/A	CLR	Viaduct Junction to North Acton built by GWR 1917
EAST BRIXTON	32 / 3B	1866	1976	LBSCR	Renamed 'Loughborough Park & Brixton' 1870, then 'East Brixton' 1894
Loughborough Park & Brixton					
Loughborough Park					
EASTCOTE	8 / 4B	1906	N/A	MET	Served by District Line Trains 1910-1933, Piccadilly Line thereafter. Goods yard closed 1964
EAST CROYDON	47 / 1B	1841	N/A	L&BR	East Croydon and New Croydon nominally 2 separate stations, combined 1909
New Croydon					Goods yard closed 1973. Croydon Tramlink opened 2000
Croydon East					
Croydon					
EAST DULWICH	32 / 4B	1868	N/A	LBSCR	Renamed 1888
Champion Hill					
Eastern Junction (Stratford)	53	1846	1973	ECR	Eastern Curve at Stratford dismantled 1973
EAST FINCHLEY (GNR)	11 / 3B	1867	1941	GNR	Nominally opened by Edgware, Highgate & London Railway, but operated by GNR from opening
East End Finchley					Became terminus of LNER service from Finsbury Park 1939, Withdrawn 1941
EAST FINCHLEY (LT)	11 / 3B	1939	N/A	LT (NOR)	Terminus of LT Northern Line extension from Archway 1939-1940. Goods yard closed 1962
East Finchley Junction	11 / 3B	1939	N/A	LT (NOR) & LNER	Junction of Northern Line with former LNER route to Finsbury Park (now depot access)
EAST GOODS YARD (FINSBURY PARK)	15 / 3B	1875	1960	GNR	
EAST HAM (LTSR)	24 / 2B	1858	1962	LTSR	Main line services non-stopped since 1962, and 'Fast' platforms abandoned
EAST HAM (MDR)	24 / 2B	1902	N/A	MDR	First served by District Railway 1902, line quadrupled 1908, District Trains using Slow Lines
					Served by Metropolitan Line since 1936 ('Hammersmith & City Line' since 1990)
					Bay Platform for Kentish Town via T&FG and T&H abandoned 1958. Goods yard closed 1962
EAST HAM DEPOT	24 / 2B	1961	N/A	BR	On Site of former District Line Little Ilford Depot
East Ham Loop North Junction	24 / 2B	1894	1958	T&FG	East Ham Loop dismantled when services diverted to Barking

NAME: (Previous names indented below)	PAGE / GRID:	YEAR OPENED:	YEAR CLOSED:	OPENED BY:	NOTES:
East Ham Loop South Junction	24 / 2B	1894	1958	T&FG	East Ham Loop dismantled when services diverted to Barking
EAST INDIA	24 / 4A & 57	1994	N/A	DLR	
EAST INDIA DOCKS GOODS	24 / 4A & 57	1859	1961	GER	
EAST LONDON WASTE TERMINAL	26 / 3A	?	N/A	PRIV	Shanks & McEwan
EAST PUTNEY (MDR)	31 / 4A	1889	N/A	LSWR	Putney Bridge to Wimbldeon built by LSWR but operated by District Railway from opening
EAST PUTNEY (LSWR)	31 / 4A	1889	1941	LSWR	Last regular passenger service withdrawn 1941, although Main Line services called on occasions until 1969. Point Pleasant Jcn to Wimbledon still used for empty stock working and diversions.
East Putney Junction	31 / 4A	1889	N/A	LSWR	
East Putney Tunnel	31 / 4A	1889	N/A	LSWR	
EAST SIDINGS (ACTON TOWN)	30 / 1A & 40 / 1A	1932	N/A	UERL (DIS & PIC)	Current layout since 1932
EAST SIDINGS (SOUTHALL)	28 / 1B	1884	N/A	GWR	Originally Engine Shed, expanded 1954, later became DMU Shed until 1986. Used by Railway Preservation societies since 1988
EAST SMITHFIELD / LONDON DOCKS GOODS	23 / 4A & 7 / 3A	1864	1966	GER	
EAST YARD (TEMPLE MILLS)	23 / 1B	1959	N/A	BR	
EDEN PARK	43 / 4B	1882	N/A	SER	
EDGWARE (GNR)	10 / 2A	1867	1939 (1964)	GNR	Nominally opened by Edgware, Highgate & London Railway, but operated by GNR from opening Closed to passengers 1939 and freight 1964
EDGWARE (UERL)	10 / 2A	1924	N/A	UERL (CCE&HR)	Built for through running to Bushey Heath, but extension abandoned 1940
EDGWARE ROAD (MET)	21 / 4B	1863	N/A	MET	Rebuilt 1926
EDGWARE ROAD (BS&WR)	21 / 4B	1907	N/A	BS&WR	
EDGWARE SIDINGS	10 / 2A	1924	N/A	UERL (CCE&HR)	Northern Line stabling sidings. Southern fan on site of intended curve to GNR branch
EDMONTON GREEN	13 / 1A	1872	N/A	GER	
Lower Edmonton					
Lower Edmonton (High Level)					
Edmonton (High Level)					
Edward Street Junction	52	?	N/A	SER	
ELEPHANT & CASTLE	32 / 1B	1862	N/A	LCDR	C&SLR Station opened 1890 (closed 1923-1924), BS&WR Station opened 1906 (closed 1996-1997)
ELMERS END	43 / 3A	1864	N/A	SER	Goods yard closed 1964. Croydon Tramlink opened 2000
Elmers End Junction	43 / 3A	1882	1997	SER	Resited south 1956 (platform extension). Elmers End to Addiscombe closed 1997
ELM PARK	26 / 2B	1935	N/A	LMS	Opened on 1932 'Slow' lines built by the LMS. Served by District Line from opening
ELMSTEAD WOODS	44 / 2B	1904	N/A	SECR	Renamed 1908
Elmstead					
ELSTREE SOUTH	9 / 1B	N/A	N/A	LT (NOR)	On Northern Line extension to Bushey Heath from Edgware. Construction abandoned 1940
ELTHAM	34 / 3B	1985	N/A	BR	Replaced Eltham Well Hall and Eltham Park Stations
ELTHAM PARK	34 / 3B	1908	1985	SECR	Renamed 1927. Replaced by Eltham Station 1985
Shooters Hill & Eltham Park					
ELTHAM WELL HALL	34 / 3B	1895	1985	SER	Renamed 1927. Goods yard expanded 1915, closed 1968. Replaced by Eltham Station 1985
Well Hall & North Eltham					
Well Hall					
ELVERSON ROAD	33 / 3B	1999	N/A	DLR	
EMBANKMENT	32 / 1A & 28 / 2A	1870	N/A	MDR	Baker Street & Waterloo platforms added 1906. CCE&HR Loop platform added 1914, southbound platform on Kennington extension opened 1926. Renamed 'Charing Cross Embankment' 1974, shortened to 'Embankment' 1976.
Charing Cross Embankment					
Charing Cross					
EMERSON PARK	16 / 2A	1909	N/A	GER	
Emerson Park & Great Nelmes					
Engine Shed Junction	22 / 2A & 57	1900	1981	MID	Eliminated when curve used by Barking Trains abandoned
ENFIELD	4 / 3B	1871	1910	GNR	Original terminus of GNR Enfield Branch from Alexandra Palace
ENFIELD CHASE	4 / 3B	1910	N/A	GNR	
ENFIELD GOODS	4 / 3B	1910	1974	BR	Goods station on site of original GNR Enfield terminus. Carriage Sidings in use until 1979
ENFIELD LOCK	5 / 2B	1855	N/A	GER	
Ordnance Factory					
ENFIELD TOWN	4 / 3B	1849	N/A	GER	Goods yard closed 1959
Enfield					
EPPING (GER)	6 / 2A	1865	1970	GER	Majority of passenger services transferred to LT in 1949. First Trains in the morning remained British Rail services until 1970
EPPING (LT)	6 / 2A	1949	N/A	LT (CEN)	First served by Central Line Trains 1949. Goods yard closed 1966
EPSOM	45 / 3B	1859	N/A	LSWR	Originally LSWR only, platforms opened on LBSCR line 1929. Goods yard closed 1928
EPSOM DOWNS (1st)	46 / 4A	1865	1989	LBSCR	Resited East and land sold for housing development
EPSOM DOWNS (2nd)	46 / 4A	1989	N/A	BR	Replaced original station to West
EPSOM TOWN	45 / 3B	1847	1929 (1965)	LBSCR	Terminus 1847-1859. Became 'Epsom Town' 1923. Closed when platforms opened at Epsom on former LBSCR line 1929. Goods yard remained open until 1965
Epsom					
ERITH	36 / 2B	1849	N/A	SER	
ERITH WHARF	36 / 2B	?	?	SER	
ESSEX ROAD	22 / 2B	1904	N/A	GN&CR	Opened by GN&CR, bought by Metropolitan Railway 1913, transferred to Northern Line 1939, closed by London Underground 1975, re-opened by British Rail 1976. 'Canonbury' prefix 1922-1948
Canonbury & Essex Road					
Essex Road					
EUROPEAN METAL RECYCLING (BRENTFORD)	29 / 2B	?	N/A	PRIV	Formerly Perry Metals
EUSTON	22 / 3A	1837	N/A	L&B	C&SLR platforms opened 1907 (closed 1922-1924), CCE&HR platforms 1907, Victoria Line platforms 1968
EUSTON SQUARE	22 / 3A	1863	N/A	MET	Renamed 1909
Gower Street					
EWELL EAST	45 / 3B	1847	N/A	LBSCR	Renamed 1923. Goods yard closed 1960
Ewell for Worcester Park					

NAME: (Previous names indented below)	PAGE / GRID:	YEAR OPENED:	YEAR CLOSED:	OPENED BY:	NOTES:
EWELL WEST	45 / 2B	1859	N/A	LSWR	Goods yard closed 1961
Ewell					
EWER STREET DEPOT	55	1899	1962	SECR	Also known as Southwark Depot. Became EMU stabling sidings after 1962
EXPRESS DAIRY (MORDEN)	41 / 4A	1954	1978	PRIV	

F

NAME: (Previous names indented below)	PAGE / GRID:	YEAR OPENED:	YEAR CLOSED:	OPENED BY:	NOTES:
Factory Junctions	32 / 3A & 51	1862	N/A	LCDR	
FAIRFIELD YARD	47 / 1B	1890	1933	LBSCR	Permanent Way yard on truncated Croydon Central Branch
FAIRLOP (GER)	15 / 3A	1903	1947	GER	Fairlop Loop closed 1947 to allow electrification and transfer to LT Central Line. Freight traffic remained until 1965
FAIRLOP (LT)	15 / 3A	1948	N/A	LT (CEN)	First served by LT Central Line Trains 1948. Goods yard closed 1965
Falcon Junction	31 / 4B	1863	N/A	LBSCR & WLER	
FALCON LANE GOODS	31 / 3B	1869	1968	LNWR	
FALCONWOOD	35 / 3A	1936	N/A	SR	
FARRINGDON	22 / 4B & 55	1865	N/A	MET	City Widened Lines platforms added 1868 (now Thameslink). 'Farringdon Street' became 'Farringdon & High Holborn' 1922, suffix dropped 1936
Farringdon & High Holborn					Platforms for 'Crossrail 1' proposed to open 2017
Farringdon Street					
FARRINGDON GOODS	22 / 4B & 55	1909	1952	MID	
Farringdon Junction	55	1866	2009	BR	Junction severed 1969-1988 and again 2009
FARRINGDON STREET	22 / 4B & 55	1863	1865	MET	Original City terminus of Metropolitan Railway, abandoned when line extended to Moorgate
FARRINGDON STREET GOODS	22 / 4B & 55	1865	196?	GNR	On site of former passenger terminus
FELTHAM	38 / 1A	1848	N/A	LSWR	
Feltham Junction	28 / 4B	1850	N/A	LSWR	
FELTHAM LOCO SHED	28 / 4B & 61	1922	1967	LSWR	
FELTHAM MARSHALLING YARD	28 / 4B & 61	1922	1969	LSWR	
FENCHURCH STREET	22 / 4B & 7 / 3A	1841	N/A	LBR	
FERME PARK DOWN SIDINGS	12 / 4B	1888	N/A	GNR	Former Ferme Park Yard, opened 1888
FIELDWAY	48 / 2B	2000	N/A	CTL	
FINCHLEY (CHURCH END)	11 / 3A	1867	1939	GNR	Nominally opened by Edgware, Highgate & London Railway, but operated by GNR from opening
Finchley					Opened as 'Finchley & Hendon', '& Hendon' suffix dropped 1872, 'Church End' added 1896
Finchley & Hendon					Closed in 1939 to enable electrification and transfer to LT Northern Line, re-opened as 'Central'
FINCHLEY CENTRAL	11 / 3A	1940	N/A	LT (NOR)	On site of former GNR 'Church End' station. Goods / Coal yard closed 1962
Finchley Central Junction	11 / 3A	1872	N/A	GNR	Divergence of High Barnet Branch from original Edgware Line (now Mill Hill East Branch)
FINCHLEY ROAD (MID)	21 / 2B	1868	1927	MID	
Finchley Road & St John's Wood					
FINCHLEY ROAD (MET)	21 / 2B	1879	N/A	MET	'South Hampstead' suffix 1885-1914. Served by Bakerloo Line 1939-1979, Jubilee Line thereafter
Finchley Road (South Hampstead)					Goods yard opened 1894, closed 1941
Finchley Road					
FINCHLEY ROAD & FROGNAL	21 / 2B	1860	N/A	HJR	Renamed 1880. Goods yard open 1870-1967. Closed 1995-1996
Finchley Road St John's Wood					
FINSBURY PARK	22 / 1B & 15 / 3B	1861	N/A	GNR	Opened as 'Seven Sisters Road', renamed 'Finsbury Park' 1869
Seven Sisters Road					Great Northern & City Line opened 1904 (Closed 1964), Piccadilly Line opened 1906, Victoria Line opened 1968. Southbound Victoria & Piccadilly Lines use former GN&C tunnel
FINSBURY PARK DIESEL DEPOT	22 / 1A & 15 / 3B	1960	1981	BR	On site of former Clarence Yard Goods
FINSBURY PARK GOODS & COAL	22 / 1B & 15 / 2B	1865	1968	GNR	
Finsbury Park Junction	22 / 1B & 15 / 3B	1976	N/A	BR	Junction of Great Northern main Line with Great Northern & City route ex-Moorgate
FIRESTONE TYRES (BRENTFORD)	29 / 2B	1928	1964	PRIV	
FORD FREIGHTLINER DEPOT (DAGENHAM)	26 / 3A	?	N/A	PRIV	
FORD MOTOR WORKS (DAGENHAM)	26 / 3A	1932	N/A	PRIV	
FOREIGN CATTLE MARKET	33 / 2B	1899	1915	PRIV	Accessed via tramway along Grove Street
FOREST GATE	24 / 2A	1840	N/A	ECR	
Forest Gate Junction	24 / 2B	1854	N/A	ECR	
FOREST HILL	43 / 1A	1839	N/A	LCR	Named 'Dartmouth Arms' until 1845. East London Line projected to serve from 2010
Forest Hill for Lordship Lane					
Dartmouth Arms					
FORTY HILL	5 / 2A	1891	1919	GER	Closed 1909-1915. Site now occupied by Turkey Street Station
Fulham Bridge	31 / 3A	1889	N/A	LSWR	Built by London & Southwestern Railway but only ever used by District Railway trains
FULHAM BROADWAY	31 / 2A & 50	1880	N/A	MDR	Renamed 1952
Walham Green					
FULWELL	39 / 2A	1864	N/A	LSWR	
Fulwell for Hampton Hill					
Fulwell & Hampton Hill					
Fulwell & New Hampton					
Fulwell					
Fulwell Junction	39 / 2A	1894	N/A	LSWR	
FULWELL LOCO DEPOT	39 / 2A	1897	1916	LSWR	Replaced by Strawberry Hill EMU Depot

G

NAME: (Previous names indented below)	PAGE / GRID:	YEAR OPENED:	YEAR CLOSED:	OPENED BY:	NOTES:
GALLIONS	25 / 4A	1880	1940	PLA	Passenger services withdrawn from Gallions Branch 1940
GALLIONS REACH	25 / 4A	1994	N/A	DLR	
GANTS HILL	14 / 4B	1947	N/A	LT (CEN)	
GARSTON	2 / 2B	1966	N/A	BR	
Gas Factory Junction	23 / 4B & 57	1850	N/A	LTSR & NLR	Access to Bow Road Goods elimiated 1964, Curve to NLR eliminated 1968
George IV Tunnel	34 / 1B	1849	N/A	SER	
GEORGE LANE (WOODFORD)	14 / 3A	1856	1970	ECR	Majority of passenger services transferred to LT in 1947 (station became South Woodford)
					First Trains in the morning remained British Rail services until 1970
GEORGE STREET	47 / 1B	2000	N/A	CTL	
GIDEA PARK	16 / 4B	1910	N/A	GER	Renamed 'Gidea Park & Squirrels Heath' 1913, '& Squirrels Heath' dropped 1969
Gidea Park & Squirrels Heath					
Squirrels Heath & Gidea Park					
Gifford Street Portals	54	2007	N/A	L&CR	
GIPSY HILL	42 / 2B	1856	N/A	LBSCR	Opened by West End of London & Crystal Palace Railway, but operated by LBSCR from outset
Gipsy Hill for Upper Norwood					Goods yard closed 1969
GLOBE ROAD	23 / 3A	1884	1916	GER	
GLOUCESTER ROAD	31 / 2B & 50	1868	N/A	MET	District Railway platforms opened 1869. GNP&BR platforms opened 1906 as Gloucester Road.
Brompton (Gloucester Road)					Entire station renamed Gloucester Road 1907. Piccadilly Line platforms closed 1987-1989
Gloucester Road Junction	42 / 4B	1983	N/A	BR	
GOLDERS GREEN	11 / 4A	1907	N/A	CCE&HR	Northern terminus of Charing Cross, Euston and Hampstead Railway when opened
GOLDERS GREEN DEPOT	11 / 4A	1907	N/A	CCE&HR	Northern Line depot
GOLDHAWK ROAD	30 / 1B & 49	1914	N/A	MET & GWR	Replaced Shepherd's Bush Station to North
GOODGE STREET	22 / 4A	1907	N/A	CCE&HR	Renamed 1908
Tottenham Court Road					
GOODMANS YARD GOODS	23 / 4A & 7 / 3A	1861	1951	LBR	
GOODMAYES	25 / 1B	1901	N/A	GER	
GOODMAYES YARD	25 / 1B	1899	1962	GER	
GORDON HILL	4 / 3B	1910	N/A	GNR	
GOSPEL OAK	21 / 1B & 57	1860	N/A	HJR	Renamed 1867. Bay platform for Barking trains since 1981
Kentish Town					
Gospel Oak Junction	21 / 1B & 57	1914	N/A	T&HJ	Junction established 1914, eliminated 1920. Re-established 1940
GRAHAME-WHITE AVIATION CO. WORKS	10 / 3A	1918	1921	PRIV	Branch lifted 1930
GRAHAM ROAD GOODS	23 / 2A	1894	1965	GER	
GRANGE HILL (GER)	15 / 2A	1903	1947	GER	Fairlop Loop closed 1947 to allow electrification and transfer to LT Central Line. Freight
Grange Hill for Chigwell Row					traffic remained until 1965
GRANGE HILL (LT)	15 / 2A	1948	N/A	LT (CEN)	First served by LT Central Line Trains 1948. Goods yard closed 1965
Grange Hill Tunnel	15 / 2A	1903	N/A	GER	
GRANGE PARK	4 / 4B	1910	N/A	GNR	
GRAVEL HILL	48 / 2B	2000	N/A	CTL	
GRAYS	16 / 3B	1854	N/A	LTSR	
GREAT PORTLAND STREET	22 / 3A	1863	N/A	MET	Opened as 'Portland Road', renamed 'Great Portland Street' 1917, '& Regent's Park' suffix
Great Portland Street & Regent's Park					added 1923, dropped 1933
Great Portland Street					
Portland Road					
GREENFORD (GWR)	19 / 2A	1904	1963	GWR	Station on GWR Birmingham Line. Bay Platform between Central Line Platforms still open
GREENFORD (LT)	19 / 2A	1947	N/A	LT (CEN) & BR	Terminus of Central Line extension from North Acton 1947-48
Greenford East Junction	19 / 3A	1903	N/A	GWR	
GREENFORD GOODS	19 / 2A	1932	1980	GWR	
GREENFORD S & T	19 / 2A	?	N/A	BR	
Greenford South Junction	19 / 2A	1904	N/A	GWR	
Greenford West Junction	19 / 3A	1904	N/A	GWR	
GREEN PARK	32 / 1A	1906	N/A	GNP&BR	Renamed 1933. Victoria Line platforms opened 1969, Jubilee Line 1979
Dover Street					
GREENWICH	33 / 2B	1838	N/A	LGR	Terminus 1838-1878. DLR platforms opened 1999
GREENWICH PARK	33 / 2B	1888	1917	LCDR	Renamed 1900. Passenger service withdrawn Nunhead to Greenwich Park 1917
Greenwich					
Grosvenor Bridge	32 / 2A & 51	1860	N/A	LBSCR	
GROSVENOR DEPOT	32 / 2A & 51	1862	N/A	LCDR	
GROSVENOR ROAD	32 / 2A & 51	1867	1911	LCDR	LBSCR Platforms opened 1870, closed 1907
GROVE PARK	44 / 1A	1871	N/A	SER	
GROVE PARK CARRIAGE SERVICE SHED	44 / 1A	?	N/A	SER	
GROVE PARK DOWN (BRAMDEAN) SIDINGS	44 / 1A	1900	N/A	SECR	
Grove Park Junction	44 / 1A	1878	N/A	SER	
GROVE PARK UP (ST MILDRED'S) SIDINGS	44 / 1A	1900	N/A	SECR	
GUINNESS (PARK ROYAL)	20 / 3A	1936	2005	PRIV	Former brewery
GUNNERSBURY	30 / 2A & 40 / 2A	1869	N/A	LSWR	Renamed 1871. First served District & Metropolitan Railways 1877. Last served Metropolitan
Brentford Road					Railway 1906. Originally had 5 platforms, 3 of which were abandoned in 1930. Remodelled 1932.
Gunnersbury Junction	30 / 2A & 40 / 2A	1869	N/A	LSWR	Renamed 1932 when 'West' junction eliminated
Gunnersbury East Junction					
Gunnersbury West Junction	30 / 2A	1869	1932	LSWR	Chiswick Curve dismantled 1932

H

NAME: (Previous names indented below)	PAGE / GRID:	YEAR OPENED:	YEAR CLOSED:	OPENED BY:	NOTES:
HACKBRIDGE	47 / 1A	1868	N/A	LBSCR	
HACKNEY (1st)	23 / 2A	1850	1870	NLR	Resited to West 1870
HACKNEY (2nd)	23 / 2A	1870	1944	NLR	Replaced original station to East. Passenger service Dalston Junction to Poplar withdrawn 1944
HACKNEY CENTRAL	23 / 2A	1980	N/A	BR	On site of former NLR Hackney Station (2nd)
HACKNEY COAL	23 / 2A	?	?	NLR	
HACKNEY DOWNS	23 / 2A	1872	N/A	GER	
Hackney Downs Junction					
Hackney Downs Junctions	23 / 2A	1872	N/A	GER	
Hackney Downs Tunnel	23 / 2A	1872	N/A	GER	
HACKNEY WICK	23 / 2B	1980	N/A	BR	
HACKNEY WICK GOODS	23 / 2B	1877	1967	GNR	
HADLEY WOOD	3 / 3B	1885	N/A	GNR	
Hadley Wood North Tunnel	3 / 2B	1850	N/A	GNR	
Hadley Wood South Tunnel	3 / 3B	1850	N/A	GNR	
HAGGERSTON (NLR)	23 / 3A	1867	1940	NLR	To re-open 2010 (East London Line Extension)
HAGGERSTON (LOROL)	23 / 3A	2010	N/A	NR (LOROL)	To open 2010 as part of East London Line Extension Phase 1
HAINAULT (GER)	15 / 2A	1903	1947	GER	Closed 1908-1930. Fairlop Loop closed 1947 to allow electrification & transfer to LT Central Line
					Freight traffic remained until 1965.
HAINAULT (LT)	15 / 2A	1948	N/A	LT (CEN)	First served by LT Central Line trains 1948
HAINAULT DEPOT	15 / 2A	1943	N/A	LT (CEN)	Opened 1943-1945 for temporary wartime use, Central Line depot since 1948
Hall Farm North Junction	13 / 4A	1872	1967	GER	Junction between original Walthamstow branch and 1872 line to Hackney Downs
Hall Farm South Junction	13 / 4A	1885	1960	GER	Junction between Chingford Branch and curve to Lea Valley Line
HAMMERSMITH (District & Piccadilly Lines)	30 / 2B & 56	1874	N/A	MDR	GNP&BR terminus 1906-1932
HAMMERSMITH (Hammersmith & City Line)	30 / 2B & 56	1864	N/A	MET & GWR	Relocated south 1868. Goods yard closed 1960
HAMMERSMITH & CHISWICK	30 / 2B	1858 (1857)	1917 (1965)	N&SWJR	Opened to freight traffic 1857, passenger traffic 1858. '& Chiswick' suffix added 1880
Hammersmith					Passenger traffic withdrawn 1917, freight remaining until 1965
HAMMERSMITH DEPOT	30 / 1B	1864	N/A	MET	Hammersmith & City Line depot
HAMMERSMITH (GROVE ROAD)	30 / 2B & 56	1869	1916	LSWR	Served by Metropolitan Railway 1877-1906. Addison Road to Studland Road Jcn closed 1916.
HAMPSTEAD	21 / 1B	1907	N/A	CCE&HR	
Hampstead (Heath Street)					
HAMPSTEAD HEATH	21 / 1B	1860	N/A	HJR	Closed 1995-1996
HAMPSTEAD HEATH GOODS	21 / 1B	1860	1972	HJR	
Hampstead Heath Tunnel	21 / 2B	1860	N/A	HJR	
HAMPTON	38 / 2B	1864	N/A	LSWR	
HAMPTON COURT	39 / 3A	1849	N/A	LSWR	'Moulsey' also spelt 'Molesey' at times. Goods yard closed 1965
Hampton Court for Moulsey					
Hampton Court & East Moulsey					
Hampton Court					
Hampton Court Junction	39 / 4B	1849	N/A	LSWR	
HAMPTON WICK	39 / 3B	1863	N/A	LSWR	
HANGER LANE	19 / 3B	1947	N/A	LT (CEN)	
Hanger Lane Junction	20 / 4A	1903	N/A	MDR	Divergence of District Railway South Harrow Branch from line to Ealing Broadway
HANSON AGGREGATES (DAGENHAM DOCK)	26 / 4A	?	N/A	PRIV	
HANSON AGGREGATES (WEST DRAYTON)	27 / 1B	?	N/A	PRIV	
HANWELL	19 / 4A	1838	N/A	GWR	Served by District Railway trains 1883-1885
Hanwell & Elthorne					
Hanwell					
Hanwell Junction	19 / 4A	1903	N/A	GWR	
HARLESDEN	20 / 3A	1912	N/A	LNWR	Served by Bakerloo Line trains since 1917
HARLESDEN (FOR WEST WILLESDEN & STONEBRIDGE PARK)	20 / 3B	1875	1902	MID	Closed 1888-1893
Stonebridge Park for West Willesden & Harlesden					
Harrow Road for Stonebridge Park & Harlesden					
Harrow Road for Stonebridge & Harlesden					
Harrow Road					
Harrow Road for Stonebridge Park & Harlesden					
Harrow Road for Stonebridge Park & West Willesden					
HARLESDEN GOODS	20 / 3A	?	?	MID	
Harlesden Junction	20 / 3B	1868	N/A	MID & LNWR	
HAROLD WOOD	16 / 1A	1868	N/A	GER	
HARRINGAY	12 / 4B	1885	N/A	GNR	
Harringay West					
Harringay					
HARRINGAY GREEN LANES	12 / 4B	1880	N/A	T&HJ	Opened as 'Green Lanes' 1880, Goods yard opened 1882, 'Harringay Park' prefix added 1884,
Harringay East					'Green Lanes' suffix dropped 1951, renamed 'Harringay Stadium' 1958, Goods yard closed 1964,
Harringay Stadium					renamed 'Harringay East' 1990, renamed 'Harringay Green Lanes' 1991
Harringay Park					
Harringay Park, Green Lanes					
Green Lanes					
Harringay Junction	12 / 4B	1868	N/A	GNR	Junction with curve to Tottenham & Hampstead Junction Railway. Lifted 1881-1916 & 1920-1940
Harringay Park Junction	12 / 4B	1868	N/A	T&HJ	Junction with curve to GNR Main Line. Curve lifted 1881-1916 & 1920-1940
HARRINGTON ROAD	43 / 3A	2000	N/A	CTL	

NAME: (Previous names indented below)	PAGE / GRID:	YEAR OPENED:	YEAR CLOSED:	OPENED BY:	NOTES:
HARROW LANE SIDINGS	57	1866	1981	NLR & LBR	
Harrow North Junction	9 / 4A	1904	N/A	MET	
HARROW-ON-THE-HILL	9 / 4A	1880	N/A	MET	Country terminus of Metropolitan Railway 1880-1885. Renamed 1894. Served by GCR since 1899
Harrow					Goods yard closed 1967
HARROW-ON-THE-HILL GOODS	9 / 4A	1880	1967	MET	
HARROW & WEALDSTONE	9 / 3A	1837	N/A	L&B	Renamed 1897. Terminus for London Underground Bakerloo Line Trains since 1984
Harrow					Goods yard closed 1967
Harrow Weald					
HARVEY'S SIDING	34 / 2A	?	?	PRIV	
HATCH END	8 / 2B	1844	N/A	LNWR	Served by London Underground Bakerloo Line Trains 1917-1982. 'Pinner & Hatch End' became
Hatch End (For Pinner)					'Hatch End (for Pinner)' 1920, suffix dropped 1956
Pinner & Hatch End					
Pinner					
HATCH END GOODS	8 / 3B	?	1966	LNWR	
HATTON CROSS	28 / 4A	1975	N/A	LT (PIC)	Terminus 1975-1977
HAVERSTOCK HILL	21 / 2B	1868	1916	MID	
Hawkswood Junctions	44 / 3B	1904	N/A	SECR	
HAYDON SQUARE GOODS	23 / 4A & 7 / 2A	1853	1962	LNWR	
Haydon Square Junction	23 / 4A & 7 / 3A	1853	1962	LNWR	
HAYDONS ROAD	41 / 2B	1868	N/A	LSWR & LBSCR	Closed 1917-1923
Haydens Lane					
HAYES	44 / 4A	1882	N/A	SER	Goods yard closed 1965
HAYES & HARLINGTON	28 / 1A	1864	N/A	GWR	Served by District Railway trains 1883-1885
Hayes					
HEADSTONE LANE	9 / 3A	1913	N/A	LNWR	Served by London Underground Bakerloo Line trains 1917-1982. Goods yard closed 1966
Heathrow Airport Junction	28 / 1A	1998	N/A	RT (HEX)	
HEATHROW EXPRESS DEPOT	20 / 4B & 60	1998	N/A	HEX	
HEATHROW JUNCTION	27 / 1B	1998	1998	HEX	Temporary terminus open January - May 1998 due to delayed opening of HEX tunnel (collapse)
HEATHROW TERMINALS 1, 2 & 3	27 / 3B	1977	N/A	LT (PIC)	Terminus 1977-1986. Heathrow Express platforms opened 1998
Heathrow Central					
HEATHROW TERMINAL 4	27 / 4B	1986	N/A	LUL (PIC)	Heathrow Express opened 1998. Closed 2005-2006 in connection with Terminal 5 Extension
HEATHROW TERMINAL 5	27 / 3A	2008	N/A	LUL & RT (HEX)	
Heathrow Tunnel Junction	27 / 1B	1998	N/A	RT (HEX)	
HENDON	10 / 4B	1868	N/A	MID	
HENDON CENTRAL	10 / 4B	1923	N/A	UERL (CCE&HR)	Terminus of extension from Golders Green 1923-1924
HENDON FACTORY PLATFORM	10 / 3B	1918	1919	PRIV	Possibly never used
HERNE HILL	32 / 4B	1862	N/A	LCDR	
Herne Hill North Junction	32 / 4B	1862	N/A	LCDR	
Herne Hill South Junction	32 / 4B	1869	N/A	LCDR	
HERNE HILL YARD	32 / 4B	1855	?	LCDR	
HERON QUAYS	33 / 1B	1987	N/A	DLR	Closed 2001-2002
HIGHAMS PARK	14 / 2A	1873	N/A	GER	Renamed from 'Hale End' to 'Highams Park (Hale End)' 1894. Goods yard closed 1965
Highams Park & Hale End					
Highams Park (Hale End)					
Hale End					
HIGH BARNET (LT)	3 / 4A	1940	N/A	LT (NOR)	Original GNR branch re-opened by LT after electrification. Goods yard closed 1962
HIGH BARNET (GNR)	3 / 4A	1872	1939	GNR	Former GNR High Barnet Branch closed 1939 for transfer to LT
HIGH BARNET SIDINGS	3 / 4A	1941	N/A	LT (NOR)	Stabling sidings for Northern Line
HIGHBURY GOODS & COAL	22 / 2B	1850	1969	NLR	
HIGHBURY & ISLINGTON	22 / 2B	1850	N/A	NLR	Opened as 'Islington', renamed 'Highbury or Islington' 1864, 'Highbury & Islington' 1872
Highbury (Great Northern & City Railway)					GN&CR station opened 1904 (= Highbury), Victoria Line platforms opened 1968
Highbury or Islington (North London Railway)					
Islington (North London Railway)					
Highbury Vale Junction	22 / 2A	1904	N/A	GN&CR	
HIGHBURY VALE GOODS	22 / 2B & 15 / 3B	1876	1971	GNR	
HIGHGATE	12 / 4A	1941	N/A	LT (NOR)	Line through station opened 1939, but station itself did not open until 1941
Highgate East Tunnel	12 / 4A	1867	1970	GNR	Remained open for Northern Line Stock transfer until 1970
HIGHGATE HIGH LEVEL	12 / 4A	1867	1954	GNR	Nominally opened by Edgware, Highgate & London Railway, but operated by GNR from opening
Highgate					Closed when Alexandra Palace to Finsbury park service withdrawn 1954. Had been intended
					for electrification and transfer to LT Northern Line, but works abandoned post-WW2
HIGHGATE ROAD HIGH LEVEL	22 / 1A & 57	1868	1915	T&HJ	
Highgate Road for Parliament Hill					
Highgate Road					
Highgate Road Junction	22 / 1A & 57	1870	1964	T&HJ	Junction between Tottenham & Hampstead Junction Railway and curve to Kentish Town
HIGHGATE ROAD LOW LEVEL	22 / 1A & 57	1900	1918	MID	
Highgate West Tunnel	12 / 4A	1867	1970	GNR	Remained open for Northern Line Stock transfer until 1970
HIGHGATE WOOD DEPOT	11 / 4B	1962	N/A	LT (NOR)	On site of GNR Wellington Sidings. Remodelled 1970, closed 1984-1989
High Meadows Junction	23 / 2B & 53	1862	N/A	GER	
HIGH STREET KENSINGTON	31 / 1A & 50	1868	N/A	MET	Metropolitan District Railway platforms opened 1871. Renamed gradually by 1880
Kensington (High Street)					
HIGH STREET KENSINGTON GOODS & COAL	31 / 1A & 50	1878	1963	MID	
HILLINGDON (1st)	17 / 2B	1923	1992	MET	Served by District Line Trains 1923-1933, Piccadilly Line trains thereafter. 'Swakeleys' suffix
Hillingdon (Swakeleys)					after 1934, gradually dropped. Goods yard closed 1964
Hillingdon					

NAME: (Previous names indented below)	PAGE / GRID:	YEAR OPENED:	YEAR CLOSED:	OPENED BY:	NOTES:
HILLINGDON (2nd)	17 / 2B	1992	N/A	LUL (MET)	Relocated due to road scheme
HITHER GREEN	34 / 4A	1895	N/A	SER	
Hither Green Junction	34 / 4A	1866	N/A	SER	
HOGSMILL MILLS	45 / 2B	1890	1950	PRIV	Siding serving mills on Hogsmill River
HOLBORN	22 / 4A	1906	N/A	GNP&BR	Central Line platforms opened and 'Kingsway' suffix added 1933, suffix gradually dropped
Holborn (Kingsway)					
Holborn					
HOLBORN VIADUCT	22 / 4B & 55	1874	1990	LCDR	Suffix 'High Level' 1912-1916
Holborn Viaduct (High Level)					
Holborn Viaduct					
HOLBORN VIADUCT (LOW LEVEL)	22 / 4B & 55	1874	1916	LCDR	Renamed 1912
Snow Hill					
HOLLAND PARK	31 / 1A	1900	N/A	CLR	
HOLLOWAY & CALEDONIAN ROAD	22 / 2A	1852	1915	GNR	
Holloway					
HOLLOWAY CATTLE	22 / 2A	?	?	GNR	
HOLLOWAY ROAD	22 / 2A	1906	N/A	GNP&BR	
HOMERTON (1st)	23 / 2A	1868	1944	NLR	Passenger service Dalston Junction to Poplar withdrawn 1944
HOMERTON (2nd)	23 / 2A	1985	N/A	BR	On site of former NLR Homerton Station
HONOR OAK	33 / 4A	1865	1954	LCDR	Closed 1917-1919 and 1944-1946. Nunhead to Crystal Palace (High Level) closed 1954
HONOR OAK PARK	33 / 4A	1886	N/A	LBSCR	East London Line projected to serve from 2010
HORNCHURCH (LTSR)	16 / 2A	1885	1962	LTSR	Served by District Railway trains 1902-1905. British Rail services withdrawn 1962 and 'Fast' platforms abandoned
HORNCHURCH (MDR)	16 / 2A	1902	N/A	DIS	1902 date denotes first time District railway served original LTSR platforms at Hornchurch. District trains withdrawn East Ham to Upminster 1905, reinstated Barking to Upminster 1932. Current District platforms constructed 1932 during LMS quadrupling of route. Ownership of 'Slow' platforms transferred to LT 1970. Goods yard closed 1982
HORNSEY	12 / 3A	1850	N/A	GNR	
HORNSEY EMU DEPOT	12 / 4B	1976	N/A	BR	On site of former Ferme Park 'Up' Yard, opened 1888
HORNSEY ROAD (FOR HORNSEY RISE)	22 / 1A	1872	1943	T&HJ	
Hornsey Road					
HORNSEY STEAM SHED	12 / 4B	?	1961	GNR	
HORNSEY UP CARRIAGE SIDINGS	12 / 3A	?	N/A	GNR	
Hotel Curve	54	1863	1977	GNR	Last regular service 1976
HOUNSLOW	29 / 4A	1850	N/A	LSWR	Goods yard closed 1967
Hounslow & Whitton					
Hounslow					
HOUNSLOW CENTRAL	29 / 3A	1886	N/A	MDR	Opened by District Railway. Renamed 'Hounslow Central' 1925.
Heston-Hounslow					First served by Piccadilly Line 1933. Last served by District Line 1964
HOUNSLOW EAST	29 / 3A	1909	N/A	MDR	Opened to replace Hounslow Town terminal station 1909. Renamed Hounslow East 1925.
Hounslow Town					First served by Piccadilly Line 1933. Last served by District Line 1964
Hounslow Junction	28 / 4B	1883	N/A	LSWR	
HOUNSLOW TOWN	29 / 3A	1883	1909	MDR	Original terminus of District Railway Hounslow Branch. Renamed 'Town' 1884
Hounslow					Closed 1886 but re-opened 1905, closed for good 1909 and branch dismantled.
HOUNSLOW WEST	28 / 3B	1884	1975	MDR	Opened by District Railway, renamed 'Hounslow West' 1925. First served Piccadilly Line 1933,
Hounslow Barracks					Last served by District Line 1964. Closed 1975 and replaced by new station at lower level
HOUNSLOW WEST	28 / 3B	1975	N/A	LT (PIC)	Through station built on extension to Hatton Cross 1975, replacing original terminus
HOWARD TENENS DISTRIBUTION CENTRE	25 / 3B	?	N/A	PRIV	Formerly 'Stora'
HOXTON	23 / 3A	2010	N/A	NR (LOROL)	Projected to open 2010 as part of East London Line Extension Phase 1
HYDE PARK CORNER	31 / 1B	1906	N/A	GNP&BR	

I

NAME: (Previous names indented below)	PAGE / GRID:	YEAR OPENED:	YEAR CLOSED:	OPENED BY:	NOTES:
ICKENHAM	17 / 2B	1905	N/A	MET	Served by District Line Trains 1910-1933, Piccadilly Line trains thereafter
ILFORD	24 / 1B	1839	N/A	ECR	
ILFORD DEPOT	25 / 1A	1949	N/A	BR	'New Shed' opened 1959 on site of West Curve to Newbury Park
ILFORD GOODS & COAL	25 / 1A	?	1968	GER	
Ilford Carriage Sidings Junction	25 / 1A	1903	1948	GER	Western Curve dismantled 1948 and Ilford Depot built on route
IMPERIAL WHARF	31 / 3B & 50	2009	N/A	NR (LOROL)	New Network Rail station, projected opening late 2009
International Junction	32 / 1B	1994	N/A	RT	Divergence of lines into platforms 20-24. Disused since 2007, track in situ for future use
ISLAND GARDENS (1st)	33 / 2B	1987	1999	DLR	Closed and re-opened in tunnel due to Lewisham Extension
ISLAND GARDENS (2nd)	33 / 2B	1999	N/A	DLR	Replaced original station
ISLE OF DOGS	33 / 1B & 57	2017	N/A	NR (XRAIL)	Proposed station on Crossrail 1 Abbey Wood branch
ISLEWORTH	29 / 3A	1850	N/A	LSWR	Replaced Smallberry Green to East. 'Spring Grove & Isleworth' 1855-1911
Spring Grove & Isleworth					
Isleworth					
IVER	27 / 1A	1924	N/A	GWR	

J

NAME: (Previous names indented below)	PAGE / GRID:	YEAR OPENED:	YEAR CLOSED:	OPENED BY:	NOTES:
JUNCTION ROAD	22 / 1A & 57	1872	1943	T&HJ	
Junction Road for Tufnell Park					
Junction Road Junction	22 / 1A & 57	1883	N/A	T&HJ	Junction between Tottenham & Hampstead Junction and Midland Railways

K

NAME: (Previous names indented below)	PAGE / GRID:	YEAR OPENED:	YEAR CLOSED:	OPENED BY:	NOTES:
KEMPTON PARK	38 / 2B	1878	N/A	LSWR	Race Days only
KENLEY	47 / 4B	1856	N/A	CR	Renamed 1856
Coulsdon					
KENNINGTON	32 / 2B	1890	N/A	C&SLR	Closed 1923-1925
Kennington New Street					
Kennington					
KENSAL GREEN	20 / 3B & 60	1916	N/A	LNWR	Served by Bakerloo Line trains since 1917
KENSAL GREEN & HARLESDEN	20 / 3B	1861	1873	HJR	
Kensal Green Junction	20 / 3B & 60	1860	N/A	HJR	
Kensal Green Tunnel	20 / 3B & 60	1837	N/A	L&B	
KENSAL RISE	20 / 3B	1873	N/A	LNWR	Renamed 1890. Closed 1995-1996
Kensal Green					
KENSINGTON	31 / 1A & 50	1844	1844	WLR	Original WLR Station, open for 6 months. Passenger service withdrawn from WLR 1844 to 1862
Kensington Junction	49	1864	1940	MET & GWR	Metropolitan Line services between Latimer Road and Addison Road withdrawn 1940
KENSINGTON (OLYMPIA)	31 / 1A & 50	1862	N/A	WLR	WLR re-opened to passengers from Willesden Junction to Addison Road 1862. First served by
Addison Road					Metropolitan Railway 1864, District Railway services commenced 1872. All services withdrawn and
					station closed 1940. Station re-opened 1946 for shuttle service to Clapham Junction
					and exhibition traffic to Earl's Court station. Regular District Line service provided since 1986.
					Through Mainline service re-introduced 1994.
KENSINGTON OLYMPIA MOTORAIL TERMINAL	31 / 1A	1965	1982	BR	
KENSINGTON SIDINGS	31 / 3B	1863	N/A	LSWR	
KENT HOUSE	43 / 3A	1884	N/A	LCDR	
KENTISH TOWN	22 / 2A & 57	1868	N/A	MID	CCE&HR station opened 1907
Kentish Town Junction	22 / 2A & 57	1870	1964	MID	Junction between Midland main Line and curve to Highagte Road High Level
KENTISH TOWN WEST	22 / 2A	1867	N/A	HJR	'West' suffix added 1924. Closed 1971-1981 (arson) and again 1995-1996 (engineering works)
Kentish Town					
KENTON	9 / 4B	1912	N/A	LNWR	Served by London Underground Bakerloo Line trains 1917-1982
Kenton (for Northwick Park)					Goods yard opened 1911, closed 1965
Kenton					
KEW	30 / 2A	1853	1862	N&SWJR	Closed when services diverted along 1862 Kew Curve to new Kew station
KEW BRIDGE	30 / 2A	1849	N/A	LSWR	
Kew					
KEW BRIDGE	30 / 2A	1862	1940	N&SWJR	Passenger services between South Acton and Kew Bridge withdrawn 1940
Kew					
Kew East Junction	30 / 2A	1862	N/A	N&SWJR	
KEW GARDENS	30 / 3A	1869	N/A	LSWR	First served District & Metropolitan Railways 1877. Last served Metropolitan Railway 1906.
					Sidings and Bay platform in use until 1931
KEW GOODS (LSWR)	30 / 2A	1849	1964	LSWR	
KEW GOODS (MID)	30 / 2A	?	1977	MID	
KEW GOODS (SR)	30 / 2A	1929	1967	SR	
KIDBROOKE	34 / 3A	1895	N/A	SER	Goods yard closed 1968
Kidbrooke Tunnel	34 / 3A	1895	N/A	SER	
KILBURN	21 / 2A	1879	N/A	MET	'& Brondesbury' until 1950. Served by Bakerloo Line 1939-1979, Jubilee thereafter
Kilburn & Brondesbury					Last served Metropolitan Line 1940
KILBURN HIGH ROAD	21 / 3A	1851	N/A	LNWR	Closed 1917, re-opened and renamed 'Kilburn High Road' 1922
Kilburn & Maida Vale					
Kilburn					
KILBURN PARK	21 / 3A	1915	N/A	UERL (BAK)	
KING GEORGE V	34 / 1B	2005	N/A	DLR	Terminus of DLR extension 2005-2009
KING HENRY'S DRIVE	48 / 3B	2000	N/A	CTL	
KINGSBURY	10 / 4A	1932	N/A	MET	Opened by Metropolitan Railway. Transferred to Bakerloo Line 1939, Jubilee Line 1979
KINGS CROSS	22 / 3A & 54	1852	N/A	GNR	
KINGS CROSS GOODS	22 / 3A & 54	1852	1973	GNR	
KINGS CROSS ST PANCRAS (MET)	22 / 3A & 54	1863	1941	MET	Original Metropolitan Railway station. '& St Pancras' after 1925, '&' dropped 1933
Kings Cross & St Pancras					Closed when new station opened to the West in 1941
Kings Cross					
KINGS CROSS ST PANCRAS (LT)	22 / 3A & 54	1906	N/A	C&SLR	GNP&BR (Piccadilly) Platforms opened 1906 as 'King's Cross', 'for St Pancras' added 1927
Kings Cross for St Pancras					C&SLR (later Northern Line) Platforms opened 1907 as 'King's Cross for St Pancras', closed
King's Cross					1922-1924, 1987-1989 and 1995-1996. Both lines renamed 'King's Cross St Pancras' 1933
					Relocated Metropolitan Line platforms opened 1941, Victoria Line platforms opened 1968
KINGS CROSS SUBURBAN PLATFORM 16	22 / 3A & 54	1866	1976	GNR	Northbound only. Service withdrawn when trains diverted along Great Northern & City Line

NAME: (Previous names indented below)	PAGE / GRID:	YEAR OPENED:	YEAR CLOSED:	OPENED BY:	NOTES:
KINGS CROSS THAMESLINK	22 / 3A & 54	1868	2007	MET	'Thameslink' after 1988. Closed 2007 when St Pancras International Station opened
Kings Cross Midland City					
Kings Cross Midland					
Kings Cross					
KINGS CROSS YORK ROAD	22 / 3A & 54	1866	1976	GNR	Southbound only. Service withdrawn when trains diverted along Great Northern & City Line
KINGSLAND	23 / 2A & 18 / 3A	1850	1865	NLR	Re-opened 1983 as Dalston Kingsland
KINGSLAND GOODS	23 / 2A & 18 / 3B	?	?	NLR	
Kingsley Road Junction	29 / 3A	1905	1909	MDR	
KINGSTON	39 / 4B	1869	N/A	LSWR	Rebuilt and expanded 1935. Goods yard closed 1966
Kingston High Level					
KINGSTON LOW LEVEL	39 / 4B	1863	1935	LSWR	Original terminus 1863-1869. Closed when High Level Station rebuilt 1935
Kingston					
KINGSWOOD	47 / 3A	1897	N/A	SECR	Goods yard closed 1962
Kingswood & Burgh Heath					
Kingswood Tunnel	47 / 3A	1900	N/A	SECR	
KING WILLIAM STREET	22 / 4B	1890	1900	C&SLR	Original terminus of C&SLR from Stockwell. Abandoned when line extended to Moorgate
KNIGHTSBRIDGE	31 / 1B	1906	N/A	GNP&BR	
KNIGHTS HILL GOODS	32 / 4B	1892	1968	LNWR	
KUEHNE + NAGEL LOGISTICS	26 / 3A	?	N/A	PRIV	Replaced 'Hays Distribution'

L

NAME: (Previous names indented below)	PAGE / GRID:	YEAR OPENED:	YEAR CLOSED:	OPENED BY:	NOTES:
LADBROKE GROVE	21 / 4A	1864	N/A	MET & GWR	Opened as 'Notting Hill', '& Ladbroke Road' suffix added 1880, renamed
					'Ladbroke Grove (North Kensington)' 1919, suffix dropped 1938
Ladbroke Grove (North Kensington)					
Notting Hill & Ladbroke Grove					
Notting Hill					
LADYWELL	33 / 4B	1857	N/A	SER	Built by the Mid Kent Railway, but operated by SER from opening
Lady Well					
Ladywell Junction	33 / 4B	1866	N/A	SER	
LAFARGE AGGREGATES (WEST DRAYTON)	27 / 1A	?	N/A	PRIV	On site of former coal yard
LAMBETH NORTH	32 / 1B	1906	N/A	BS&WR	Opened as 'Kennington Road', renamed 'Westminster Bridge Road' 1906, renamed
Lambeth (North)					Lambeth (North)' 1917, renamed 'Lambeth North' c.1928, closed 1996-1997
Westminster Bridge Road					
Kennington Road					
Lampton Junction	29 / 3A	1884	1909	MDR	
LANCASTER GATE	21 / 4B	1900	N/A	CLR	
LANGDON PARK	23 / 4B	2007	N/A	DLR	
Latchmere Junctions Nos. 1, 2 & 3	31 / 3B	1863	N/A	WLER	
LATIMER ROAD	21 / 4A & 49	1868	N/A	MET & GWR	
LEA BRIDGE	23 / 1B	1840	1985	ECR	Closed when Tottenham Hale to North Woolwich service withdrawn
Lea Bridge Road					
Lea Bridge Junction	23 / 1B	1870	1967	GER	Southern junction of Hall Farm Curve
Lea Junction	23 / 2B & 53	1862	N/A	GER	
LEBANON ROAD	47 / 1B	2000	N/A	CTL	
LEE	34 / 4A	1866	N/A	SER	Goods yard closed 1968
Lee Loop Junction	34 / 4A	1900	N/A	SER	
Lee Spur Junction	34 / 4A	1900	N/A	SER	
LEICESTER SQUARE	22 / 4A	1906	N/A	GNP&BR	CCE&HR platforms opened 1907
Leigham Court Tunnel	42 / 1A	1856	N/A	LBSCR	Opened by West End of London & Crystal Palace Railway, but operated by LBSCR from outset
Leigham Junction	42 / 1B	1868	N/A	LBSCR	
Leigham Tunnel	42 / 1A	1868	N/A	LBSCR	
LEMAN STREET	23 / 4A & 7 / 3B	1877	1941	LTSR	Closed 1916-1919
LEWISHAM	33 / 3B	1849	N/A	SER	Suffix 'Junction' 1865-1929
Lewisham Junction					
Lewisham					
LEWISHAM	33 / 3B	1999	N/A	DLR	
Lewisham Crossover	33 / 3B	1929	N/A	SR	
LEWISHAM ROAD	33 / 3B	1871	1917	LCDR	Passenger service withdrawn Nunhead to Greenwich Park 1917
Lewisham Vale Junction	33 / 3B	1976	N/A	BR	
LEY STREET YARD SIDINGS	25 / 1A	?	N/A	GER	
LEYTON (ECR)	23 / 1B	1856	1970	ECR	'Low' prefix dropped 1867. Majority of passenger services transferred to LT in 1947.
Low Leyton					First Trains in the morning remained British Rail services until 1970
LEYTON (LT)	23 / 1B	1947	N/A	LT (CEN)	First served by LT Central Line trains in 1947. Goods yard closed 1968
LEYTON MIDLAND ROAD	13 / 4B	1894	N/A	T&FG	Renamed 1949
Leyton					
LEYTONSTONE (ECR)	24 / 1A	1856	1970	ECR	Majority of passenger services transferred to LT in 1947. First trains in the morning
					remained British Rail services until 1970
LEYTONSTONE (LT)	24 / 1A	1947	N/A	LT (CEN)	First served by LT Central Line trains in 1947. Goods yard closed 1955
LEYTONSTONE HIGH ROAD	24 / 1A	1894	N/A	T&FG	Renamed 1949
Leytonstone					
Leytonstone Junction	14 / 4A	1947	N/A	LT (CEN)	Divergence of 1947 route to Newbury Park from Epping Line
LILLIE BRIDGE DEPOT	31 / 2A & 50	1872	N/A	MDR	Originally built by District Railway. Used by GNP&BR (Piccadilly Line) 1906-1932.
					Used for engineering purposes (now 'Transplant') since 1932

NAME: (Previous names indented below)	PAGE / GRID:	YEAR OPENED:	YEAR CLOSED:	OPENED BY:	NOTES:
LIMEHOUSE (1st)	23 / 4B	1840	1926	LBR	Passenger service to Blackwall and North Greenwich withdrawn 1926
LIMEHOUSE (2nd)	23 / 4B	1840	N/A	LBR	Opened as 'Stepney', renamed 'Stepney East' in 1923. DLR platforms opened and Main Line
Stepney East					station further renamed 'Limehouse' in 1987
Stepney					
Limehouse Junction	23 / 4B	1880	1951	LBR	
Linford Street Junction	32 / 3A & 51	1994	N/A	RT	Disused since 2007 (diversion of Eurostar to St Pancras), but chord still in situ
LITTLE ILFORD DEPOT	24 / 2B	1905	1958	MDR	District Railway depot. Closed when Upminster Depot opened, replaced by East Ham BR Depot
LIVERPOOL STREET	22 / 4B & 59	1874	N/A	GER	First served by Metropolitan Railway February 1875 (direct into GER station). Separate
Bishopsgate (Metropolitan Railway only)					Metropolitan Railway platforms opened as 'Bishopsgate' July 1875, CLR platforms opened 1912
					Platforms for 'Crossrail 1' proposed to open 2017
LLOYD PARK	48 / 2A	2000	N/A	CTL	
LONDON BRIDGE	32 / 1B	1836	N/A	LGR	C&SLR Platforms opened 1900 (closed 1923-1924), Jubilee Line 1999
LONDON CITY AIRPORT	34 / 1B	2005	N/A	DLR	
LONDON FIELDS	23 / 2A	1872	N/A	GER	Closed during World War I, re-opening 1919
LONDON INTERNATIONAL FREIGHT TERMINAL	53	1967	1996	BR	
LONDON ROAD DEPOT	32 / 1B	1906	N/A	BS&WR	Bakerloo Line depot
LONG GROVE HOSPITAL	45 / 2A	1905	1950	PRIV	Horton Estate Light Railway opened to supply building materials, later fuel, to hospitals
Longhedge Junctions	32 / 3A & 51	1862	N/A	LCDR	
LONGHEDGE LOCO WORKS	51	1862	1904	LCDR	Locomotive production ceased 1904
LORD'S	21 / 3B	1868	1939	MET	Opened as 'St John's Wood Road', 'Road' suffix dropped 1925, renamed 'Lord's' June 1939,
St John's Wood					closed November 1939
St John's Wood Road					
LORDSHIP LANE	43 / 1A	1865	1954	LCDR	Closed 1917-1919 and 1944-1946. Nunhead to Crystal Palace (High Level) closed 1954
LOUGHBOROUGH JUNCTION (1st)	32 / 3B	1864	1916	LCDR	Renamed 'Loughborough Road' July 1872, then 'Junction' December 1872
Loughborough Road					
Brixton Junction					
LOUGHBOROUGH JUNCTION (2nd)	32 / 3B	1872	N/A	LCDR	Opened July 1872, renamed December 1872. Platforms on curve to Denmark Hill closed 1925
Loughborough Road					
LOUGHTON (ECR)	6 / 3B	1856	1865	ECR	Original terminus of branch from Stratford. Closed when line extended to Ongar.
LOUGHTON (GER)	6 / 4B	1865	1970	GER	Relocated East 1940. Majority of passenger services transferred to LT in 1948
					First trains in the morning remained British Rail services until 1970
LOUGHTON (LT)	6 / 4B	1948	N/A	LT (CEN)	First served by Central Line trains 1948
LOUGHTON GOODS	6 / 3B	1858	1966	GER	On site of original ECR Loughton Station
Loughton Junction	23 / 1B	1856	1972	ECR	Divergence of ECR Loughton Branch. Last passenger train 1970, lifted 1972
LOUGHTON SIDINGS	6 / 4B	1948	N/A	LT (CEN)	Stabling Sidings for Central Line
LOWER EDMONTON (LOW LEVEL)	13 / 1A	1872	1939	GER	Station on original GER Enfield Branch from Angel Road. Closed to passengers 1939 .
					Angel Road to Lower Edmonton Junction remained open for freight, closing in 1964
					Goods yard in use 1900-1965
Lower Edmonton Junction	13 / 1A	1872	1964	GER	Angel Road to Lower Edmonton Junction closed in 1964
LOWER SYDENHAM (1st)	43 / 2B	1857	1906	SER	Built by the Mid Kent Railway, but operated by SER from opening. Resited South 1906
LOWER SYDENHAM (2nd)	43 / 2B	1906	N/A	SECR	Goods yard closed 1966
LOWER SYDENHAM GASWORKS	43 / 1A	1878	1971	PRIV	
LUDGATE HILL	22 / 4B & 55	1864	1929	LCDR	Terminus 1864-1866
Ludgate Hill Junction	55	1874	1969	LCDR	
Ludgate Junction	31 / 3B	1862	N/A	LCDR & LSWR	

M

MAIDA VALE	21 / 3B	1915	N/A	UERL (BAK)	
MAIDEN LANE	22 / 2A & 54	1887	1917	NLR	
Maiden Lane Curve	54	1863	1865	GNR	Possibly never used
MAIDEN LANE GOODS	54	1866	1965	NLR	
MALDEN MANOR	40 / 4B	1938	N/A	SR	
MANOR HOUSE	12 / 4B	1932	N/A	UERL (PIC)	
MANOR PARK	24 / 2B	1873	N/A	GER	
Manor Park & Little Ilford					
MANOR ROAD GOODS	22 / 1B	1872	1965	GER	
MANOR SIDINGS	16 / 3A	?	?	BR	Disused
MANOR WAY	25 / 4A	1880	1940	PLA	Passenger services withdrawn from Gallions Branch 1940
Royal Albert Dock Manor Way					
Royal Albert Dock Manor Road					
MANSION HOUSE	22 / 4B & 55	1871	N/A	MDR	Terminus of District Railway 1871-1884. Closed 1989-1991
MARBLE ARCH	21 / 4B	1900	N/A	CLR	
MARCON STONE TERMINAL (ANGERSTEIN WHARF)	34 / 1A	?	N/A	PRIV	
MARCON STONE TERMINAL (PADDINGTON)	21 / 4A & 62	?	N/A	PRIV	
MARCON STONE TERMINAL (PARK ROYAL)	20 / 3A	?	N/A	PRIV	
MARLBOROUGH ROAD	21 / 3B	1868	1939	MET	
MARYLAND	24 / 2A	1873	N/A	GER	
Maryland Point					
MARYLEBONE	21 / 4B	1899	N/A	GCR	Terminus of Great Central Railway. Served by Bakerloo Line since 1907
Great Central					
MARYLEBONE CARRIAGE SIDINGS	21 / 3B	1899	N/A	GCR	
MARYLEBONE GOODS & COAL	21 / 3B	1898	1967	GCR	

NAME: (Previous names indented below)	PAGE / GRID:	YEAR OPENED:	YEAR CLOSED:	OPENED BY:	NOTES:
MAYER-PARRY SCRAP (WILLESDEN)	20 / 3B & 60	?	N/A	PRIV	Car-crushing plant. Opened in 1960's on site of former carriage sidings
MAZE HILL	34 / 2A	1873	N/A	SER	
Maze Hill (for National Maritime Museum)					
Maze Hill (East Greenwich) for National Maritime Museum					
Maze Hill & East Greenwich					
Maze Hill & Greenwich Park					
Maze Hill & East Greenwich					
Greenwich (Maze Hill)					
Maze Hill Tunnel	34 / 2A	1878	N/A	SER	
MCVITIE & PRICE'S SIDING	20 / 3A	1902	?	PRIV	Later United Biscuits
Merstham Tunnel	48 / 4A	1841	N/A	L&BR	
MERTON ABBEY	41 / 3B	1868	1929 (1975)	LSWR & LBSCR	Closed 1917-1923. Merton Park to Tooting Junction closed to passengers 1929
					Junction at Tooting severed 1934 with freight traffic accessing from the Merton Park end
					Freight ceased 1968 (Tooting) and 1975 (Merton Abbey)
MERTON PARK (LBSCR & LSWR)	41 / 3A	1868	1997	LSWR & LBSCR	Platform for Wimbledon to Croydon trains not opened until 1870. Renamed 1887
Lower Merton					Wimbledon to West Croydon closed 1997 prior to conversion to Tramlink
MERTON PARK (CTL)	41 / 3A	2000	N/A	CTL	On site of former Merton Park Station
Metropolitan Junctions	32 / 1B & 55	1866	N/A	SER	
METROPOLITAN WATER BOARD RAILWAY (HAMPTON)	38 / 2B & 3B	1915	1947	PRIV	A self-contained Narrow Gauge (2 foot) Railway supplying Pumping Stations with Coal
MIDDLESEX OIL & CHEMICAL WORKS	17 / 4A	1966	1979	PRIV	Last section of GWR Uxbridge (Vine Street) Branch to close
MILDMAY PARK	22 / 2B	1880	1934	NLR	
MILEAGE YARD (GOODS & COAL)	21 / 4A & 62	?	?	GWR	
MILE END (ECR)	23 / 3A	1843	1872	ECR	Replaced by Bethnal Green Junction to West
MILE END (MDR)	23 / 4B	1902	N/A	MDR & LTSR	Served by Metropolitan Line since 1936. Central Line platforms opened 1946
MILE END COAL	23 / 3A	?	?	GER	
MILE END GOODS	23 / 3A	?	?	GER	
MILITARY SIDING (FELTHAM)	38 / 1A	?	?	PRIV	
MILL HILL BROADWAY	10 / 2A	1868	N/A	MID	Renamed 1950
Mill Hill					
MILL HILL EAST (GNR)	11 / 2A	1867	1939	GNR	Nominally opened by Edgware, Highgate & London Railway, but operated by GNR from opening
Mill Hill East for Mill Hill Barracks					Closed in 1939 to enable doubling and electrification of Finchley Central to Edgware prior
Mill Hill					to transfer to LT Northern Line. Doubling abandoned and Mill Hill East became terminus
MILL HILL EAST (LT)	11 / 2A	1941	N/A	LT (NOR)	On site of former GNR station. Goods yard closed 1962
MILL HILL (THE HALE)	10 / 2A	1906	1939	GNR	Originally opened as 'The Hale Halt', renamed 'Mill Hill (The Hale)' 1928
The Hale Halt					Closed in 1939 to enable doubling and electrification of Finchley Central to Edgware prior
					to transfer to LT Northern Line. Works abandoned and station did not re-open.
					Goods yard open 1910 - 1964
MILLWALL DOCKS	33 / 1B	1871	1926	LBR	Terminus 1871-1872. Passenger service to Blackwall and North Greenwich withdrawn 1926
MILLWALL GOODS	33 / 2B	1872	1925	LBR	
MILLWALL JUNCTION	23 / 4B & 57	1871	1926	LBR	Rebuilt & resited 1888. Passenger service to Blackwall and North Greenwich withdrawn 1926
MINORIES	23 / 4A & 7 / 3A	1840	1853	LBR	
Minories Junction	23 / 4A & 7 / 2A	1884	N/A	MDR	
MITCHAM (WCR)	41 / 4B	1855	1997	WCR	Wimbledon to West Croydon closed 1997 prior to conversion to Tramlink
MITCHAM (CTL)	41 / 4B	2000	N/A	CTL	On site of former Mitcham Station
MITCHAM EASTFIELDS	41 / 3B	2008	N/A	NR	
MITCHAM JUNCTION	41 / 4B	1868	N/A	LBSCR	Croydon Tramlink platforms opened 2000
MITRE BRIDGE EXCHANGE PLATFORMS	60	1844	1844	GWR & WLR	Exchange platforms between GWR and WLR, in operation 1844 only
MITRE BRIDGE GOODS	20 / 4B & 60	?	?	LNWR	
Mitre Bridge Junction	20 / 4B & 60	1860	N/A	HJR	
MONUMENT	22 / 4B	1884	N/A	MDR & MET	Opened as 'Eastcheap' October 1884, renamed 'The Monument' November 1884, 'The' prefix
The Monument					gradually dropped
Eastcheap					
MOORGATE	22 / 4B	1865	N/A	MET	City Widened Lines platforms opened 1866, closed 2009, C&SLR platforms opened 1900, GN&C
Moorgate Street					(later Northern Line, then British Rail) platforms opened 1904. Renamed 1924
MOOR PARK	8 / 2A	1910	N/A	MET	Opened as 'Sandy Lodge', 'Moor Park' prefix after 1923, 'Sandy Lodge' suffix dropped 1950
Moor Park & Sandy Lodge					Goods yard closed 1938
Sandy Lodge					
MORDEN	41 / 3A	1926	N/A	UERL (NOR)	
MORDEN DEPOT	41 / 3A	1926	N/A	UERL (NOR)	
MORDEN ROAD (WCR)	41 / 3A	1857	1997	WCR	Road' suffix added 1951
Morden Road Halt					Wimbledon to West Croydon closed 1997 prior to conversion to Tramlink
Morden Halt					
Morden					
MORDEN ROAD (CTL)	41 / 3A	2000	N/A	CTL	On site of former Morden Road Station
MORDEN SOUTH	41 / 4A	1930	N/A	SR	
MORNINGTON CRESCENT	22 / 3A	1907	N/A	CCE&HR	Closed 1992-1998 for lift replacement works
Mortimer Street Junction	22 / 1A & 57	1900	1981	MID	Junction of curve to Kentish Town, abandoned 1981 after diversion of Barking Trains
MORTLAKE	30 / 3A	1846	N/A	LSWR	Renamed 1948
Mortlake & East Sheen					
Mortlake					
Mortlake Junction	30 / 3B	1862	1881	LSWR	Barnes Curve disused since 1869 but not dismantled until 1881
MOTSPUR PARK	40 / 4B	1925	N/A	SR	
Motspur Park Junction	40 / 4B	1938	N/A	SR	

NAME: (Previous names indented below)	PAGE / GRID:	YEAR OPENED:	YEAR CLOSED:	OPENED BY:	NOTES:
MOTTINGHAM	44 / 1B	1866	N/A	SER	Renamed 'Mottingham' 1927. Goods yard used by United Dairies after 1948, closed 1968
Eltham & Mottingham					
Eltham for Mottingham					
Eltham & Mottingham					
Eltham					
Mount Street Tunnel	34 / 1B	1849	N/A	SER	
MUDCHUTE (1st)	33 / 2B	1987	1999	DLR	Closed and re-opened at lower level due to Lewisham Extension
MUDCHUTE (2nd)	33 / 2B	1999	N/A	DLR	Replaced original station
MUSWELL HILL	12 / 3A	1873	1954 (1956)	GNR	Nominally opened by Edgware, Highgate & London Railway, but operated by GNR from opening
Alexandra Park (Muswell Hill)					Closed to passengers 1873-1875 and again 1951-1952 along with entire branch, finally
					closed when Alexandra Palace to Finsbury Park service withdrawn 1954. Had been intended
					for electrification and transfer to LT Northern Line, but works abandoned post-WW2.
					Remained open for freight traffic until 1956

N

NAME: (Previous names indented below)	PAGE / GRID:	YEAR OPENED:	YEAR CLOSED:	OPENED BY:	NOTES:
Navarino Road Junction	23 / 2A	1986	N/A	BR	Curve opened due to closure of Broad Street. Passenger service withdrawn 1992
NEASDEN	20 / 2B	1880	N/A	MET	Opened as 'Kingsbury & Neasden', renamed 'Neasden & Kingsbury' 1910, suffix dropped 1932
Neasden & Kingsbury					Goods yard opened 1894, closed 1958. Served by Bakerloo Line 1939-1979, Jubilee thereafter
Kingsbury & Neasden					Last served Metropolitan Line 1940.
NEASDEN DEPOT	20 / 1B	1880	N/A	MET	Originally Metropolitan Railway Works & Power Station. Substantially rebuilt in 1930s.
					Stabled Bakerloo Line Trains 1939-1979, Jubilee Line Trains 1979-present
NEASDEN FREIGHT TERMINAL	20 / 2A	?	N/A	PRIV	Tibbett & Britten
Neasden Junction	20 / 2B	1906	N/A	GCR	
NEASDEN POWER STATION	20 / 1A	1905	1968	MET	Metropolitan Railway Power Station
Neasden South Junction	20 / 2B	1906	N/A	GCR	
NEASDEN SOUTH SIDINGS	20 / 2A	?	N/A	GCR	
NECROPOLIS	32 / 1B	1854	1941	LSWR	Station for funeral traffic to Brookwood Cemetary. Resited south 1902
NEW ADDINGTON	48 / 3B	2000	N/A	CTL	
NEW BARNET	3 / 4B	1850	N/A	GNR	
Barnet					
NEW BECKENHAM (1st)	43 / 2B	1864	1866	SER	Built by the Mid Kent Railway, but operated by SER from opening
NEW BECKENHAM (2nd)	43 / 2B	1866	N/A	SER	
New Beckenham Junction	43 / 2B	1864	N/A	SER	
NEWBURY PARK (GER)	15 / 4A	1903	1947	GER	Fairlop Loop closed 1947 to allow electrification and transfer to LT Central Line. Freight
					traffic remained until 1965
NEWBURY PARK (LT)	15 / 4A	1948	N/A	LT (CEN)	First served by LT Central Line 1947 via branch from Leytonstone. Goods yard closed 1965
Newbury Park Junction	25 / 1A	1903	1948	GER	Western Curve dismantled 1948 and Ilford Depot built on route
NEWBURY PARK SIDINGS	15 / 4A	?	?	GER	Electrified 1947 for Central Line use, but lightly used after Hainault Depot's opening
NEW CROSS (SER)	33 / 2B & 52	1850	N/A	SER	First served by Metropolitan Railway 1884 (no service 1906-1913), became 'East London Line'
					during 1980's, no service 1995-1998, last LU service 2007
NEW CROSS (ELR)	33 / 2B & 52	1869	1886	ELR	Original East London Railway terminus. Closed 1876-1884
NEW CROSS DEPOT	33 / 2B & 52	1913	2007	ELR	East London Line stabling sidings. Closed 2007.
NEW CROSS GATE	33 / 2A & 52	1839	N/A	LCR	First served District and Metropolitan Railways 1884, last served District 1905. No service
New Cross					Metropolitan Railway 1906-1913. 'Gate' suffix added 1923. East London Line closed 1995-1998,
					last LU service 2007
NEW CROSS GATE DEPOT	33 / 2B & 52	2010	N/A	NR (LOROL)	LOROL depot being constructed for East London Line extensions, replacing New Cross Depot
NEW CROSS GOODS & COAL	52	1904	1967	GER	On site of original ELR terminus
NEW CROSS LOCO WORKSHOPS	52	1844	1947	LBSCR	
NEW ELTHAM	35 / 4A	1878	N/A	SER	Prefix 'New Eltham' added 1886, suffix 'Pope Street' dropped 1927. Goods yard closed 1965
New Eltham & Pope Street					
Pope Street					
New Guildford Line Junction	39 / 4B	1885	N/A	LSWR	
NEWINGTON ROAD & BALLS POND	22 / 2B	1858	1870	NLR	
New Kew Junction	30 / 2A	1862	N/A	N&SWJR	
NEW MALDEN	40 / 3B	1846	N/A	LSWR	Renamed 'Malden for Coombe' 1955, then 'New Malden' from 1957
Malden					
Malden for Coombe					
Coombe & Malden					
New Malden & Coombe					
Malden					
NEW MALDEN GOODS	40 / 3A	1869	1964	LSWR	
New Malden Junction	40 / 3B	1869	N/A	LSWR	
NEW SOUTHGATE	12 / 2A	1850	N/A	GNR	Suffix dropped 1871
New Southgate & Friern Barnet					
New Southgate for Colney Hatch					
New Southgate & Colney Hatch					
Southgate & Colney Hatch					
Colney Hatch & Southgate					
NEW WANDSWORTH	31 / 4B	1858	1867	LBSCR	
NEW WANDSWORTH GOODS & COAL	31 / 4B	1858	1968	LBSCR	
NINE ELMS	32 / 2A	1838	1848 (1968)	LSWR	LSWR London terminus until Waterloo opened 1848. Used for goods traffic until 1968
NINE ELMS DEPOT	32 / 3A	1885	1967	LSWR	
Nine Elms Junction	32 / 2A	1994	N/A	RT	Disused since 2007 (diversion of Eurostar to St Pancras), but chord still in situ

NAME: (Previous names indented below)	PAGE / GRID:	YEAR OPENED:	YEAR CLOSED:	OPENED BY:	NOTES:
NINE ELMS SOUTH GOODS	32 / 2A	?	1968	LSWR	
NOEL PARK & WOOD GREEN	12 / 3B	1878	1963	GER	Renamed 'Green Lanes & Noel Park' 1884, renamed 'Noel Park & Wood Green' 1902
Green Lanes & Noel Park					Palace Gates Branch closed to passengers 1963, freight remaining until 1965
Green Lanes					Goods yard in use 1883-1964
NORBITON	40 / 3A	1869	N/A	LSWR	Goods yard closed 1965
Nortbiton for Kingston Hill					
NORBURY	42 / 3A	1878	N/A	LBSCR	
NORTH ACTON (CLR)	20 / 4A	1923	N/A	CLR	North Acton to Ealing Broadway opened by Great Western Railway 1920
NORTH ACTON (GWR)	20 / 4A	1904	1913	GWR	
North Acton Junction (1)	20 / 4A	1947	N/A	LT (CEN)	Junction between Central Line and extension to Greenford (later West Ruislip)
North Acton Junction (2)	20 / 4A	1917	1964	GWR	Junction between GWR Birmingham Main Line and route ex-Viaduct Junction
NORTH DULWICH	32 / 4B	1868	N/A	LBSCR	
NORTH EALING	20 / 4A	1903	N/A	MDR	First served Piccadilly Line 1932, last served District Line 1933
NORTH END (or BULL & BUSH)	21 / 1B	N/A	N/A	CCE&HR	Platforms built but station buildings and platform access never completed
NORTHFIELDS	29 / 1B	1932	N/A	UERL (DIS)	Replaced Northfields & Little Ealing due to construction of Northfields Depot
					Goods yard closed 1932. First served by Piccadilly Line 1933. Last served by District Line 1964
NORTHFIELDS DEPOT	29 / 1B	1932	N/A	UERL (DIS & PIC)	Ceased to be regularly used by District Line Trains after 1964.
NORTHFIELDS & LITTLE EALING	29 / 1B	1908	1932	MDR	Renamed 1911, replaced by Northfields Station 1932
Northfield (Ealing)					
NORTH GREENWICH & CUBITT TOWN	33 / 2B	1872	1926	LBR	Passenger service to Blackwall and North Greenwich withdrawn 1926
North Greenwich					
NORTH GREENWICH	34 / 1A	1999	N/A	LUL (JUB)	
NORTH HARROW	9 / 4A	1915	N/A	MET	
North Junction (Mitcham)	41 / 4B	1868	1997	LBSCR & WCR	Junction eliminated when Wimbldeon to Croydon line closed 1997
North Kent East Junction	33 / 2B & 52	1849	N/A	SER	
North Kent West Junction	52	1844	1983	LGR & LCR	
NORTH MIDDLESEX GASWORKS	11 / 2A	1886	1956	PRIV	
NORTHOLT (GWR)	18 / 2B	1907	1948	GWR	
Northolt (for West End) Halt					
Northolt Halt					
NORTHOLT (LT)	18 / 2B	1948	N/A	LT (CEN)	
Northolt Junction	18 / 2B	1906	N/A	GCR & GWR	
NORTHOLT PARK	19 / 2A	1906	N/A	GCR	Opened as 'South Harrow & Roxeth', renamed 'Northolt Park for Northolt Village' 1929
Northolt Park for Northolt Village					'for Northolt Village' suffix dropped 1955
South Harrow & Roxeth					
NORTH POLE DEPOT	20 / 4B & 60	1994	2007	ES	Eurostar Depot. Closed when Temple Mills Depot opened 2007. Mothballed for future use
North Pole Junction	20 / 4B & 60	1860	N/A	WLR	Formerly provided connection to GWR Main Line, now only North Pole Depot
NORTHUMBERLAND PARK	13 / 3A	1840	N/A	ECR	
Marsh Lane					
NORTHUMBERLAND PARK DEPOT	13 / 3A	1968	N/A	LT (VIC)	Sole Depot for Victoria Line
NORTH SHED (QUEENS PARK)	21 / 3A	1915	N/A	UERL (BAK)	Stabling Shed for Bakerloo Line
NORTH SHEEN	30 / 3A	1930	N/A	SR	
NORTH WEALD	6 / 2A	1865	1994	GER	Epping to Ongar transferred to LT 1949, Electrified 1956, Closed 1994. Goods yard closed 1964
NORTH WEMBLEY	19 / 2B	1912	N/A	LNWR	Served by Bakerloo Line Trains 1917-1982, 1984-Present
NORTHWICK PARK	9 / 4B	1923	N/A	MET	Renamed 1937
Northwick Park & Kenton					
NORTHWOOD	8 / 2A	1887	N/A	MET	Goods yard closed 1966
NORTHWOOD HILLS	8 / 3A	1933	N/A	MET	
NORTH WOOLWICH	35 / 1A	1847	2006	ECR	Goods yard closed 1970. Stratford to North Woolwich closed 2006
Norwood Fork Junction	43 / 4A	1862	N/A	LBSCR	
NORWOOD (JOLLY SAILOR)	43 / 3A	1839	1859	LCR	Resited South 1859 (Norwood Junction)
NORWOOD JUNCTION	43 / 3A	1859	N/A	LBSCR	Renamed 1955. East London Line projected to serve from 2010
Norwood Junction & South Norwood for Woodside					
Norwood Junction					
NORWOOD JUNCTION LOCO SHED	43 / 3A	1935	1964	SR	
NOTTING HILL GATE	31 / 1A	1868	N/A	MET	Central London Railway platforms opened 1900. Served by District Line since 1926
					Interchange facilites between Central and Circle / District Lines not provided until 1959
NUNHEAD (1st)	33 / 3A	1871	1925	LCDR	Originally 3 through tracks. Relocated West 1925
NUNHEAD (2nd)	33 / 3A	1925	N/A	SR	Replaced original station to East
Nunhead Junction	33 / 3A	1892	N/A	LCDR	Crystal Palace (High Level) branch eliminated 1954

O

OAKLEIGH PARK	3 / 4B	1873	N/A	GNR	
OAKWOOD	4 / 4A	1933	N/A	LT (PIC)	Opened as 'Enfield West', 'Oakwood' suffix added 1934, renamed 'Oakwood' 1946
Enfield West (Oakwood)					
Enfield West					
OCKENDON	16 / 2B	1892	N/A	LTSR	Goods yard closed 1968
OLD FORD	23 / 3B	1867	1944	NLR	Passenger service Dalston Junction to Poplar withdrawn 1944
OLD FORD GOODS	23 / 3B	1868	1967	NLR	
OLD KENT ROAD & HATCHAM	33 / 2A & 52	1866	1917	LBSCR	Renamed 1870
Old Kent Road					
Old Kent Road Junction	52	1871	1964	LBSCR	Projected to re-open as part of East London Line Extension Phase 2 in 2011

NAME: (Previous names indented below)	PAGE / GRID:	YEAR OPENED:	YEAR CLOSED:	OPENED BY:	NOTES:
Old Kew Junction	30 / 2A	1853	N/A	N&SWJR	
Old Oak Common Flyover	60	?	N/A	GWR	
OLD OAK COMMON LOCO SHED	20 / 4B & 60	1906	1964	GWR	
OLD OAK COMMON SIDINGS	20 / 4B & 60	?	N/A	GWR	
Old Oak Common West Junction	20 / 4B & 60	1903	N/A	GWR	
OLD OAK LANE HALT	20 / 4B & 60	1906	1947	GWR	
OLD OAK SIDINGS	20 / 4B & 60	?	N/A	N&SWJR	
OLD STREET	22/ 3B	1901	N/A	C&SLR	GN&C (later Northern Line, later British Rail) platforms opened 1904
ONGAR	6 / 2B	1865	1994	GER	Epping to Ongar transferred to LT 1949, Electrified 1956, Closed 1994
					Goods yard closed 1966
ORIENT WAY SIDINGS	23 / 1B	2008	N/A	NR	On site of Stratford Traction Maintenance Depot. Replaced Thornton Field Sidings
OSTERLEY	29 / 2A	1934	N/A	LT (DIS & PIC)	Replaced Osterley & Spring Grove Station. Last served by District Line 1964.
OSTERLEY & SPRING GROVE	29 / 2A	1883	1934	MDR	Served by Piccadilly Line after 1933. Replaced by Osterley Station.
OVAL	32 / 2B	1890	N/A	C&SLR	Renamed c.1894. Closed 1923-1924
The Oval					
Kennington Oval					
OXFORD CIRCUS	22 / 4A	1900	N/A	CLR	BS&WR platforms opened 1906, Victoria Line platforms opened 1969

P

PADDINGTON (1st)	21 / 4B & 62	1838	1854	GWR	Original terminus 1838-1854. Became Paddington Goods Station after 1854
PADDINGTON (2nd)	21 / 4B & 62	1854	N/A	GWR	Metropolitan Railway Platforms opened 1863 (= 'Bishops Road'), renamed 'Paddington' 1933
Bishops Road (Metropolitan Railway only)					
PADDINGTON (MET)	21 / 4B & 62	1868	N/A	MET	Platforms on District / Circle Lines. Bakerloo Line platforms added 1913. Renamed 1948
Paddington (Praed Street)					
PADDINGTON GOODS	21 / 4B & 62	1854	1975	GWR	On site of original Paddington Station
PALACE GATES	12 / 3A	1878	1963	GER	Palace Gates Branch closed to passengers 1963, freight remaining until 1965
PALACE GATES COAL CONCENTRATION DEPOT	12 / 3A	1954	1984	PRIV	Charringtons Ltd. On site of former Goods Yard at Palace Gates
PALACE OF ENGINEERING	20 / 2A	1924	1925	PRIV	Goods station remained open until 1965
PALMERS GREEN	12 / 2A	1871	N/A	GNR	Suffix dropped 1971. Goods yard closed 1962
Palmers Green & Southgate					
Palmer's Green					
Park Junction	11 / 4B	1873	1957	GNR	Junction between GNR Alexandra Palace Branch and line to Edgware. All traffic ceased on
					Alexandra Palace Branch 1957 and junction eliminated.
PARK ROYAL (GWR)	20 / 4A	1903	1937	GWR	
PARK ROYAL (MDR)	20 / 4A	1931	N/A	LT (DIS)	Served by District Line 1931-1933, Piccadilly Line from 1932 onwards. 'Hanger Hill' suffix
Park Royal (Hanger Hill)					in use 1936-1947
Park Royal					
PARK ROYAL GOODS	20 / 3A	1903	1982	GWR	
PARK ROYAL & TWYFORD ABBEY	20 / 3A	1903	1931	MDR	
Park Royal					
PARK ROYAL WEST HALT	20 / 3A	1932	1948	GWR	
Parks Bridge Junction	33 / 3B	1866	N/A	SER	
Park Street Tunnels	22 / 3A	1837	N/A	L&B	
PARSONS GREEN	31 / 3A	1880	N/A	MDR	
PARSONS GREEN SIDINGS	31 / 3A	1880	N/A	MDR	District Line stabling sidings
Paxton Tunnel	43 / 2A	1865	1954	LCDR	Closed 1917-1919. Nunhead to Crystal Palace (High Level) closed 1954 (Passengers and Goods)
PECKHAM COAL	33 / 3A	1891	1958	LNWR & MID	
PECKHAM RYE	33 / 3A	1865	N/A	LCDR	East London Line extension phase 2 (LOROL) projected to serve from 2011
PECKHAM RYE DEPOT	33 / 3A	1909	1961	LBSCR	Originally built to accommodate stock for LBSCR South London Line overhead electrification
Peckham Rye Junction	33 / 3A	1868	N/A	LBSCR	
PENGE EAST	43 / 2A	1863	N/A	LCDR	Renamed 'Penge East' 1923. Goods yard closed 1966
Penge Lane					
Penge					
Penge Junction	43 / 3B	1863	N/A	LCDR	
Penge Tunnel	43 / 2A	1863	N/A	LCDR	
PENGE WEST	43 / 2A	1839	N/A	LBSCR	Opened as 'Penge' 1839, closed 1841. Re-opened as 'Penge Bridges' 1863, renamed 'Penge' 1879
Penge Bridges					suffix 'West' added 1923, goods yard closed 1964. East London Line projected to serve from 2010
Penge					
PERIVALE HALT	19 / 3B	1904	1947	GWR	Closed 1915-1920
PERIVALE	19 / 3B	1947	N/A	LT (CEN)	
Perry Street Fork Junction	36 / 3B	1895	N/A	SER	
PETTS WOOD	44 / 3B	1928	N/A	SR	
Petts Wood Junctions	44 / 3B	1902	N/A	SECR	
PHIPPS BRIDGE	41 / 3B	2000	N/A	CTL	
PICCADILLY CIRCUS	22 / 4A	1906	N/A	BS&WR	GNP&BR platforms opened December 1906
PIG HILL SIDINGS	31 / 3B	1863	N/A	WLER	
PIMLICO (LBSCR)	32 / 2A & 51	1858	1860	LBSCR	Opened by West End of London & Crystal Palace Railway, but operated by LBSCR from outset
PIMLICO (LT)	32 / 2A	1972	N/A	LT (VIC)	
PINNER	8 / 4B	1885	N/A	MET	Goods yard closed 1967
PLAISTOW (LTSR)	24 / 3A	1858	1962	LTSR	Main Line services non-stopped since 1962, and 'Fast' Platforms abandoned
PLAISTOW (MDR)	24 / 3A	1902	N/A	MDR	First served by District Railway 1902, line quadrupled 1908, District Trains using Slow Lines
					Served by Metropolitan Line since 1936 ('Hammersmith & City Line' since 1990)

NAME: (Previous names indented below)	PAGE / GRID:	YEAR OPENED:	YEAR CLOSED:	OPENED BY:	NOTES:
PLAISTOW DEPOT	24 / 3A	1911	1962	LTSR	
PLAISTOW LOCO WORKS	24 / 3A	1858	1925	LTSR	
PLAISTOW & WEST HAM GOODS	24 / 4A	1906	?	GER	
PLANT DEPOT (HITHER GREEN)	34 / 4A	?	N/A	PRIV	
PLASSER WORKS (WEST EALING)	19 / 4A	?	N/A	PRIV	
PLUMSTEAD	35 / 1A	1859	N/A	SER	
PLUMSTEAD YARD	35 / 1A	?	N/A	SER	
Point Pleasant Junction	31 / 4A	1889	N/A	LSWR	'Up' line and flyover dismantled 1990, 'Down' line now bi-directional
PONDERS END	5 / 4B	1840	N/A	GER	
PONTOON DOCK	34 / 1B	2005	N/A	DLR	
POPLAR (LBR)	23 / 4B & 57	1840	1926	LBR	Passenger service to Blackwall withdrawn 1926
POPLAR (NLR - Did Not Open)	57	N/A	N/A	NLR	Platforms constructed 1851 but station did not open
POPLAR (NLR)	23 / 4B & 57	1866	1944	NLR	Passenger service Dalston Junction to Poplar withdrawn 1944
Poplar (East India Road)					
POPLAR (DLR)	23 / 4B & 57	1987	N/A	DLR	
POPLAR DEPOT	23 / 4B & 57	1987	N/A	DLR	DLR Depot
POPLAR DOCK GOODS	57	1882	1951	MID	
POTTERS BAR	3 / 1A	1850	N/A	GNR	
Potters Bar Tunnel	3 / 2A	1850	N/A	GNR	
Pouparts Junction	31 / 3B	1867	N/A	LBSCR & LSWR	
POYLE ESTATE HALT	27 / 3A	1954	1965	BR	Passenger service West Drayton to Staines West withdrawn 1965
POYLE FOR STANWELL MOOR HALT	27 / 3A	1927	1965	GWR	Renamed 1927. Passenger service West Drayton to Staines West withdrawn 1965
Stanwell Moor & Poyle Halt					
PRE-ASSEMBLY DEPOT (HITHER GREEN)	34 / 4A	?	N/A	PRIV	Balfour Beatty
PRESTON ROAD (FOR UXENDON)	19 / 1B	1908	1931 / 1932	MET	Southbound / Up platform closed 1931, Northbound / Down closed 1932
PRESTON ROAD	19 / 1B	1931 / 1932	N/A	MET	Southbound / Up platform opened 1931, Northbound / Down opened 1932
PRIMROSE HILL	21 / 2B & 61	1851	1992	LNWR	Closed 1917-1922. Chalk Farm renamed Primrose Hill 1950
Chalk Farm					Closed when Watford Junction to Liverpool Street service withdrawn 1992
Hampstead Road					
Primrose Hill Junction	61	1851	N/A	LNWR	
Primrose Hill Tunnels	21 / 2B & 61	1837	N/A	L&B	2nd tunnel added 1879, 3rd tunnel added 1922
PRINCE REGENT	24 / 4B	1994	N/A	DLR	
PRINCESS ROYAL DISTRIBUTION CENTRE	20 / 3A	1996	N/A	PRIV	Royal Mail depot
PUDDING MILL LANE	23 / 3A	1996	N/A	DLR	
PURFLEET	16 / 3A	1854	N/A	LTSR	
PURFLEET FOSTER YEOMAN STONE TERMINAL	16 / 3A	?	N/A	PRIV	Deep Water Wharf
PURFLEET RIFLE RANGE HALT	16 / 3A	1911	1948	LTSR	
PURFLEET THAMES TERMINAL	16 / 3A	?	N/A	PRIV	Deep Water Wharf
PURLEY	47 / 4B	1841	N/A	L&BR	Opened as Godstone Road, closed 1847-1856. Re-opened 1856 as 'Caterham Junction'
Caterham Junction					Renamed 'Purley' 1888
Godstone Road					
Purley Chipstead Line Junction	47 / 4B	1897	N/A	SER	
Purley North Junction	47 / 3B	?	N/A	LBSCR	
PURLEY OAKS	47 / 3B	1899	N/A	LBSCR	
Purley South Junction	47 / 4B	1856	N/A	SER	
PUTNEY	31 / 4A	1846	N/A	LSWR	
PUTNEY BRIDGE	31 / 3A	1880	N/A	MDR	Opened as Putney Bridge & Fulham 1880 as terminus of extension from West Brompton.
Putney Bridge & Hurlingham					Extension to Wimbledon opened 1889 (LSWR), '& Fulham' replaced by '& Hurlingham'
Putney Bridge & Fulham					1902, '& Hurlingham' suffix dropped 1932.

Q

NAME: (Previous names indented below)	PAGE / GRID:	YEAR OPENED:	YEAR CLOSED:	OPENED BY:	NOTES:
QUAKER OATS (SOUTHALL)	28 / 1B	?	?	PRIV	
Quarry Tunnel	48 / 4A	1900	N/A	LBSCR	
QUEENSBURY	10 / 4A	1934	N/A	LT (MET)	Opened by LT Metropolitan Line. Transferred to Bakerloo Line 1939, Jubilee Line 1979
QUEENS PARK	21 / 3A	1879	N/A	LNWR	Served by Bakerloo Line since 1915, terminus 1915-1917. Renamed 1954
Queens Park (West Kilburn)					
QUEENS ROAD	23 / 1A	N/A	N/A	GER	Platforms built 1872 but station did not open
QUEENS ROAD GOODS	13 / 4B	1894	1968	MID	
Boundary Road Goods					
QUEENS ROAD PECKHAM	33 / 3A	1866	N/A	LBSCR	East London Line extension phase 2 (LOROL) projected to serve from 2011
Peckham					
QUEENSTOWN ROAD BATTERSEA	32 / 3A & 51	1877	N/A	LSWR	Renamed 1980
Queens Road Battersea					
QUEENSWAY	21 / 4A	1900	N/A	CLR	Renamed 1946. Closed 2005-2006 for lift replacement
Queens Road					

R

NAME: (Previous names indented below)	PAGE / GRID:	YEAR OPENED:	YEAR CLOSED:	OPENED BY:	NOTES:
RAINHAM	26 / 3B	1854	N/A	LTSR	
RAVENSBOURNE	44 / 2A	1892	N/A	LCDR	
RAVENSCOURT PARK	30 / 2B	1873	N/A	LSWR	Opened by LSWR. First served District and Metropolitan railways 1877, renamed 1888.
Shaftesbury Road					Last served Metropolitan Railway 1906, last served LSWR 1916.
RAYNERS LANE	8 / 4B	1906	N/A	MET	Served by District Line Trains 1910-1933, Piccadilly Line thereafter. Goods yard open 1929-1964
RAYNES PARK	40 / 3B	1871	N/A	LSWR	
RAYNES PARK GOODS	40 / 3B	1871	1983	LSWR	Closed as goods yard 1969, remained in use as Permanent way yard until 1983
Raynes Park Junction	40 / 3B	1859	N/A	LSWR	
Ray Street Gridiron	55	1868	N/A	MET	Widened Lines dive-under, replaced by a concrete raft 1960
Reading Lane Junction	23 / 2A	1986	N/A	BR	Curve opened due to closure of Broad Street. Passenger service withdrawn 1992
RECTORY ROAD	23 / 1A	1872	N/A	GER	
REDBRIDGE	14 / 4B	1947	N/A	LT (CEN)	
REEDHAM	47 / 4A	1911	N/A	SECR	Closed 1917-1919. 'Halt' dropped 1936
Reedham Halt					
REEDHAM SIDINGS	47 / 4A	?	N/A	LBSCR	
REEVES CORNER	47 / 1B	2000	N/A	CTL	
REGENT'S PARK	22 / 4A	1906	N/A	BS&WR	
RICHMOND (1st)	29 / 4A	1846	1848 (1936)	LSWR	Terminus 1846-1848, later became Goods station, closing 1936
RICHMOND (2nd)	29 / 4A	1848	N/A	LSWR	Replaced 1846 terminus. First served District & Metropolitan Railways 1877. Last served Metropolitan Railway 1906. Extensively rebuilt 1936-1937
Richmond Bridge	29 / 4B	1848	N/A	LSWR	
RICHMOND GASWORKS	30 / 3A	1882	1933	PRIV	
RICHMOND GOODS	29 / 4B	1848	1936	LSWR	Demolished when station rebuilt
Richmond Junction (1)	29 / 3A	1869	1972	LSWR	Physical connection eliminated 1972
Richmond Junction (2)	31 / 1A & 49	1869	1916	LSWR	Service withdrawn between Addison Road and Studland Road Junction 1916
RICKMANSWORTH	1 / 4A	1887	N/A	MET	Goods yard closed 1966
Rickmansworth High Street					
Rickmansworth					
RICKMANSWORTH (CHURCH STREET)	7 / 1B	1862	1952 (1966)	LNWR	Branch from Watford Junction; closed to passengers 1952 and freight in 1966
Rickmansworth					
RICKMANSWORTH NORTH SIDINGS	1 / 4A	?	N/A	MET	Stabling Sidings for Metropolitan Line
RICKMANSWORTH SOUTH SIDINGS	1 / 4B	1966	N/A	MET	Stabling Sidings for Metropolitan Line, On site of former goods yard
RIDDLESDOWN	47 / 4B	1927	N/A	SR	
Riddlesdown Tunnel	47 / 4B	1884	N/A	LBSCR & SER	
RIPPLE LANE FREIGHTLINER TERMINAL	25 / 3B	1972	N/A	BR	
RIPPLE LANE YARD	25 / 3B	1937	N/A	LMS	
RODING VALLEY (LNER)	14 / 1B	1936	1947	LNER	Fairlop Loop closed 1947 to allow electrification and transfer to LT Central Line. Freight traffic remained until 1965
RODING VALLEY (LT)	14 / 1B	1948	N/A	LT (CEN)	First served by LT Central Line Trains 1948
ROMFORD	16 / 4B	1839	N/A	ECR	
Romford for Hornchurch, Upminster & Corbet's Tey					
Romford					
ROMFORD FACTORY	16 / 1A	1843	?	ECR	Locomotive Works until 1847 then wagon cover factory after 1854
ROTHERHITHE	33 / 1A	1869	N/A	ELR	First served District and Metropolitan Railways 1884, last served District 1905. No service Metropolitan Railway 1906-1913. Became 'East London Line' in 1980s. Closed 1995-1998. Again closed 2007 due to East London Line extension works, to re-open 2010
ROYAL AGRICULTURAL SHOW SIDING	20 / 3A	?	?	PRIV	
ROYAL ALBERT	24 / 4B	1994	N/A	DLR	
ROYAL BETHLEM HOSPITAL	43 / 4B	1928	1930	PRIV	3/4 Mile siding from Eden Park in use during construction of the Hospital
ROYAL DOCKYARD (WOOLWICH)	34 / 1B	?	?	PRIV	
ROYAL MINT STREET GOODS	23 / 4A & 7 / 3A	1858	1951	LBR	
Royal Mint Street Junction	23 / 4A & 7 / 3A	1991	N/A	DLR	
ROYAL OAK	21 / 4A & 62	1871	N/A	MET & GWR	
ROYAL VICTORIA	24 / 4A	1994	N/A	DLR	
RUGBY ROAD	30 / 1B	1909	1917	N&SWJR	Passenger services withdrawn from Hammersmith & Chiswick Branch 1917
RUISLIP	18 / 1A	1904	N/A	MET	Served by District Line Trains 1910-1933, Piccadilly Line thereafter. Goods yard closed 1964
RUISLIP DEPOT	18 / 1A	1948	N/A	LT (CEN)	Depot for Central Line and Transplant (Engineering)
RUISLIP GARDENS (GCR / GWR)	18 / 1A	1934	1958	GCR / GWR	
RUISLIP GARDENS (LT)	18 / 1A	1948	N/A	LT (CEN)	
RUISLIP GOODS	18 / 1A	1905	1964	MET	
RUISLIP MANOR	18 / 1A	1912	N/A	MET	Served by District Line Trains 1912-1933, Piccadilly Line trains thereafter. Closed 1917-1919
RUSSELL SQUARE	22/ 4A	1906	N/A	GNP&BR	

S

NAME	PAGE / GRID	YEAR OPENED	YEAR CLOSED	OPENED BY	NOTES
Salmons Lane Junction	23 / 4B	1880	1962	LTSR	
SANDERSTEAD	47 / 2B	1884	N/A	LBSCR & SER	
SANDILANDS	48 / 1A	2000	N/A	CTL	
Sandilands Tunnels	48 / 1A	1885	N/A	SER	Closed 1983 along with Woodside to Selsdon, but re-opened 2000 by Croydon Tramlink
SELHURST	42 / 4B	1865	N/A	LBSCR	

NAME: (Previous names indented below)	PAGE / GRID:	YEAR OPENED:	YEAR CLOSED:	OPENED BY:	NOTES:
SELHURST DEPOT	42 / 4B	1911	N/A	LBSCR	
Selhurst Junctions	42 / 4B	1862	N/A	LBSCR	
SELSDON	47 / 2B	1885	1983	LBSCR & SER	Woodside to Selsdon closed 1916-1935, 'Road' dropped 1935, Oxted Line platforms closed 1959
Selsdon Road					Woodside platforms closed for good 1983. Goods yard closed 1968, oil terminal until 1993
SEVEN KINGS	25 / 1A	1899	N/A	GER	
Seven Kings West Junction	25 / 1A	1903	1956	GER	Link between Newbury Park and Seven Kings dismantled 1956
SEVEN SISTERS	12 / 4B	1872	N/A	GER	Victoria Line station opened 1968
SEVEN SISTERS (Palace Gates Platforms)	12 / 4B	1878	1963	GER	Platforms for Palace Gates Branch, closed to passengers 1963
Seven Sisters Junction	12 / 4B	(1879) 1880	N/A	GER	Junction with curve to Tottenham & Hampstead Junction Railway.
					Curve opened to goods 1879, passengers 1880. No passenger services 1963-1989, singled 1977
Shacklegate Junction	39 / 2A	1894	N/A	LSWR	
SHADWELL & ST GEORGES EAST	23 / 4A	1840	1941	LBR	Renamed 1900. Closed 1916-1919
Shadwell					
SHADWELL	23 / 4A	1876	N/A	ELR	First served District and Metropolitan Railways 1884, last served District 1905. No service
Shadwell & St Georges-in-the-East					Metropolitan Railway 1906-1913. Became 'East London Line' in 1980s. DLR platforms opened
					1987. East London Line platforms closed 1995-1998 & 2007-2010
Sheet Factory Junction	53	1846	1973	ECR	Eastern Curve at Stratford dismantled 1973
SHELL MEX & BP (ANGERSTEIN WHARF)	34 / 1A	?	?	PRIV	
SHEPHERD'S BUSH (CLR)	31 / 1A & 49	1900	N/A	CLR	Terminus of Central London Railway 1900-1908. Sometimes has suffix 'Green' added
SHEPHERD'S BUSH (GWR & MET)	49	1864	1869	MET & GWR	Station opened on 1864 Spur from Metropolitan and Great Western Railways' line to
					Hammersmith. Replaced by Uxbridge Road Station to South in 1869
SHEPHERD'S BUSH (LSWR)	30 / 1B & 49	1869	1916	LSWR	Addison Road to Studland Road Junction abandoned 1916
SHEPHERD'S BUSH (MET) (1st)	30 / 1B & 49	1864	1914	MET & GWR	Replaced by Shepherd's Bush (2nd) to North and Goldhawk Road to South
SHEPHERD'S BUSH (NR)	31 / 1A & 49	2008	N/A	NR	On site of former Uxbridge Road Station
SHEPHERD'S BUSH (WLR)	49	1844	1844	WLR	Initial passenger service on West London Railway withdrawn after 6 months
					When services resumed in 1862 original 1844 Shepherd's Bush Station did not re-open
SHEPHERD'S BUSH MARKET	30 / 1B & 49	1914	N/A	MET & GWR	Replaced Shepherd's Bush (1st) to South. Renamed 2008
Shepherd's Bush (MET) (2nd)					
Shepherd's Lane Junction	32 / 3A	1991	N/A	BR	Connection built for Eurostar access to North Pole Depot
SHEPPERTON	37 / 4B	1864	N/A	LSWR	
Shepperton for Halliford					
SHERN HALL STREET WALTHAMSTOW	13 / 3B	1870	1873	GER	Terminus of branch from Stratford 1870-1873
SHERWOOD HOSPITAL & POWER STATION	45 / 3A	1918	1950	PRIV	Horton Estate Light Railway opened to supply building materials, later fuel, to hospitals
SHOREDITCH (NLR)	22 / 3B	1865	1941	NLR	
SHOREDITCH (ELR)	23 / 4A & 59	1876	2006	ELR	Closed 2006 to allow extension work to commence. Line beyond platforms severed 1966.
					Closed 1995-1998.
SHOREDITCH (DUNLOE STREET) GOODS DEPOT	23 / 3A	1893	1968	NLR	
SHOREDITCH HIGH STREET	23 / 4A & 59	2010	N/A	NR (LOROL)	To open 2010 as part of East London Line Extension Phase 1
SHORTLANDS	44 / 3A	1858	N/A	LCDR	
New Bromley					
Shortlands Junction	44 / 3A	1892	N/A	LCDR	Remodelled as a 'flying' junction 2003
SIDCUP	35 / 4B	1866	N/A	SER	Goods yard closed 1966
Silk Stream Junctions	10 / 3B	?	N/A	MID	Junction between Midland Main Line and freight flyover
SILVER STREET	13 / 2A	1872	N/A	GER	
SILVERTOWN & LONDON CITY AIRPORT	34 / 1B	1863	2006	ECR	Stratford to North Woolwich closed 2006
Silvertown					
SLADE GREEN	36 / 3B	1900	N/A	SECR	Renamed 1953
Slades Green					
SLADE GREEN DEPOT	36 / 3B	1901	N/A	SECR	Converted for EMU use 1924 (previously Steam depot)
Slade Green Junction	36 / 3B	1895	N/A	SER	
SLOANE SQUARE	31 / 2B	1868	N/A	MDR	
SMALLBERRY GREEN	29 / 3A	1849	1850	LSWR	Opened as 'Hounslow'. Terminus 1849-1850. Replaced by Isleworth Station to West.
Hounslow					
SMITHAM	47 / 4A	1904	N/A	SECR	Closed 1917-1919. Goods yard closed 1962
SMITHFIELD GOODS	22 / 4B & 55	1869	1962	GWR	
Smithfield Sidings	55	1990	N/A	BR	On site of former sidings (x 4), re-laid as part of 'Thameslink' project
Smithfield Tunnel	55	1866	2009	MET	Farringdon to Moorgate (NR) closed 2009 due to platform lengthening at Farringdon
SMITHS SIDING (FELTHAM)	38 / 1A	?	?	PRIV	
SNARESBROOK (ECR)	14 / 4A	1856	1970	ECR	Majority of passenger services transferred to LT in 1947. First trains in the morning
Snaresbrook for Wanstead					remained British Rail services until 1970
Snaresbrook & Wanstead					
Snaresbrook					
SNARESBROOK (LT)	14 / 4A	1947	N/A	LT (CEN)	First served by LT Central Line trains in 1947. Goods yard closed 1949
Snow Hill Tunnel	55	1866	N/A	LCDR	Track lifted through tunnel between 1969 and 1988, no passenger service 1916 - 1988
SOMERS TOWN GOODS	22 / 3A & 54	1887	1968	MID	British Library now on site
St Pancras New Goods					
SOUTH ACTON (N&SWJR)	30 / 1A & 40 / 1A	1880	N/A	N&SWJR	
South Acton Junction	30 / 1A & 40 / 1A	1869	N/A	N&SWJR	
SOUTH ACTON (MDR)	30 / 1A & 40 / 1A	1905	1959	MDR	South Acton curve opened 1899 in connection with construction of South Harrow extension.
					First passenger trains 1905, last freight trains 1914. Passenger service withdrawn 1959.
SOUTH BERMONDSEY (1st)	33 / 1A & 52	1869	1928	LBSCR	Renamed December 1869. Closed 1917-1919
Rotherhithe					
SOUTH BERMONDSEY (2nd)	33 / 2A & 52	1928	N/A	SR	
South Bermondsey Junction	52	1869	N/A	LBSCR	

NAME: (Previous names indented below)	PAGE / GRID:	YEAR OPENED:	YEAR CLOSED:	OPENED BY:	NOTES:
SOUTHALL	28 / 1B	1839	N/A	GWR	
Southall West Junction	28 / 1B	1859	N/A	GWR	
SOUTH BROMLEY	23 / 4B	1884	1944	NLR	Passenger service Dalston Junction to Poplar withdrawn 1944
SOUTHBURY	5 / 4A	1960	N/A	BR	Opened 1960 on site of former Churchbury Station. Goods yard closed 1970
SOUTH CROYDON	47 / 2B	1865	N/A	LBSCR	
South Croydon Junction	47 / 2B	1884	N/A	LBSCR & SER	
SOUTH DOCK	33 / 1B	1871	N/A	LBR	
South West India Dock					
South Dock					
SOUTH EALING	29 / 1B	1883	N/A	MDR	First served by Piccadilly Line 1933. Last served by District Line 1964
SOUTH EASTERN GAS WORKS	34 / 1A	1889	1978	PRIV	
Southern Junction (Stratford)	53	1847	1981	ECR	Western Curve at Stratford dismantled 1981
SOUTHFIELDS	41 / 1A	1889	N/A	LSWR	Putney Bridge to Wimbldeon built by LSWR but operated by District Railway from opening. Last regular main line passenger service withdrawn 1941, although services called on occasions until 1969. Point Pleasant Jcn to Wimbledon still used for empty stock working and diversions.
SOUTHGATE	12 / 1A	1933	N/A	LT (PIC)	
SOUTH GREENFORD	19 / 3A	1926	N/A	GWR	
South Greenford Halt					
SOUTH HAMPSTEAD	21 / 2B	1879	N/A	LNWR	Closed in 1917, re-opened and renamed 1922
Loudoun Road					
SOUTH HAREFIELD HALT	17 / 1B	1928	1931	GCR & GWR	
Harefield Halt					
SOUTH HARROW (1st)	19 / 1A	1903	1935	MDR	Terminus 1903-1910. First served Piccadilly Line 1932. Last served District Line 1933.
SOUTH HARROW (2nd)	19 / 1A	1935	N/A	LT (PIC)	Station relocated 1935
SOUTH HARROW SIDINGS	19 / 1A	1903	N/A	MDR	Stabling sidings (formerly depot) for Piccadilly Line (previously District Railway)
South Harrow Tunnel	19 / 2A	1906	N/A	GCR	
South Junction (Mitcham)	42 / 4A	1855	1997	LBSCR & WCR	Junction eliminated when Wimbldeon to Croydon line closed 1997
SOUTH KENSINGTON	31 / 2B & 56	1868	N/A	MDR	Initial section of Metropolitan District Railway Gloucester Road to Westminster (Bridge) opened 1868 but operated by Metropolitan Railway. Separate District platforms opened 1871. GNP&BR platforms opened 1907.
SOUTH KENTISH TOWN	22 / 2A	1907	1924	CCE&HR	
SOUTH KENTON	19 / 1B	1933	N/A	LNWR	Served by Bakerloo Line Trains 1917-1982, 1984-Present
SOUTH LAMBETH FREIGHT DEPOT	32 / 2A & 51	1863	1980	GWR	
SOUTH MERTON	41 / 3A	1929	N/A	SR	
SOUTH METROPOLITAN GAS COMPANY	34 / 1A	?	?	PRIV	
SOUTH QUAY	33 / 1B	1987	N/A	DLR	
SOUTH RUISLIP	18 / 2B	1908	N/A	GCR & GWR	First served by Central Line Trains 1948
South Ruislip & Northolt Junction					
Northolt Junction					
SOUTH SHED (QUEENS PARK)	21 / 3A	1915	N/A	UERL (BAK)	Stabling Shed for Bakerloo Line
SOUTH TOTTENHAM	13 / 4A	1871	N/A	T&HJ	
South Tottenham & Stamford Hill					
South Tottenham Junction	13 / 4A	(1879) 1880	N/A	GER	Junction between Tottenham & Hampstead Junction Railway and curve to GER. Curve opened to goods 1879, passenger 1880. No passenger services 1963-1989, singled 1977
SOUTHWARK	32 / 1B	1999	N/A	LUL (JUB)	
SOUTHWARK PARK	33 / 1A & 52	1902	1915	SECR	
Corbett's Lane					
SOUTH WEST SIDINGS	20 / 3B & 60	?	N/A	N&SWJR	
SOUTH WIMBLEDON	41 / 2A	1926	N/A	UERL (NOR)	(Merton) suffix added 1928, but gradually dropped
South Wimbledon (Merton)					
South Wimbledon					
SOUTH WOODFORD	14 / 3A	1947	N/A	LT (CEN)	First served by LT Central Line Trains 1947. On site of George Lane (Woodford) Station
South Woodford (George Lane)					'George Lane' suffix dropped 1950. Goods yard closed 1964
SPA ROAD, BERMONDSEY	33 / 1A	1843	1915	LGR	Replaced original station to West
Spa Road & Bermondsey					
SPA ROAD & BERMONDSEY	33 / 1A	1836	1843	LGR	Temporary terminus of London & Greenwich Railway during 1836. Resited East 1843.
SPENCER ROAD HALT	47 / 2B	1906	1915	SER	
SPITALFIELDS GOODS	23 / 4A	?	1967	GER	
SQUARE GRIP REINFORCEMENTS LTD (COLNBROOK)	27 / 2A	1957	?	PRIV	
Spur Junction	43 / 3A	1862	1972	LCDR	Bromley Spur disused since 1966 but not dismantled until 1972
STAINES	37 2A & 3B	1849	N/A	LSWR	Suffix 'Junction' 1885-1923, suffix 'Central' 1923-1966
Staines Central					Goods yard closed 1973
Staines Junction					
Staines Old					
Staines					
Staines Bridge	37 / 4A	1856	N/A	LSWR	
STAINES CARRIAGE SIDINGS	37 / 2A	?	N/A	LSWR	
Staines East Junction	37 / 3B	1856	N/A	LSWR	
STAINES HIGH STREET	37 / 2A & 3B	1887	1916	LSWR	Proposed to re-open 2014 as part of 'Airtrack' project
STAINES LINOLEUM WORKS	37 / 3B	1887	1957	PRIV	
Staines Moor Junction	37 / 3A	1940	1947	SR	Established during World War II to provide an alternative route in case of bomb damage
STAINES WEST	37 / 2A & 3A	1885	1965	GWR	'West' suffix added 1949. Passenger service West Drayton to Staines West withdrawn 1965
Staines					
Staines West Curve	37 / 3B	1877	1965	LSWR	Proposed to re-open 2014 as part of 'Airtrack' project

NAME: (Previous names indented below)	PAGE / GRID:	YEAR OPENED:	YEAR CLOSED:	OPENED BY:	NOTES:
STAINES WEST GOODS	37 / 3A	1885	1953	GWR	Later became oil terminal
Staines West Junction	37 / 3A	1981	1991	BR	Established for access to Staines West oil terminal after M25 severed route to West Drayton
					Still in situ but disused
STAINES WEST OIL TERMINAL (SHELL / BP)	37 / 3A	1964	1991	PRIV	
STAMFORD BROOK	30 / 2B	1912	N/A	MDR	Platforms only built for District Line
STAMFORD HILL	12 / 4B	1872	N/A	GER	
STANMORE	9 / 2B	1932	N/A	MET	Opened by Metropolitan Railway. Transferred to Bakerloo Line 1939, Jubilee Line 1979
					Goods yard closed 1936 (Now sidings). Platform 3 to open 2009.
STANMORE SIDINGS	9 / 2B	1932	N/A	MET	Stabling sidngs for Jubilee Line (previously Metropolitan Railway then Bakerloo Line)
STANMORE VILLAGE	9 / 2B	1890	1952 *(1964)*	LNWR	'Village' suffix added 1950. Stanmore Village to Belmont closed to passengers 1952,
Stanmore					Freight remained until 1964
ST ANNS ROAD	12 / 4B	1882	1942	T&HJ	
STAR LANE	24 / 4A	2010	N/A	DLR	Canning Town to Stratford International DLR extension to open 2010
STEPNEY GREEN	23 / 4A	1902	N/A	MDR & LTSR	Served by Metropolitan Line since 1936 ('Hammersmith & City Line' since 1990)
STEWARTS LANE (LBSCR)	32 / 3A & 51	1858	1858	LBSCR	Opened by West End of London & Crystal Palace Railway, but operated by LBSCR from outset
STEWARTS LANE (LCDR)	32 / 3A & 51	1863	1866	LCDR	
STEWARTS LANE DEPOT	32 / 3A & 51	1862	N/A	LCDR	
STEWARTS LANE GOODS	32 / 3A & 51	1862	1970	LCDR	
Stewarts Lane Junction	51	1862	N/A	LCDR	
ST HELIER	41 / 4A	1930	N/A	SR	Goods yard closed 1963
St James Road Junction	42 / 4B	1862	1984	LBSCR	
ST JAMES'S PARK	32 / 1A	1868	N/A	MDR	Also spelt 'St James' Park'
ST JAMES STREET WALTHAMSTOW	13 / 4B	1870	N/A	GER	
ST JOHN'S	33 / 3B	1873	N/A	SER	
ST JOHN'S WOOD	21 / 3B	1939	N/A	LT (BAK)	Opened by Bakerloo Line, transferred to Jubilee Line 1979
STOKE NEWINGTON	23 / 1A	1872	N/A	GER	
ST MARGARETS	29 / 4B	1876	N/A	LSWR	
St Mary Cray Junctions	44 / 3B	1904	N/A	SECR	
ST MARY'S (WHITECHAPEL ROAD)	23 / 4A & 59	1884	1938	MDR & MET	Renamed 1923. Closed due to Aldgate East being relocated eastwards
St Mary's					
St Mary's Curve	59	1884	1939 *(2007)*	MDR	Last passenger service 1939, stock transfer until 2007
St Mary's Junction	59	1884	1939 *(2007)*	MDR	Last passenger service 1939, stock transfer until 2007
STOAT'S NEST	47 / 4A	1841	1856	L&BR	
Stoat's Nest Junction	47 / 4A	1899	N/A	LBSCR	
STOAT'S NEST QUARRY	48 / 3A	?	?	PRIV	
Stockley Park Flyover	27 / 1B	1998	N/A	RT (HEX)	
STOCKWELL	32 / 3A	1890	N/A	C&SLR	Terminus of City & South London Railway 1890-1900. Closed 1923-1924
					Victoria Line platforms opened 1971
STONEBRIDGE PARK	20 / 2A	1912	N/A	LNWR	Served by Bakerloo Line Trains since 1917. Terminus of Bakerloo services 1982-1984
STONEBRIDGE PARK DEPOT	20 / 2A	1982	N/A	LT (BAK)	Bakerloo Line Depot
STONEBRIDGE PARK GOODS	20 / 2A	?	?	LNWR	
STONELEIGH	45 / 2B	1932	N/A	SR	
ST PANCRAS INTERNATIONAL	22 / 3A & 54	1868	N/A	MID	Extensively rebuilt for Eurostar services, 'Thameslink' platforms and 'International'
St Pancras					suffix added 2007
ST PANCRAS GOODS	22 / 3A & 54	1862	1968	MID	Initial access via GNR, full opening in 1868
ST PAUL'S	22 / 4B	1900	N/A	CLR	Renamed 1937
Post Office					
ST QUINTIN PARK & WORMWOOD SCRUBS (1st)	20 / 4B	1871	1893	WLR	Relocated North 1893
Wormwood Scrubs					
ST QUINTIN PARK & WORMWOOD SCRUBS (2nd)	20 / 4B	1893	1940	LNWR	Replaced original station to South
Strand-on-the-Green Bridge	30 / 2A	1869	N/A	LSWR	
STRATFORD	24 / 2A	1839	N/A	ECR	Central Line platforms opened 1946, DLR 1987, Jubilee Line 1999. 'Low Level' NR platforms
Stratford (West Ham)					replaced by platforms 12a & 12b 2009 for terminating LOROL services, then being converted for
Stratford					DLR use (Stratford International extension), re-opening 2010
Stratford Central Junction East	53	1840	N/A	ECR	
Stratford Central Junction West	53	1854	N/A	ECR	
STRATFORD FREIGHTLINER TERMINAL	23 / 2B & 53	?	1998	BR	Closed 1998
STRATFORD GOODS	24 / 2A & 53	?	?	GER	
STRATFORD HIGH STREET	24 / 3A	2010	N/A	DLR	Canning Town to Stratford International DLR to open 2010. On site of Stratford Market
STRATFORD INTERNATIONAL	23 / 2B & 53	2009	N/A	L&CR	Canning Town to Stratford International DLR extension to open 2010
STRATFORD MARKET	24 / 3A	1847	1957	ECR	'Stratford Bridge' until 1880
Stratford Market (West Ham)					
Stratford Market					
Stratford Bridge					
STRATFORD MARKET	24 / 3A	1879	1988	GER	Fruit & Vegetable Market, Closed 1984. Sidings retained for engineering use until 1988
STRATFORD MARKET DEPOT	24 / 3A	1999	N/A	LUL (JUB)	Jubilee Line Depot, on site of former Stratford Market
STRATFORD TRACTION MAINTENANCE DEPOT (TMD)	53	1841	2001	ECR	Relocated to Temple Mills due to Channel Tunnel Rail Link works at Stratford
STRATFORD TRACTION MAINTENANCE DEPOT (TMD)	23 / 1B	2001	2007	EWS	Relocated depot closed and replaced by Orient Way Sidings 2007
STRAWBERRY HILL	39 / 1A	1873	N/A	LSWR	
STRAWBERRY HILL DEPOT	39 / 2A	1916	N/A	LSWR	On site of Fulwell Loco Depot. Last used for steam locos 1923
Strawberry Hill Junction	39 / 1A	1864	N/A	LSWR	
STREATHAM	42 / 2A	1868	N/A	LBSCR	
STREATHAM COMMON	42 / 2A	1862	N/A	LBSCR	'Greyhound Lane' suffix dropped 1870
Streatham Common (Greyhound Lane)					
Streatham Common					

NAME: (Previous names indented below)	PAGE / GRID:	YEAR OPENED:	YEAR CLOSED:	OPENED BY:	NOTES:
STREATHAM COMMON GOODS	42 / 2A	?	?	LBSCR	
Streatham Common Junction	42 / 2A	1886	N/A	LBSCR	
STREATHAM HILL	42 / 1A	1856	N/A	LBSCR	Opened by West End of London & Crystal Palace Railway, but operated by LBSCR from outset
Streatham & Brixton Hill					'Streatham' until 1868
Streatham					
STREATHAM HILL DEPOT	42 / 1A	1936	N/A	SR	
Streatham Junction	42 / 2A	1886	N/A	LBSCR	
Streatham North Junction	42 / 2A	1868	N/A	LBSCR	
Streatham South Junctions A & B	42 / 2A	1868	N/A	LBSCR	
Streatham South Junction C	42 / 2A	1868	N/A	LSWR & LBSCR	
Streatham Tunnel	42 / 1A	1868	N/A	LBSCR	
STROUD GREEN	12 / 4A	1881	1954	GNR	Closed when Alexandra Palace to Finsbury Park service withdrawn 1954. Had been intended
					for electrification and transfer to LT Northern Line, but works abandoned post-WW2
Studland Road Junction	30 / 2B	1877	1916	LSWR & MDR	Addison Road to Studland Road Junction abandoned 1916
SUDBURY & HARROW ROAD	19 / 2B	1906	N/A	GCR	Goods yard closed 1965
SUDBURY HILL	19 / 2A	1903	N/A	MDR	First served Piccadilly Line 1932, last served District Line 1933
Sudbury Hill for Greenford Green					
SUDBURY HILL HARROW	19 / 2A	1906	N/A	GCR	Renamed 1926. Goods yard closed 1965
South Harrow					
Sudbury Junction	20 / 3A	?	N/A	LNWR	
SUDBURY TOWN	19 / 2B	1903	N/A	MDR	First served Piccadilly Line 1932, last served District Line 1933
Sudbury Town for Horsendon					
SUNBURY	38 / 3A	1864	N/A	LSWR	
SUNDRIDGE PARK	44 / 2A	1878	N/A	SER	Renamed 1894
Plaistow					
SURBITON	39 / 4B	1838	N/A	LSWR	
Surbiton & Kingston					
Kingston Junction					
Kingston					
SURREY CANAL ROAD	33 / 2A & 52	2011	N/A	NR (LOROL)	Projected to open as part of East London Line Extension Phase 2
SURREY QUAYS	33 / 1A & 52	1869	N/A	ELR	First served District and Metropolitan Railways 1884, last served District 1905. No service
Surrey Docks					Metropolitan Railway 1906-1913. Renamed 'Surrey Docks' 1911. Became 'East London Line' in
Deptford Road					1980s. Renamed 'Surrey Quays' 1989. Closed 1995-1998. Again closed 2007 for extension work
					to re-open 2010
SUTTON	46 / 2B	1847	N/A	LBSCR	
SUTTON COMMON	46 / 1A	1930	N/A	SR	
Sutton East Junction	46 / 2B	1868	N/A	LBSCR	
Sutton West Junction	46 / 2A	1930	N/A	SR	
SWISS COTTAGE (MET)	21 / 2B	1868	1940	MET	Terminus of branch from Baker Street 1868-1879
SWISS COTTAGE (JUB)	21 / 2B	1939	N/A	LT (BAK)	Opened by Bakerloo Line, transferred to Jubilee Line 1979
SYDENHAM	43 / 2A	1839	N/A	LCR	East London Line projected to serve from 2010
Sydenham Down Junction	43 / 2A	1854	N/A	LBSCR	
SYDENHAM GASWORKS	43 / 1B	1878	1971	PRIV	Gasworks ceased production in late 1960's but railway connection not removed until 1971
SYDENHAM HILL	43 / 1A	1863	N/A	LCDR	
Sydenham Up Junction	43 / 2A	1854	N/A	LBSCR	
SYON LANE	29 / 2B	1931	N/A	SR	

T

NAME:	PAGE / GRID:	YEAR OPENED:	YEAR CLOSED:	OPENED BY:	NOTES:
TADWORTH	47 / 3A	1900	N/A	SECR	Goods yard closed 1962
Tadworth & Walton on the Hill					
Tanners Hill Junction	33 / 3B	1976	N/A	BR	
TARMAC STONE TERMINAL (HAYES)	28 / 1A	?	N/A	PRIV	
TARMAC STONE TERMINAL (STEWARTS LANE)	32 / 3A & 51	?	N/A	PRIV	
TATTENHAM CORNER	47 / 2A	1901	N/A	SECR	Closed 1914-1928. Goods yard closed 1962
TEDDINGTON	39 / 2B	1863	N/A	LSWR	'Bushey' also spelt 'Bushy' at times. Goods yard closed 1965
Teddington for Bushey Park					
Teddington & Bushey Park					
Teddington (Bushey Park)					
TEMPLE	22 / 4A	1870	N/A	MDR	'The' prefix dropped gradually
The Temple					
Temple Mills East Junction	23 / 2B & 53	1862	N/A	GER	
TEMPLE MILLS EUROSTAR DEPOT	23 / 1B	2007	N/A	NR (ES)	Partly on site of Temple Mills Marshalling Yard.
TEMPLE MILLS YARD	23 / 1B	1959	N/A	BR	No longer used as a Marshalling yard; some engineering use.
THAMES DITTON	39 / 4A	1851	N/A	LSWR	
Thames Tunnel (1)	16 / 3B	2007	N/A	L&CR	
Thames Tunnel (2)	33 / 1A	1843	N/A	ECR	Opened to pedestrian traffic 1843, first trains ran through tunnel 1869
THAMES WHARF	24 / 4A	1846	1965	ECR	Midland Railway goods yard opened 1870
THAMES WHARF	34 / 1A	N/A	N/A	DLR	Proposed station
Thames Wharf Junction	24 / 4A	1847	1965	ECR	
THEOBALDS GROVE (1st)	5 / 1A	1891	1919	GER	Closed 1909-1915
THEOBALDS GROVE (2nd)	5 / 1A	1960	N/A	BR	Opened 1960 on site of former Theobalds Grove Station. Goods yard closed 1967
THERAPIA LANE	42 / 4A	2000	N/A	CTL	

NAME: (Previous names indented below)	PAGE / GRID:	YEAR OPENED:	YEAR CLOSED:	OPENED BY:	NOTES:
THERAPIA LANE DEPOT	42 / 4A	2000	N/A	CTL	Maintenance and stabling for London Tramlink Croydon
THEYDON BOIS (GER)	6 / 3A	1865	1970	GER	Majority of Passenger services transferred to LT in 1949. First Trains in the morning
Theydon					remained British Rail services until 1970
THEYDON BOIS (LT)	6 / 3A	1949	N/A	LT (CEN)	First served by Central Line Trains 1949. Goods yard closed 1966
THORNEY MILL SIDINGS	27 / 1A	1943	N/A	GWR	Formerly used for Coal, Oil, Scrap metal and Stone traffic, today only Stone traffic remains.
THORNEY MILL STONE TERMINAL (BARDON)	27 / 1A	1986	N/A	PRIV	
THORNTON FIELD CARRIAGE SIDINGS	23 / 3B & 53	1928	2008	GER	Site cleared for 2012 Olympic park. Replaced by Orient Way Sidings
THORNTON HEATH	42 / 3B	1862	N/A	LBSCR	
TIDAL BASIN	24 / 4A	1858	1943	ECR	
Tilbury Junction	23 / 3B & 57	1869	1959	NLR	Junction between NLR and curve to LTSR at Bromley
TOLWORTH	45 / 1A	1938	N/A	SR	
TOOTING	41 / 2B	1894	N/A	LSWR & LBSCR	Replaced Tooting Junction Station to West. Closed 1917-1923, renamed 1938
Tooting Junction					Junction severed 1934 and line to Merton Park became a siding accessed from that station
TOOTING BEC	41 / 1B	1926	N/A	UERL (NOR)	Renamed 1950
Trinity Road (Tooting Bec)					
TOOTING BROADWAY	41 / 2B	1926	N/A	UERL (NOR)	
TOOTING JUNCTION	41 / 2B	1868	1894	LSWR & LBSCR	Resited to East (Tooting Station)
TOTTENHAM COURT ROAD	22 / 4A	1900	N/A	CLR	CCE&HR platforms opened 1907 as 'Oxford Street', renamed 1908
Oxford Street (CCE&HR only)					Platforms for 'Crossrail 1' proposed to open 2017
Tottenham Curve Tunnels 1, 2 & 3	57	1883	N/A	MID	
TOTTENHAM HALE	13 / 3A	1840	N/A	ECR	Victoria Line station opened and 'Hale' suffix added 1968
Tottenham					
Tottenham North Junction	13 / 4A	1868	1961	T&HJ	North curve to Lea Valley Line dismantled 1961
Tottenham South Junction	13 / 4A	1868	N/A	T&HJ	Junction between Tottenham & Hampstead Junction Railway and Lea Valley Line
Tottenham West Junction	13 / 4A	1868	1961	T&HJ	North curve to Lea Valley Line dismantled 1961
TOTTERIDGE & WHETSTONE (GNR)	11 / 1B	1872	1939	GNR	Closed in 1939 to enable electrification and transfer to LT Northern Line
Totteridge					
TOTTERIDGE & WHETSTONE (LT)	11 / 1B	1940	N/A	LT (NOR)	On site of former GNR station. Goods yard closed 1962
TOWER GATEWAY	23 / 4A & 7 / 3A	1987	N/A	DLR	Closed 2008-2009 (rebuilding)
TOWER HILL	22 / 4B	1884	1967	MDR & MET	Replaced former 'Tower of London' Station to East. Renamed 1946, relocated East 1967
Mark Lane					
TOWER HILL	23 / 4A & 7 / 3A	1967	N/A	LT (DIS)	Replaced Tower Hill (formerly Mark Lane) Station to West. On site of former 'Tower of London'
TOWER OF LONDON	23 / 4A & 7 / 3A	1882	1884	MET	Terminus of Metropolitan Railway extension from Aldgate 1882-1884, replaced by Mark Lane
					(later Tower Hill [1st]) station to West. Present Tower Hill Station on site of 'Tower of London'
TRIANGLE SIDINGS	31 / 2A & 50	1957	N/A	LT (DIS)	Built partially on site of Cromwell Curve. Stabling sidings for District and Circle Lines
TRUMPER'S CROSSING HALTE	29 / 1A	1904	1926	GWR	Closed 1915-1920
Trumper's Crossing Halte for South Hanwell and Osterley Park					
TUFNELL PARK	22 / 1A & 57	1907	N/A	CCE&HR	
TUFNELL PARK GOODS	22 / 1A	1886	1968	T&HJ	
TULSE HILL	42 / 1B	1868	N/A	LBSCR	
Tulse Hill North Junction	42 / 1B	1869	N/A	LBSCR	
Tulse Hill South Junction	42 / 1B	1870	N/A	LBSCR	
TURKEY STREET	5 / 2A	1960	N/A	BR	Opened 1960 on site of former Forty Hill Station. Goods yard closed 1966
TURNHAM GREEN	30 / 2B & 40 / 1B	1869	N/A	LSWR	Opened by LSWR. First served District and Metropolitan railways 1877, last served Metropolitan
					Railway 1906, last served LSWR 1916. Restricted Piccadilly Line service since 1963
TURNPIKE LANE	12 / 3B	1932	N/A	LT (PIC)	
TWICKENHAM (1st)	29 / 4B	1849	1954	LSWR	Relocated east 1954
TWICKENHAM (2nd)	29 / 4B	1954	N/A	BR	Replaced earlier station to west. Goods yard closed 1967
Twickenham Junction	29 / 4A	1863	N/A	LSWR	
TWYFORD ABBEY HALT	20 / 3A	1904	1911	GWR	

U

NAME:	PAGE / GRID:	YEAR OPENED:	YEAR CLOSED:	OPENED BY:	NOTES:
UNITED GLASS	34 / 2A	?	?	PRIV	
UPMINSTER	16 / 2B	1885	N/A	LTSR	Served by District Railway since 1902, no service 1905-1932. Goods yard closed 1964
UPMINSTER BRIDGE	16 / 2A	1934	N/A	LMS	Station on new Slow Lines opened between Barking and Upminster 1932. Served by District
					Line trains from opening, Main line services ceased 1962.
UPMINSTER DEPOT	16 / 2B	1958	N/A	LT (DIS)	District Line depot
UPNEY	25 / 2A	1932	N/A	LMS	Barking to Upminster quadrupled by the LMS in 1932 and Upney station opened.
					Served by District Line from opening. Ownership transferred to LT in 1970.
UPPER HALLIFORD	38 / 3A	1944	N/A	SR	
Upper Halliford Halt					
Halliford Halt					
UPPER HOLLOWAY	22 / 1A	1868	N/A	T&HJ	Renamed with 'for St Johns Park and Highgate Hill' suffix 1871, 'and Highgate Hill' dropped 1875
Upper Holloway for St John's Park					suffix 'for St Johns Park' dropped 1903
Upper Holloway for St Johns Park and Highgate Hill					
Upper Holloway					
UPPER SYDENHAM	43 / 1A	1884	1954	LCDR	Closed 1917-1919 and 1944-1946. Nunhead to Crystal Palace (High Level) closed 1954
UPPER WARLINGHAM	48 / 3B	1884	N/A	LBSCR & SER	
Upper Warlingham for Riddlesdown					
Upeer Warlingham & Whyteleafe					
Upper Warlingham					
UP SIDINGS (HAYES)	28 / 1A	?	N/A	GWR	S&T Sidings - Disused

NAME: (Previous names indented below)	PAGE / GRID:	YEAR OPENED:	YEAR CLOSED:	OPENED BY:	NOTES:
Up Slow Flyover (Wimbledon)	41 / 1A	1937	N/A	SR	
UPTON PARK (LTSR)	24 / 3B	1877	1962	LTSR	Main Line services non-stopped since 1962, and 'Fast' platforms abandoned
UPTON PARK (MDR)	24 / 3B	1902	N/A	MDR	First served by District Railway 1902, line quadrupled 1908, District Trains using 'Slow' lines
					Served by Metropolitan Line since 1936 ('Hammersmith & City Line' since 1990)
UPTON PARK GOODS	24 / 3B	1895	1989	LTSR	
UXBRIDGE (1st)	17 / 2A	1904	1938	MET	Served by District Line 1910-1933, served by Piccadilly Line trains 1933-1938
UXBRIDGE (2nd)	17 / 2A	1938	N/A	LT (MET & PIC)	
UXBRIDGE GOODS (MET)	17 / 2A	1905	1939	MET	
UXBRIDGE HIGH STREET	17 / 2A	1907 (1914)	1939 (1962)	GCR & GWR	Goods yard open 1914-1962. No passenger service 1917-1920, withdrawn for good 1939
UXBRIDGE ROAD	31 / 1A & 49	1869	1940	WLR	Passenger service withdrawn Willesden Jcn to Clapham Jcn 1940. Re-opened as 'Shepherd's
					Bush' in 2008
UXBRIDGE ROAD GOODS	31 / 1A & 49	1869	1967	LNWR	
Uxbridge Road Junction	49	1864	1940	WLR & MET	
UXBRIDGE SIDINGS	17 / 2A	1938	N/A	LT (MET)	Metropolitan Line stabling sidings. On site of first station and former Goods yard
UXBRIDGE VINE STREET	17 / 3A	1856	1962 (1964)	GWR	'Vine Street' suffix added 1907. Passenger services withdrawn from
Uxbridge					Uxbridge Vine Street Branch 1962, freight in 1964

V

NAME:	PAGE / GRID:	YEAR OPENED:	YEAR CLOSED:	OPENED BY:	NOTES:
VAN DEN BURGHS & JURGENS (PURFLEET)	16 / 3A	?	?	PRIV	Margerine manufacturers, disused
VAN OMMEREN (PURFLEET)	16 / 3A	?	?	PRIV	
VAUXHALL	32 / 2A	1848	N/A	LSWR	Victoria Line station opened 1971
Vauxhall Bridge					
Ventnor Road	46 / 3A	1982	N/A	BR	Point where single track commences on Epsom Downs Branch
VESTRY DEPOT	32 / 2B	?	?	LCDR	
Viaduct Junction	20 / 4B	1917	1964	GWR	
VICKERS WORKS (ERITH)	36 / 1A	?	?	PRIV	
VICKERS WORKS (CRAYFORD)	36 / 4B	1915	?	PRIV	
VICTORIA	32 / 2A	1860	N/A	LBSCR	LCDR Station opened alongside LBSCR Station 1862. District Railway station opened 1868.
					Two Mainline stations unified 1924 by Southern Railway. Victoria Line platforms opened 1969
VICTORIA PARK (1st)	23 / 2B	1856	1866	NLR	Renamed 1859, resited South 1866
Victoria Park Hackney Wick					
VICTORIA PARK (2nd)	23 / 2B	1866	1943	NLR	
VICTORIA PARK & BOW	23 / 3B & 57	1849	1850	BER & ECR	Blackwall Extension Railway opened to passengers 1849, closed 1850
Victoria Park Junction	23 / 2B	1854	1984	NLR & ECR	Junction eliminated and NLR Poplar Branch dismantled 1984
Voltaire Road Junction	32 / 3A & 51	?	N/A	LCDR & LBSCR	

W

NAME:	PAGE / GRID:	YEAR OPENED:	YEAR CLOSED:	OPENED BY:	NOTES:
WADDON	47 / 2B	1863	N/A	LBSCR	Goods yard closed 1968
WADDON MARSH (SR)	47 / 1B	1930	1997	SR	Wimbledon to West Croydon closed 1997 prior to conversion to Tramlink
Waddon Marsh Halt					
WADDON MARSH (CTL)	47 / 1B	2000	N/A	CTL	On site of former Waddon Marsh Station
WALLINGTON	47 / 2A	1847	N/A	LBSCR	Renamed 1868. Goods yard closed 1963
Carshalton					
WALTHAM CROSS (1st)	5 / 1B	1840	1885	GER	Relocated South 1885
Waltham					
WALTHAM CROSS (2nd)	5 / 1B	1885	N/A	GER	
Waltham Cross (& Abbey)					
Waltham Cross					
WALTHAMSTOW CENTRAL	13 / 4B	1870	N/A	GER	Victoria Line station opened and mainline station renamed 1968. Goods yard closed 1964
Hoe Street, Walthamstow					
WALTHAMSTOW QUEENS ROAD	13 / 4B	1894	N/A	T&FG	Renamed 1958
Walthamstow					
WALWORTH ROAD	32 / 2B	1862	1916	LCDR	Renamed 1865
Camberwell Gate					
WALWORTH ROAD COAL	32 / 2B	1871	1973	MID	
WANDLE PARK	47 / 1B	2000	N/A	CTL	
WANDSWORTH COMMON (1st)	31 / 4B	1856	1858	LBSCR	Opened by West End of London & Crystal Palace Railway, but operated by LBSCR from outset
					Temporary terminus on North side of Wandsworth Common
WANDSWORTH COMMON (2nd)	31 / 4B	1858	N/A	LBSCR	Replaced temporary station to North. Coal yard closed 1964
WANDSWORTH ROAD	32 / 3A & 51	1863	N/A	LCDR	LBSCR platforms opened 1867, LCDR platforms closed 1916
					East London Line extension Phase 2 (LOROL) projected to serve from 2011
WANDSWORTH ROAD GOODS	32 / 3A & 51	?	?	LNWR	
WANDSWORTH TOWN	31 / 4A	1846	N/A	LSWR	Renamed 1903
Wandsworth					
WANSTEAD	14 / 4A	1947	N/A	LT (CEN)	
WANSTEAD PARK	24 / 2A	1894	N/A	T&FG	
WAPPING	33 / 1A	1869	N/A	ELR	First served District and Metropolitan Railways 1884, last served District 1905. No service
Wapping & Shadwell					Metropolitan Railway 1906-1913. Became 'East London Line' in 1980s. Closed 1995-1998.
					Again closed 2007 due to East London Line extension works, to re-open 2010

NAME: (Previous names indented below)	PAGE / GRID:	YEAR OPENED:	YEAR CLOSED:	OPENED BY:	NOTES:
WARREN STREET	22 / 3A	1907	N/A	CCE&HR	Renamed 1908. Victoria Line platforms opened 1968
Euston Road					
WARWICK AVENUE	21 / 4B & 62	1915	N/A	UERL (BAK)	
WARWICK ROAD GOODS	31 / 2A & 50	1863	1967	LNWR & GWR	
Warwick Road Junction	31 / 2A & 50	1872	N/A	MDR	Curve to Addison Road built 1869, no regular use until 1872
WATERLOO	32 / 1B	1848	N/A	LSWR	Waterloo & City Line platforms opened 1898, Baker Street & Waterloo Railway 1906,
					Northern Line 1926, Jubilee Line 1999. Eurostar services terminated here 1994-2007
WATERLOO EAST	32 / 1B & 55	1869	N/A	SER	Connection to Waterloo LSWR station removed 1911 and 'Junction' suffix dropped
Waterloo Eastern					'Eastern' suffix added after 1935, shortened to 'East' 1977
Waterloo					
Waterloo Junction					
WATFORD (L&B)	2 / 3B	1837	1858	L&B	Replaced by Watford Junction Station to South
WATFORD (MET & GCR)	2 / 4A	1925	N/A	MET & LNER	Goods yard closed 1966
WATFORD HIGH STREET	2 / 4B	1913	N/A	LNWR	Served by London Underground Bakerloo Line Trains 1917-1982
Watford East Junction	1 / 4B	1925	N/A	MET & LNER	
WATFORD JUNCTION	2 / 3B	1858	N/A	LNWR	Replaced earlier Watford Station. Served by London Underground Bakerloo Line Trains 1917-1982
WATFORD NORTH	2 / 2B	1910	N/A	LNWR	
Callowland					
Watford North Junction	1 / 4B	1925	N/A	MET & LNER	
Watford South Junction	1 / 4B	1925	N/A	MET & LNER	
WATFORD STADIUM	2 / 4A	1982	1996	BR	Opened using funds from Watford FC. Only served on Match Days.
					Not intended to re-open if Metropolitan Line extended to Watford Junction.
Watford Tunnels	2 / 2A	1837	N/A	L&B	
WATFORD WEST	2 / 4A	1912	1996	LNWR	Croxley Green Branch service suspended 1996. Metroploitan Line proposed to re-open
					line along with Watford West Station
WELLESLEY ROAD	47 / 1B	2000	N/A	CTL	
WELLING	35 / 3B	1895	N/A	SER	Goods yard closed 1962
WELLINGTON SIDINGS	11 / 4A	1867	1962	GNR	Freight & Carriage Sidings. Used by Northern Line Trains post-1940, now Highgate Wood Depot
WELSH HARP	20 / 1B	1870	1903	MID	For excursion traffic to Brent Reservoir (Welsh Harp)
WEMBLEY CENTRAL	19 / 2B	1842	N/A	L&B	Served by Bakerloo Line Trains 1917-1982, 1984-Present. Renamed 'Wembley Central' 1948
Wembley (For Sudbury)					
Sudbury & Wembley					
Sudbury					
WEMBLEY DEPOT	20 / 2A	2005	N/A	NR	Chiltern Railways depot
WEMBLEY PARK	20 / 1A	1894	N/A	MET	Served by Bakerloo Line Trains 1939-1979, Jubilee Line 1979-Present
WEMBLEY PARK GOODS	20 / 1A	1894	1965	MET	Transferred to LNER 1937
WEMBLEY PARK SIDINGS	20 / 1A	?	N/A	MET	Stabling sidings for Metropolitan Line
WEMBLEY STADIUM (1st)	20 / 2A	1923	1968	LNER	Renamed 'Stadium' 1927. Wembley Stadium Loop last used 1968, officially closed 1969,
Wembley Exhibition					dismantled 1970
Exhibition Station, Wembley					
WEMBLEY STADIUM (2nd)	20 / 2A	1906	N/A	GCR	Opened as 'Wembley Hill', renamed 'Wembley Complex' 1978, renamed 'Wembley Stadium' 1987
Wembley Complex					
Wembley Hill					
WEST ACTON	20 / 4A	1923	N/A	CLR	North Acton to Ealing Broadway opened by Great Western Railway 1920
WESTBOURNE PARK & KENSAL GREEN	21 / 4A & 62	1866	1871	MET & GWR	
WESTBOURNE PARK (GWR)	21 / 4A & 62	1871	1992	GWR	
WESTBOURNE PARK (MET)	21 / 4A & 62	1871	N/A	MET & GWR	
WEST BROMPTON	31 / 2A & 50	1866	N/A	WLER	District Railway platforms opened 1869. Main line platforms closed 1940 but re-opened 1999.
WESTCOMBE PARK	34 / 2A	1879	N/A	SER	
Coombe Farm Lane					
WEST CROYDON	47 / 1B	1839	N/A	LCR	Original terminus of London & Croydon Railway 1839-1847. Tramlink station opened 2000.
Croydon					Projected terminus of East London Line Extension Phase 1 (2010)
WEST DRAYTON (1st)	27 / 1B	1838	1884	GWR	Served by District Railway 1883-1884. Relocated East 1884.
WEST DRAYTON (2nd)	27 / 1B	1884	N/A	GWR	Served by District Railway 1884-1885, Renamed 1974
West Drayton & Yiewsley					
WEST DRAYTON COAL	27 / 1A	1963	1999	PRIV	Lafarge stone terminal now on site
WEST DULWICH	42 / 1B	1863	N/A	LCDR	
Dulwich					
WEST EALING	19 / 4B	1871	N/A	GWR	Opened as 'Castle Hill', renamed 'Castle Hill & Ealing Dean' 1875
Castle Hill & Ealing Dean					Served by District Railway Trains 1883-1885. Renamed 'West Ealing' 1899
Castle Hill					'Old' Goods yard closed in mid-1960's, Milk Traffic ceased 1978
West Ealing Junction	19 / 4B	1903	N/A	GWR	
WEST EALING NEW GOODS	19 / 4B	1908	1980	GWR	'Old' Goods yard on south side of station
WEST END SIDINGS	21 / 2A	1868	1968	MID	
Western Junction (Stratford)	53	1847	1981	ECR	Western Curve at Stratford dismantled 1981
WEST FINCHLEY (LNER)	11 / 2A	1933	1939	LNER	Closed in 1939 to enable electrification and transfer to LT Northern Line
Finchley West					
WEST FINCHLEY (LT)	11 / 2A	1940	N/A	LT (NOR)	On site of former GNR station
WESTFERRY	23 / 4B	1987	N/A	DLR	
WEST GREEN	12 / 3B	1878	1963	GER	Palace Gates Branch closed to passengers 1963, freight 1965. Goods yard closed 1964
WEST HAM	24 / 3A	1901	N/A	LTSR	Served by District Railway since 1902. Served by Metropolitan Line since 1936
West Ham Manor Road					('Hammersmith & City Line' since 1990). 'Fast' platforms abandoned 1940. Low Level
West Ham					(North London Line) Platforms opened 1979. 'Fast' (LTS) Platforms re-built 1998.
					Jubilee Line Platforms opened 1999. 'Manor Road' suffix in use 1924-1969
WEST HAMPSTEAD (MET)	21 / 2A	1879	N/A	MET	Last served Metropolitan Line 1940. Served by Bakerloo Line 1939-1979, Jubilee thereafter

NAME: (Previous names indented below)	PAGE / GRID:	YEAR OPENED:	YEAR CLOSED:	OPENED BY:	NOTES:
WEST HAMPSTEAD (LNWR)	21 / 2A	1888	N/A	LNWR	Goods yard open 1870-1967. Renamed 1975. Closed 1995-1996
West End Lane					
WEST HAMPSTEAD THAMESLINK	21 / 2A	1871	N/A	MID	'Thameslink' suffix added 1988
West Hampstead Midland					
West Hampstead					
West End & Brondesbury					
West End (For Kilburn & Hampstead)					
WEST HAM SOUTH GOODS	24 / 4B	1892	1964	GER	
WEST HARROW	9 / 4A	1913	N/A	MET	
WEST INDIA DOCKS	23 / 4B	1840	1926	LBR	Passenger service to Blackwall and North Greenwich withdrawn 1926
WEST INDIA QUAY	33 / 1B & 57	1987	N/A	DLR	
WEST KENSINGTON	31 / 2A & 50	1874	N/A	MDR	Renamed 1877
North End (Fulham)					
WEST KENSINGTON GOODS & COAL	31 / 2A & 50	1878	1965	MID	
West Kensington Junction	50	1874	N/A	MDR	
West London Junction (1)	31 / 3B	1993	N/A	BR	Sheepcote Lane Curve originally opened 1863 but dismantled 1936. Re-opened 1993
					to allow Eurostar trains access to North Pole Depot from Waterloo
West London Junction (2)	60	1844	N/A	WLR	
WEST LONDON WASTE TRANSFER STATION	18 / 2B	?	N/A	PRIV	
WESTMINSTER	32 / 1A	1868	N/A	MDR	Renamed 1907. Jubilee Line platforms opened and station rebuilt 1999
Westminster Bridge					
WEST NORWOOD	42 / 1B	1856	N/A	LBSCR	Opened by West End of London & Crystal Palace Railway, but operated by LBSCR from outset
Lower Norwood					Renamed 1886
West Norwood Junction	42 / 1B	1870	N/A	LBSCR	
WEST PARK HOSPITAL	45 / 3A	1918	1950	PRIV	Horton Estate Light Railway opened to supply building materials, later fuel, to hospitals
WEST RUISLIP	17 / 1B	1906	N/A	GCR & GWR	First served by LT Central Line Trains 1948
West Ruislip (For Ickenham)					
Ruislip & Ickenham					
WEST SIDINGS (SOUTHALL)	28 / 1B	1838	N/A	GWR	Disused
WEST SILVERTOWN	34 / 1A	2005	N/A	DLR	
WEST SUTTON	46 / 2A	1930	N/A	SR	
West Thurrock Junction	16 / 3B	1892	N/A	LTSR	Junction between original Tilbury Line and loop via Ockendon
WEST WICKHAM	43 / 4B	1882	N/A	SER	Goods yard closed 1963
WEST YARD (RIPPLE LANE)	25 / 3B	?	N/A	?	
Whipps Cross Tunnel	14 / 4A	1856	N/A	ECR	
WHITECHAPEL	23 / 4A & 59	1876	N/A	ELR	District Railway platforms opened 1884 (terminus until 1902). 'Whitechapel (Mile End)' until 1901,
Whitechapel (Mile End)					suffix then dropped. Served by Metropolitan Railway 1906-1913 then again 1936-present
					('Hammersmith & City Line' since 1990). East London Railway platforms first served by
					Metropolitan Railway 1913, later became 'East London Line', closed 1995-1998 and 2007-2010
					Platforms for 'Crossrail 1' proposed to open 2017
Whitechapel Junction	59	1884	1939 (2007)	MDR	Last passenger service 1939, stock transfer until 2007
WHITE CITY (CEN)	20 / 4B & 49	1947	N/A	LT (CEN)	Replaced Wood Lane Station
WHITE CITY (MET)	30 / 1B & 49	1908	1959	MET	Opened as 'Wood Lane (Exhibition)' 1908, closed 1914. Re-opened as 'Wood Lane (White City)'
Wood Lane (White City)					1920, renamed 'White City' 1947, closed 1959
Wood Lane (Exhibition)					
WHITE CITY DEPOT	30 / 1B & 49	1949	N/A	LT (CEN)	Replaced earlier Wood Lane Depot. Re-sited 2007
WHITECROSS STREET GOODS	55	?	?	MID	
WHITE HART LANE	13 / 2A	1872	N/A	GER	Goods yard closed to public traffic 1965, saw some private traffic until 1977
WHITTON	29 / 4A	1930	N/A	SR	
Whitton Junction	28 / 4B	1883	N/A	LSWR	
WHYTELEAFE	48 / 3B	1900	N/A	SECR	
WHYTELEAFE SOUTH	48 / 3B	1856	N/A	CR	Renamed 'Whyteleafe South' 1956
Warlingham					
Warlingham & Cane Hill					
WILLESDEN BRENT SIDINGS	20 / 3A	?	N/A	LNWR	
WILLESDEN DEPOT	20 / 3B & 60	1965	N/A	BR	
WILLESDEN FREIGHTLINER TERMINAL	20 / 3B & 60	?	N/A	BR	
WILLESDEN "F" SIDINGS	20 / 3A	?	N/A	LNWR	
WILLESDEN GREEN	20 / 2B	1979	N/A	MET	'& Cricklewood' 1894-1938. Served by Bakerloo Line 1939-1979, Jubilee thereafter
Willesden Green & Cricklewood					Last served Metropolitan Line 1940.
Willesden Green					
WILLESDEN GREEN GOODS	20 / 2B	?	1966	MET	
WILLESDEN HIGH LEVEL	20 / 3B & 60	1866	1885	N&SWJR	Second High level station. Abandoned when new spur built from first High level Station
					to Acton Wells Junction 1885
WILLESDEN JUNCTION (1st)	20 / 3B & 60	1842	1962	L&B	Low Level Platforms on West Coast Main Line. Rebuilt & resited 1866
WILLESDEN JUNCTION (2nd)	20 / 3B & 60	1866	N/A	HJR	Low Level Platforms on LNWR DC Lines added 1912, served by Bakerloo Line since 1917
WILLOW WALK GOODS	33 / 1A & 62	1849	1932	SER	Amalgamated with Bricklayers Arms by SR 1932, but fabric of depot remained in use
WIMBLEDON	41 / 2A	1838	N/A	LSWR	First served by District Railway 1889. Rebuilt 1929. Goods yard closed 1970
Wimbledon & Merton					
WIMBLEDON BOROUGH COUNCIL SIDING	41 / 1B	1898	1965	PRIV	
WIMBLEDON CHASE	41 / 3A	1929	N/A	SR	
Wimbledon East "A" Junctions	41 / 2A	1868	N/A	LSWR & LBSCR	
Wimbledon North Junction	41 / 2A	1889	N/A	LSWR	

NAME: (Previous names indented below)	PAGE / GRID:	YEAR OPENED:	YEAR CLOSED:	OPENED BY:	NOTES:
WIMBLEDON PARK	41 / 1A	1889	N/A	LSWR	Putney Bridge to Wimbldeon built by LSWR but operated by District Railway from opening. Last regular Main Line passenger service withdrawn 1941, although services called on occasions until 1969. Point Pleasant Jcn to Wimbledon still used for empty stock working and diversions.
WIMBLEDON PARK SIDINGS	41 / 1A	?	N/A	SR	Part of Wimbledon Traincare Depot (SWT)
Wimbledon South "B" Junction	41 / 2A	1855	1997	LSWR & WCR	Wimbldeon to Croydon line closed 1997 in preparation for Tramlink construction
WIMBLEDON S&T SIDINGS	41 / 2A	1916	N/A	LSWR	Disused, originally Durnsford Road Goods
Wimbledon West "C" Junctions	41 / 2A	1929	N/A	SR	
WINCHMORE HILL	12 / 1B	1871	N/A	GNR	Goods yard closed 1962
Windmill Bridge Junctions	42 / 4B	1862	N/A	LBSCR	
WOODFORD (ECR)	14 / 2A	1856	1970	ECR	Majority of passenger services transferred to LT in 1947. First trains in the morning remained British Rail services until 1970
WOODFORD (LT)	14 / 2A	1947	N/A	LT (CEN)	First served by LT Central Line Trains 1947. Terminus for Central Line 1947-1948 Goods yard closed 1966
Woodford Junction	14 / 2B	1903	N/A	GER	Divergence of Fairlop Loop (= Hainault Loop) from Epping Line
WOODFORD SIDINGS	14 / 2A	1947	N/A	LT (CEN)	Central Line stabling sidings
WOODGRANGE PARK	24 / 2B	1894	N/A	T&FG	
Woodgrange Park Junction	24 / 2B	1894	N/A	T&FG	
WOOD GREEN	12 / 3A	1932	N/A	UERL (PIC)	
Wood Green North Junction	12 / 2A	1871	N/A	GNR	Divergence of GNR Enfield Branch (now Hertford Loop) from main Line
Wood Green Tunnels	12 / 2A	1850	N/A	GNR	
WOOD LANE (CLR)	20 / 4B & 49	1908	1947	CLR	Terminus of CLR 1900-1908 (on terminal loop). Replaced by White City 1947
WOOD LANE (H&C)	20 / 4B & 49	2008	N/A	LUL (H&C)	
WOOD LANE DEPOT	30 / 1B & 49	1900	1949	CLR	Original Central London Railway depot, replaced by White City Depot 1949
Wood Lane Junction	20 / 4B & 49	1920	1938	GWR & LT (CEN)	Junction between GWR (Viaduct Jcn to North Acton) and Central Line from Wood Lane
WOODMANSTERNE	47 / 3B	1932	N/A	SR	
WOODSIDE (SER)	43 / 4A	1871	1997	SER	Goods yard in use 1871-1963
Woodside & South Norwood					Elmers End to Addiscombe closed 1997 prior to opening of Croydon Tramlink
WOODSIDE (CTL)	43 / 4A	2000	N/A	CTL	On site of former Woodside Station
Woodside Junction	43 / 4A	1883	1983	SER	Woodside to Selsdon closed 1983
WOODSIDE PARK (GNR)	11 / 2B	1872	1939	GNR	Closed in 1939 to enable electrification and transfer to LT Northern Line
Woodside Park for North Finchley					
Torrington Park, Woodside					
Torrington Park					
WOODSIDE PARK (LT)	11 / 2B	1940	N/A	LT (NOR)	On site of former GNR station. Goods yard closed 1962
WOODSTOCK ROAD	30 / 1B	1909	1917	N&SWJR	Passenger services withdrawn from Hammersmith & Chiswick Branch 1917
WOOD STREET	13 / 3B	1873	N/A	GER	Goods yard in use 1893-1968, Carriage Sidings abandoned 1986
Wood Street (Walthamstow)					
WOOLWICH	35 / 1A	2017	N/A	NR (XRAIL)	Proposed station on Crossrail 1 Abbey Wood branch
WOOLWICH ARSENAL	35 / 1A	1849	N/A	SER	DLR platforms opened 2009
WOOLWICH ARSENAL	35 / 1A	?	?	PRIV	
WOOLWICH DOCKYARD	34 / 1B	1849	N/A	SER	
Woolwich					
WORCESTER PARK	45 / 1B	1859	N/A	LSWR	Renamed 1862. Goods yard closed 1963
Old Malden & Worcester Park					
WORCESTER PARK BRICKWORKS	45 / 1B	1898	c.1950s	PRIV	

Y

NAME:	PAGE / GRID:	YEAR OPENED:	YEAR CLOSED:	OPENED BY:	NOTES:
YEOVENEY	37 / 1A	1887	1962	GWR	Renamed 'Yeoveney Halt' 1935, closed before rest of line
Yeoveney Halt					
Runemede Halt					
Runemede Range Halt					
YORK ROAD	22 / 3A & 54	1906	1932	GNP&BR	May re-open in connection with King's Cross Redevelopment
York Road Curve	54	1863	1977	GNR	Last regular service 1976